# Advance Praise for *Graduates in Wonderland*

"I loved *Graduates in Wonderland*. It made me nostalgic for the uncertainty and excitement and seemingly endless possibilities of the post-college years but also relieved to have that phase behind me. The first thing I did after reading it was pour my heart out—via e-mail, of course—to my best friend."
    —Rachel Bertsche, *New York Times* bestselling author of *MWF Seeking BFF*

"A charming epistolary tale of female friendship and early post-graduate life in all its exciting and confusing glory. Jess and Rachel's adventures will be relatable to anyone who has ventured down that strange rabbit hole we call the 'real world' and wondered just how to find her way back out again in one successful, happy piece."    —Rachel Friedman, author of *The Good Girl's Guide to Getting Lost*

"Sounding, thinking, and talking exactly like your best friends, these girls dive headfirst into the humor and heartache of life after college. They kiss a lot of foreign frogs in a lot of foreign cities. And just when they think they are in danger of becoming real live adults, they prove themselves spectacularly wrong. And I love them for it."    —Jerramy Fine, author of *Someday My Prince Will Come*

"I knew from page eight, on which one of the authors ends a letter with a piece of brutally honest advice about the other's crush, that I would love *Graduates in Wonderland*. Theirs is a best friendship I find as complex, challenging, and deeply intimate as my own—the type of dynamic, all-consuming female friendship story that is as common as it is undertold. Jess and Rachel are smart, funny, and wise, and it's a pleasure to be like a fly in their e-mails, if that were a thing."
    —Katie Heaney, author of *Never Have I Ever*

"Gloriously addictive. This book is like catching up with your best friends over two-dollar tacos and margaritas, trying to convince each other to date this guy or travel or buy weirdo heels. I've been there, babes! The two authors have perfectly captured a time in your life where you have no footing and everything is utter chaos . . . but at least you have your buddies. A warm breath of both nostalgia and reality. The kind of writing you eat with a spoon. Funny and sweet and honest, like the best kinds of friendships. Will recommend to all my ladies."
    —Alida Nugent, author of *Don't Worry, It Gets Worse*

"Rachel and Jess have done an extraordinary job, in the creation of this book, of turning an epistolary life story into something richly tender, and genuinely suspenseful. The intimacy here is not just between the writers, but with the readers. I've adventured forth now with Jess and Rachel, and I have returned with a warm, good feeling in my heart."
    —Beth Kephart, author of *Handling the Truth: On the Writing of Memoir* and *Going Over*

# Graduates in Wonderland

## THE INTERNATIONAL MISADVENTURES

## OF TWO (ALMOST) ADULTS

## JESSICA PAN
## and RACHEL KAPELKE-DALE

GOTHAM BOOKS

GOTHAM BOOKS
Published by the Penguin Group
Penguin Group (USA) LLC
375 Hudson Street
New York, New York 10014

USA | Canada | UK | Ireland | Australia | New Zealand | India | South Africa | China
penguin.com
A Penguin Random House Company

LIBRARY OF CONGRESS CATALOGING-IN-PUBLICATION DATA
has been applied for.

ISBN 978-1-592-40860-3

Printed in the United States of America
1  3  5  7  9  10  8  6  4  2

*Set in Bembo  •  Designed by Elke Sigal*

*To our parents*
*And for all good friends separated by circumstance*

# Contents

# A Note from the Authors

The experiences recounted in this book are real, but to protect the privacy and anonymity of those involved, we have changed names and identifying characteristics. In order to maintain a streamlined narrative, this book has been edited for readability and cohesion. The timeline has been altered to reflect a compressed period of time (i.e., we do not include months where we did nothing but eat Saltine crackers and watch *Gossip Girl*). For a few minor characters, we combined characteristics and incidents of different people into one composite character.

# Graduates in Wonderland

# YEAR ONE

### Jess to Rachel

Rachel,

These are some of the last courses I took at Brown:

- Behavioral Neuroscience
- Late Nineteenth-Century French Painting
- Russian Literature in Translation
- Abnormal Psychology

After my first week in Beijing, I decided that these are the courses I should have taken instead:

- Six Mandarin Phrases That Mean "No, Thank You, I Don't Eat That"
- Practical Uses for Fire
- Guess My Race: A Sociological Study
- Abnormal Psychology

Since we last spoke, I've flown thirteen hours and made it halfway across the world with my entire life packed into two suitcases and no return ticket (don't tell Chinese immigration that). First observation: Everything here is so crowded and new to me. Ancient temples sit right next to brand-new futuristic buildings; Chinese hipsters dart among elderly Chinese people who wander around in pajamas after sunset. The city is overflowing with heavy traffic and yellow-and-blue cabs, and the buildings are overwhelmingly gray and red. And it's so fucking hot—the local men here roll up their shirts in the heat in a style I like to call "the Beijing bikini."

When I got into the cab at the airport, I realized that taxi drivers here assume I'm Chinese, until I speak my broken Mandarin to them, and they crane their necks to get a better look at me, and exclaim, "Foreigner?!" Meanwhile, all the expats in China assume I'm full Chinese, not some halfie from Texas, and approach me with their own terrible, stilted Mandarin. I'm going to completely lose it on the next person who asks me, "WHERE . . . BATHROOM?"

What is going on? Am I Chinese or am I a foreigner?!

I want to perform some sort of experiment called "Where's Jess?" (à la "Where's Waldo?") to see if anyone could pick me out of a crowd here. I thought China would be full of people who look like me and understand me, but I'm in some strange backward universe. Also, if you want the really easy version of this game, play "Where's Astrid?" because she's the only blond, blue-eyed girl for miles. Last night, we wandered upon a night market where they were selling cooked worms, caterpillars, starfish, etc. A man thrust a plate in front of us and said, "Buy these testicles!" Then I turn around and see that Astrid has been kidnapped by Chinese people who want to take their picture with the exotic Norwegian girl. She's beginning to think she's famous.

So far, everything else I thought I knew was wrong. My idea of China was gleaned from what I had seen on the news (crowded Chinese streets and bird flu), kung fu movies (flying humans who wield swords), and my limited experience in Chinatown in Los Angeles visiting my dad's side of the family (eating noodles, spending hours inexplicably waiting in line at Chinese banks).

What I did not expect was to be covered in dust, sweating profusely, and writing this e-mail by candlelight. CANDLELIGHT. Like the thing they used in the Middle Ages to see in the dark. Astrid and I found a place to live through an acquaintance of an acquaintance from her German class at Brown, so we've already moved into an apartment on the sixth floor of a dusty apartment complex. But apparently, electricity costs money here too, and neither of us has a clue about how to pay the bill. Let's hope my computer doesn't die before I get to send this e-mail.

And yes, no electricity means no air-conditioning, so I've opened all the windows and am sitting here writing this in my underwear. You didn't ask, but I'm telling anyway. Since I can't communicate with 99 percent of the people I see, I'm going to overcompensate with too much information in these e-mails. For example: The smell of Beijing is like a punch in the face. The air is gray and hot and I can't even place the source of the odor. It's a mixture of Tiger Balm, burning plastic (Astrid calls this the smell of cancer), food waste and God knows what other kinds of waste, gas fumes, cigarette smoke, and grilled meat from street vendors.

I feel like anything's possible here. Even when I'm waiting in line at the bank for three hours (that part was actually true), I'm thinking, "But I'm in China, so this experience is not wasted."

My short-term plan is under way. I'm starting classes at a Mandarin language school here soon, and when my program wraps up, I'm going to start applying for journalism jobs. This is a place where absolutely anything could happen. I could become the straight, half-Chinese Anderson Cooper. I could have three-quarters-Chinese babies with the next boy I see. I could actually learn Mandarin OR I could somehow end up lost in the Chinese countryside selling eggs (this is a real fear of mine). It's more likely that I'll accidentally set my hair on fire with this candle, though.

Stranger things have happened. For instance, when was the last time you were attracted to a guy named Beard Brother?

On our first night here, Astrid and I met up with some older graduates from Brown who we found via the online alumni directory. A guy who graduated last year brought some friends and they all offered to show us around. I don't know if it's the combination of high pollution levels, a potent alcohol here called *baijiu* (tastes like rubbing alcohol), or just the intoxication of being in a foreign land, but I fell into a conversation with a guy named Maxwell and immediately took a liking to him.

He and his best friend used to teach English in a tiny town in the Chinese countryside, where they were the only foreigners in the entire place. Maxwell has a bushy beard and mustache, and had the best stories about the young Chinese kids he taught, who gave themselves English names like Tiger Dinosaur or Nightclub.

"I had one class where about a quarter of the boys and one of the girls were self-named Wolf. I think there was some kind of hierarchy involved too, because they were named Wolf One through Wolf Sixteen," Maxwell said. "I never figured out the order, though."

"But what did they call you?" I asked him.

"They named me Beard Brother. They were simultaneously amazed, intimidated, and disgusted by my beard," Maxwell said, laughing. "It was an emotional drain on them just to be around it."

The stories almost made me want to head to rural China until he explained that there was nothing to do in the city and no opportunities for anything besides teaching English.

Then Maxwell asked me what I was doing in Beijing.

Since even I don't know the answer to this question, I told him about how I wanted an adventure and how I wanted to finally visit my dad's home country and how I wanted to learn Mandarin. And also because I'd just graduated and did not have a job. When I said it out loud, it almost made sense to me.

From then, it was one of those nights that went on and on—we ended up in Beijing's bar district dancing in an '80s music club and I pulled out all the stops with my dance moves, although they were no match for Maxwell's. (I wish I were a boy so that I would be boobless and have long, sinewy arms and fluid movements like him.) We jumped around and sweated profusely under strobe lights and as Maxwell dipped me, I had that very strange sensation of not recognizing my own life.

Then we went for Chinese street food at 4 A.M. (just food here) and Maxwell walked me back to my apartment.

I mean, he walked *us* back to *our* apartment. Did I mention that Astrid was there the entire time? We're both completely charmed by him, and we've been hanging out with him nearly every day since we met. With Maxwell by our side, Astrid and I explore our neighborhood, try out used bicycles, and alternate staring into his eyes. Neither of us has dared to discuss what is happening or what it means.

Okay, I'm just going to say it. Maxwell seems completely enamored of Astrid and she of him. And, of course, it makes me resent Astrid, who is currently asleep in the bedroom next door. It's killing me because I really like him, and because I don't want something like this to come between me and Astrid. And yet . . . both are happening.

But I'm thousands of miles away from everyone else I know, and Astrid is the only familiar face here. Home feels so far away right now. When I said good-bye to my parents at the Amarillo airport, my mom hugged me and said, "You're braver than I am. Be safe." My dad hugged me and said, "Remember what I told you when we dropped you off at college? The sentiment still stands: I love you, but don't fuck up."

But I'm not sure that I won't fuck this situation up.

Remember this time last fall, when we began our senior year? You and Rosabelle and Astrid picked me up from the Providence airport, brought me bad white wine, and it was raining and we sat huddled on the front steps of our porch and drank and laughed about how we had no idea what we were doing with our lives but we had ten more months to figure it out. Those were the days, my friend! We had it so good! I miss you so much. I wish I could meet you at Ocean's Café, right now—you know the weather is perfect and we could discuss the assholes who lived upstairs, our classes, the color of your hair, and quitting smoking.

How's life stateside? I can't believe you're so far away.

I miss you more than I miss microwaveable food (which is a lot!).

Love,

Jess

## Rachel to Jess

I can't believe you and Astrid are in Beijing! So are you saying that it's possible that you are wandering night food markets and dancing to '80s music in clubs while on the other side of the world, I'm sitting on the C train commuting from Brooklyn to the gallery on the Upper East Side? And when Rosabelle and I are baking cookies after dinner in our apartment, you're having breakfast with Astrid in Beijing? The twelve-hour time difference is really doing a number on my mind!

I also wish I had a good reason for coming here—but unlike in Beijing, nobody ever questions why I chose to move to New York. New York is just where you're supposed to go after college. It's basically a rule, if you go to school on the East Coast. (You broke the cardinal rule!)

New York feels different now that I'm working here instead of just visiting. I imagined it would be really similar to when I came last summer and hung out on friends' roofs and drank umbrella drinks with Rosabelle at a tiki bar and came across the shooting locations from my favorite movies. Basically, I thought that it would be like my view of New York in the 1960s, still gritty but exciting, full of smoky nightclubs. So far, it hasn't turned out that way, but there's something about living in New York that feels like hyper-reality. Like the stakes here are higher than they are anywhere else.

Rosabelle and I live in an apartment that is a 1.5 bedroom in Fort Greene. This means one bedroom and a nursery. I live in the nursery. For $850 a month, I had to make the choice between shutting my door or having a double bed in my room. So far, I am compromising by pushing the bed diagonally when I sleep and rearranging it every morning. Rosabelle gets a real bedroom, but she's paying a lot more (and splitting the rent with Buster, who has moved in). I spend my nights trying to shut out the sounds of Buster and Rosabelle climaxing next door. No matter how much you love your friends, there's nothing worse than hearing them having sex (I know you know this, having lived with Astrid and her various boyfriends for four years at college). Any advice?

My way of coping is to escape from them via the fire escape, which I refer to as my balcony. It's been so hot this summer, and I just sit out there and read and peek through the brownstones at the tiny corner of Fort Greene Park that I can see.

I also get to listen to our neighbor, the daughter of a famous singer, bicker with her boyfriend all the time. I have to tell you, the boyfriend sounds like an asshole. To protect their privacy, let's call the father Jilly Boel. The boyfriend keeps saying, "Nobody cares that your father is Jilly Boel!"

I keep wanting to yell back, "I do! Sing me a song!"

But then I leave them to their own devices.

So . . . I finally started working with Vince at the gallery. He runs the place, talks to artists, and chooses the layout for the next show. I'm his second personal assistant, so I spend my time paging through glossy auction catalogues and successfully managing a six-line telephone.

I work in a beautiful office, all modern and glass and artworks all around and a really nice first assistant, Melanie, who trained me and also warned me about Vince. On my first day, she told me that the most important thing about being an assistant is learning to anticipate your boss's needs. She also said, "Good luck." I didn't know what she meant until one day he praised me for my new system of organizing mail and the next day threw the pile back in my face with no comment. He's also sort of obsessed with Melanie and me looking extra-crisp and professional. It doesn't seem possible that three months ago we were lazing around our backyard in cutoff shorts, drinking boxed wine.

But there are some great perks. The first week after I started, we had an opening for a young artist who was having his first solo show. He kept looking around the gallery like he couldn't believe this was happening. When I told him that we'd sold his first painting, he hugged me. He also introduced me to several of his artist friends. That part was great. But after they left, I spent the rest of the evening in the corner drinking white wine out of a plastic cup and wishing you guys were here with me.

I miss you and Astrid! Come to my openings and get drunk with me in the corner! I know you're set on staying in Beijing for at least a year, but it's my duty as one of your best friends to try and convince you to come to New York. First of all, brunch. I can't imagine Chinese brunch is any good. And everyone we know is here too. This is a good (and bad) thing about moving to New York. Sometimes it feels like the entire city came here en masse from Brown.

Tell me more about China—what is it like living surrounded by the hardest language in the world? What is your daily life even like?

I can't believe you're already in love. Oh wait, actually I can. You've fallen in love with every male barista who ever smiled at you. I don't know how you're going to handle the Astrid-Maxwell-You triangle. I think this needs to be said: You and Astrid are such completely different people that it seems to me if Maxwell is in love with her, then he could never be the guy for you.

Okay, I love and miss you and (not so) secretly want you to come home. Write back and I will tell you what happens next, just as soon as it happens to me. Does Vince find this e-mail and fire me? Will I order six cups of drip coffee from Starbucks and pour them into the coffeepot at work to make it look like I learned how to make coffee? Do I move back home to Wisconsin when I realize I can't hack it here?

Shit. I just noticed a huge run in the back of my stockings that goes from my heel to the control top . . . and it's probably been there all day. I work in a beautiful art space, but I feel like a sloppy ice-cream cone melting all over the designer carpeting.

Love always,

Rachel

**SEPTEMBER 3**

## Jess to Rachel

I can't believe Buster moved in with you and Rosabelle! I never pegged them as loud fornicators. Don't you remember that after being repeatedly woken up by Astrid's sexual escapades with her boyfriend, the play I wrote based on the experience was performed in the "Once Upon a Weekend" festival? That's my advice to you—write your angst into a play, enter it into a contest, and have it performed in front of Rosabelle and Buster. It works! Also, earplugs.

As for my daily life, I typically wake up at 6 A.M. because my Mandarin course is all the way across town. I sleep on the subway, next to a bunch of Chinese people also sleeping on their commutes, and then I have intensive Mandarin classes all morning. I'm trying to master the language's four tones (long and flat, rising, undulating, and sharp), but the only way I can pronounce them correctly is by moving my head in the direction of the word's tone while I'm speaking (for the third tone, which rises and falls, I swoop my head up and down). The language classes are fun, but lack a lot of practical information. For the vacation lesson, there's no vocabulary about boarding a plane or booking a hotel room—suddenly you're just climbing a mountain somewhere. I'm great at remarking on imaginary snow peaks, but I struggle to buy a subway ticket.

Then I come home to inevitably find Astrid and Maxwell hanging out in our apartment.

So, it's official—Astrid and I are both secretly in love with Maxwell. He's around all the time, so it's difficult to get away from it all. He's up for any adventure and can make anything into a funny situation. I wish he'd stop being so likable, so I could move on. It pisses me off that he's so great. Asshole.

I've always objectively known Astrid was beautiful, but until now, I've never felt directly threatened by it. I'd never compared our hair or our smiles, and I don't like thinking about her this way. Things are tense when it's the three of us, but when Astrid and I are alone, I'm glad she's here to navigate life with me.

I've taken to pretending that I like Maxwell's best friend, Jason, to throw everyone off. He's American also, and the rest of the group thinks he is definitely not interested in women. I just think that some people love to dance. He's not my type at all—blond, muscular, blue eyes—but he took me to an art quarter in Beijing called the 798 District. It has a million tiny galleries, and free wine, cheese, and crackers, and it was mostly foreigners, so it felt eerily like Brown. It was also like Brown because I was with a guy who is probably gay and ill suited for me. But he did give me the best moment I've had in China so far.

Last night, Jason and I were leaving Maxwell's apartment at the same time. I was just going to walk home, but Jason offered to let me ride on the back of his bicycle. Although this isn't the safest method, I managed to ride with him with some balance and by clinging on for dear life while he did all the leg work. He pedaled me back to my apartment at 3 A.M. in the misty rain. I asked him to take the long way home, and it was surreal as we silently traveled down the deserted streets with my arms wrapped around him. I swear if Wong Kar-wai could have seen us, he would have definitely re-created the scene for his next film.

Overall, Beijing is such a strange bubble. The expat community feels really small because I'm running into the same people again and again. I'm meeting French people, Italians, Russians (you wouldn't believe how many Russians there are in Beijing), Brits, other Americans, everyone. I always thought that Brown was so international—which it was, after Texas—but it seemed like there was only one person per country (examples: Beautiful Norwegian Astrid, Hot South African James, Cruel English Tristan, That One Belgian Girl).

My Mandarin program only lasts for another week, and I don't have a clue what my next move will be, but I met someone who does voices for Chinese cartoon characters and she thinks I'd be great at it. I can't wait to put that on my résumé. My parents are going to be thrilled that this is what I've done with my college education. I'm trying out next week.

Your life does sound really far away from mine, but maybe you will eventually figure Vince out. Or are you positive that he is always going to be an asshole, in which case this may be good character building? Now tell me all about New York. And send me some bagels.

Love,

That One Chinese-Texan Girl

SEPTEMBER 20

## Rachel to Jess

Jess,

I'm writing from my desk at work; outside it's getting dark. It's about 7 P.M. right now, and I'm waiting for the cleaning lady to come in—that's the glamour of the second assistant's job. Basically, I'm a million miles from you riding bicycles in Beijing.

I get Beijing being a strange bubble—New York feels smaller by the day. Rosabelle, Buster, and I went to a party this weekend that was a complete flashback to college. People from Brown congregated in the kitchen to hear a guy who graduated with us talk about his internship at the *New Yorker*. The jealousy was palpable. I got out of there before someone stabbed me out of sheer frustration.

Somehow, even though I know so many people in the city, adjusting to life here has been hard for me. My favorite thing right now is coming home to watch old movies—it's my escape from real life.

This is so hard to explain, because I can write cheerful e-mails to other people and show up at work and seem perky, and I don't think the people I see on a daily basis realize how down I really am. I don't even think Rosabelle does. I am going to tell you this because we promised that in these e-mails we would not gloss over the bad stuff, because then what's the point of staying in touch?

Over the past few weeks, I've become unable to walk into work without feeling overwhelmingly nervous. Last week when an artist Vince had been courting left him for another gallery, he calmly acquiesced on the phone and then, after hanging up, became so angry that he punched a hole in the wall. Then he walked out and said, in a soft and dangerous voice, "Cancel your plans. You're staying late tonight." When Vince does these things, Melanie laughs it off and accepts it, but my fear of him just starts to go into overdrive. Meanwhile, did you know that the cable company itemizes porn viewings by date and time? Neither did I—until Vince handed me his cable bill. So now I know what the mysterious four-hour block in his calendar last week actually was. . . .

To pass the time and to make us feel better, Melanie and I fill out quizzes to identify psychopaths online, and answer them on Vince's behalf. In case you were wondering, the answer is always yes. Although it seems like the answer would be yes for most bosses who are driven and narcissistic.

And I still have to smile and chat with him, who for the record looks and smells like Tony Soprano would (a mixture of cigars and salami), and who says things like, "Who punched the holes in this report? It looks like a retard did it! Are you sure you went to Brown?" Whatever, Vince is a psychopath, and I have the test to prove it.

It's strange to have a job where if I can get a mug full of coffee to Vince's desk, steaming hot, one minute before he arrives and slams his door, I've succeeded. I need to be invisible to be good at my job, which is hard when all we've ever been taught is the importance of standing out from the crowd.

While I know my life isn't great right now, I've had shitty jobs before and they never bothered me once I'd left for the day. I thought it was just my job, but while Melanie doesn't like her job either, she seems happy in other aspects of her life. I feel like I'm in a rut I just can't shake. Everything feels really gray right now.

I struggle to get out of bed when I'm not in the office. And on the days when I do have to go to work, when I wait on the subway platform, I find myself growing anxious and tearing up. Everyone around me stares straight ahead. Even once we're on the train and I'm crying on their shoulders (because, honestly, the C train is super crowded in the morning). Clearly, this is because it's New York and I'm just as likely to stab them as to do anything else. But still. People! Help a Wisconsinite out. We're so friendly!

My anxiety grows as I near the office. Once I'm in and I've had my first contact with Vince, I'm anxious all day—afraid of his beck and call and his inevitable criticism and fury. I count the hours until he leaves for the night and then I feel temporary relief, and then I make my way home at 8 P.M.

But I can't think of a better alternative to this. There's either back at home with nothing to do or unemployed in China with you, probably also in love with Maxwell. I am at the bottom of a HOLE.

Once I realized that this just wasn't getting any better, I got the number of a therapist here from a family friend. I am not sure I see the point of this but I'm really hoping it will pull me out of my days spent staring fearfully into the void of Vince's office and crying on the subway.

I miss you more than you miss bagels.

Love,

Debbie Downer

**SEPTEMBER 21**

## Jess to Rachel

Did you know that if you dig that hole deep enough you'll end up all the way in China?

Sorry. I don't know what to say. You know I'm a tough-love kind of person. So I guess if I were in New York right now this is what I would do: I'd turn off that Simon and Garfunkel that I know you have on repeat, I'd drag your sorry ass out to eat something that isn't frozen pizza (I know you too well), and we'd go to the movies so that you have a dark, warm place to sob your eyes out. It's cathartic and more socially acceptable than crying on the subway. (Even as I write this, I am regretting this hypothetical promise because I am still traumatized from seeing *The Notebook* with you. No, really, fellow concerned audience members, she's okay. No, she didn't lose the love of her life to dementia. She just has a lot of feelings. Okay, I'll tell her it's just a movie.) And then we'd go out and eventually the night would end with us laughing on someone else's front steps and being shushed by their neighbors.

Sometimes when I have been low, very low, I have emerged from the slump by forcing myself to go on an escapade with an outgoing friend who really listens and cares. I know that sounds too simple, but I promise it gives you perspective—more perspective than watching TV alone. Go with me on this. Just imagine skydiving with Amélie! Or solving a complicated mystery with Jon Stewart! Or just going on a weekend road trip with Rosabelle. Does she know how you're feeling yet?

And you have to remind yourself that new opportunities exist, and will always exist. Remember: You can always look for a new job. But for right now, if you're really struggling, I think seeing a therapist might be a good idea too.

I really wish you were here. I keep thinking that if you were here, we could have so much fun. Something to cheer you up:

I completely bombed my children's cartoon voice-over audition. I can't seem to fake being incredibly happy again and again and again unless I'm on drugs. I also, apparently, do not realistically react in the way that a six-year-old cartoon girl does to candy and puppies. It was pretty humiliating. I've been bombing a lot lately. We went to a bilingual improv (anybody can speak any language) that is held in the middle of a tiny bar in one of the oldest areas of the city. Let me just say that I suck at improv and everyone, including the Chinese people who don't speak English, felt really sorry for me. So that's two professions I can cross off my list: voice actor and comedian.

I know this makes me sound like a theater person, but trust me, I am still most definitely not. Remember how I was so shy in my Spanish class that I almost failed? In Beijing, I have no choice but to speak Mandarin (okay, and by that I mean miming ridiculous things like "watermelon" or "flip-flops" or "tampon"). I have to make a fool of myself daily to get anything done, including buying food and toiletries. Because of this, I'm losing my self-conscious shell, and it's so freeing.

I've started another Mandarin program, but I still have to wake up at 6 A.M. to get there on time. It doesn't help that I go to bed at 2 A.M. I have sold my soul to the Mandarin language.

But on to the big stuff.

Astrid and I ended up in a huge fight in the middle of an outdoor technology market. We spent three hours trying to buy phones and a modem for dial-up Internet—no one could understand exactly what we wanted. I wanted to just go home and ask a Chinese friend to help us but Astrid's stubborn and needed to have the Internet RIGHT NOW (we've been stealing it from neighbors, but they're onto us). The air was hot and humid and my T-shirt was slick with sweat and starting to stick to my back. I was on the verge of leaning in really close to her and saying in a low voice, "I will end you." But I knew she'd lean in closer and hiss, "I will end you first." And she would manage to end me first. You know how intense she is.

Finally, she was so fed up with the situation that she abandoned it for the moment. In typical Astrid fashion, she said, "Screw this. Let's just go get massages. We deserve them." Astrid's the best person for escapism, as I'm sure you remember. I think that's part of the problem, though. Every idea she has seems like a good one, and then suddenly days go by with her in one blink and you don't know what happened to your old life. Being with her is intoxicating but exhausting. It used to be easier, because we always wanted the same things, but it's not that simple anymore. I want my own life, and she still wants me to be the sidekick to hers.

Let's just say the Maxwell situation isn't helping.

What's confusing is that most of the time Maxwell, his friends, Astrid, and I really *are* having so much fun, more fun than I've had in a long time. We stay out late most nights, either dancing or exploring, and when we return to our neighborhood around 3 A.M., we congregate outside of our apartment building in the balmy night air.

We wander through a jungle gym to reach a handful of stone tables, which are usually covered with trash, cigarette butts, and sun-flower seeds—it's all very dilapidated. Maxwell calls the table closest to the street "the best table in town," and that's where we always sit. We drink bottles of beer and peel the lychees we've just bought off the street vendors and talk loudly and inevitably the Chinese neighbors get mad at us for waking them up. Sometimes Astrid is there, and sometimes she's not. I love both versions of these nights—because I love being silly with Astrid, making her laugh and being around someone who knows me so well. But I also love the nights alone with Maxwell, because he's the one who makes *me* laugh too.

Shouldn't it be illegal for a guy to look at you like you're the only girl in the world when he's clearly in love with someone else? I think the real betrayal is this: When you make a guy laugh and they main-tain eye contact with you while they're laughing. Please stop staring deep into my soul, Maxwell. There's an unspoken code that if you aren't romantically interested in someone, you look away from them when you're laughing—otherwise it just feels too intimate. I've spent entire first dates looking at the floor.

So there's always that weird subtext with Maxwell when we're alone: "I know you want Astrid, but we're the ones who laugh to-gether." I don't dare say anything about it. Eventually the air grows chilly, and we go our separate ways.

I am meeting a lot of other expats, but all we have in common is the fact that we are expats in China. So far, the best conversations I have are with taxi drivers. I love these guys! I love practicing my Mandarin with them. After they establish that I am an American, here is how every single conversation goes:

Cabdriver: (*gives me a good, long look*) You know, you look a little Chinese to me.

Me: My dad's Chinese.

Cabdriver: YOUR DAD IS CHINESE?!

Me: Yes.

Cabdriver: And your mother is . . . ?

Me: American.

Cabdriver: So you're a "mixed-blood." (In Mandarin, this is an acceptable thing to say.)

Me: Yes!

Cabdriver: tue fjklsio akdj woeur adsla wieur aldj ckxlz

(In this e-mail, this looks like Czech or something, but it's actually supposed to be Mandarin that is too advanced for me to understand.)

Me: Yes . . . ?

*Pause*

And then I get out, and I'm like, "It was so good to meet you!" and they're like "DON'T OPEN THE DOOR ON THAT CYCLIST!" and also, "Go slowly"—their way of saying, "Take care." I love speaking this exotic language. I feel like a completely different person when I step back and listen to myself.

Speaking of half-bloods, have I told you that I've been reading the final Harry Potter book? During my first week here, I was desperate and it was the only English book I could find. However, I made the mistake of first buying a fake one off the street. It was called *Harry Potter and Leopard Walk-Up to Dragon*. It was essentially bad translations of the Lord of the Rings, with Harry Potter characters inserted. I'll try to send one to you. Here's how it begins: "Harry doesn't know how long it will take to wash the sticky cream cake off his face. For a civilised young man it is disgusting to have dirt on any part of his body." He sounds a little OCD to me in this version.

Fucking gold. Read it and weep, J. K. Rowling.

Love,

Jess

P.S. What do you think happened when Harry Potter had sex for the first time? Like, what magical thing happened? I'm thinking when he's done, he has a full beard or something.

Let me know your thoughts, ASAP.

## Rachel to Jess

It's hard to imagine a world in which you and Astrid are competing for the same guy—you've never liked (or been able to tolerate) the same guy before. You always like guys who have approximately 3 percent body fat and are two inches taller than you, while Astrid likes beefy Eastern Europeans.

Also, I can't imagine you performing improv or voicing a cartoon. I think you are definitely becoming more extroverted in Beijing. I wonder what New York is doing to me. . . . I keep thinking that New York is what's wrong with me, but my therapist says that this is not helpful (yes, therapist). I can't control what happens to me, only what I feel about it.

So, this means that I took your advice and my dad's advice, as well as the advice of a kindly tourist on the C train, and finally called a therapist. Actually, if you want to know the truth, I called *three* therapists. The first one was the analyst, and the way I understand it is that you tell *him* what's wrong with *you*. So basically, you are also my analyst by this definition. You majored in psychology, so this makes perfect sense. Anyway, he was so nice on the phone—so, so nice. Until this:

Him: I do have a Saturday-morning slot available.

Me: Fantastic, I'll take it. Oh, and quickly—if I can ask, what's your fee?

Him: The first consultation is $750 and after that, we can discuss whether you're eligible for reduced fees.

Me: Uh. What's the lowest possible rate?

Him: $500 an hour.

Me: Thanks so much! You know, I'm so busy these days . . .

*Click.*

No insurance.

I finally found another guy through Mount Sinai and he is, like, our age. He told me that I could call him Eric.

I told him that this made me uncomfortable. Now I call him Dr. Eric.

Dr. Eric told a lot of stories about bullies. He said that the surgery interns used to bully the psychiatry interns, namely him. This just made me feel bad for him, and also like maybe my therapist was a loser. He told me to write down on a piece of paper "This is not about me," and to look at the paper every time Vince said something threatening. I started crying at this point, and he showed me that he also had a paper like this, which he keeps in his wallet. That just made me cry harder. It was so SAD.

Lately I just pick up on everyone's emotions, no matter what they are, and respond to them a million times more intensely than I normally would/is appropriate. I know I've always felt things a bit too much (*Notebook*, ugh) but all the same, this is ridiculous.

Meanwhile, I have a shiny new prescription for Xanax, so I am fully qualified to be a dissatisfied 1960s housewife.

Dr. Eric costs $250 an hour, so I still had to find somebody else— somebody cheaper. Which was good. I was cognizant of the fact that he makes me feel existentially sad.

So many feelings.

I told him I couldn't afford him anymore, and so he went through his BlackBerry and arrived at the name and number of Claudia (no last name), another therapist. So I arrived at Claudia's brownstone office in the Village, and sat in the waiting area. When she came out, she called out, "Rachel?" in a thick German accent, and when I stood up, Claudia looked from me to her clipboard and back again before inviting me into her office.

I followed her in and saw a chalkboard . . . a bucket of blocks . . . a rag doll . . .

Turns out Dr. Eric referred me to a child therapist.

After she explained this to me, Claudia asked me if I wanted to continue with her for a trial counseling session, and I did. We spent the whole time doing a basic questionnaire, in which she asked a lot of questions about my family and my past experiences. She didn't want to talk about Vince *at all*. I was like, okay, neither do I, but he's really the problem here.

All she said was, "*Is* he?"

Ugh.

I feel like I know exactly what she is trying to do, but I also kind of like her. Her office has a bunch of artwork and plants, and the kid stuff is kind of comforting. She makes me mint tea. Also, I like knowing that I am the most emotionally mature of her patients (probably). But I do have to write her a check at the end of each session ($150— am I going down the scale of therapists? Pretty soon it's just going to be me, a twenty-dollar bill, and a cheap prostitute). Paying a confidant is so unsettling.

And now, after very healthily comparing my therapist to a prostitute, I am closing the office for the evening and going to a gallery opening in Chelsea, because Claudia is making me do one thing every day that "scares me." She said that my weekly trips to the Film Forum don't count. I've also been trying to think about things in New York that I like (which makes me think that she is brainwashed, but maybe will help lure you back here?). So far I have this:

Fall finally came to New York today after holding out for way too long. When I woke up, everything smelled like fall and the leaves were starting to change and it was chilly—and I love it. From work, right now, I can see Central Park and it looks like broccoli because I'm so high up and the light is so dramatic. The tops of the trees are all streaked with sunlight.

I haven't told Rosabelle too much about Claudia. I mentioned the Xanax and she's calling them my crazy pills, so I kind of hate her right now. I'm contemplating hiding her favorite baking tray. Then we'll see who's crazy.

I love you!

Rach

P.S. I think when Harry Potter has sex for the first time, sparks fly from his penis.

---

## Jess to Rachel

I would have pursued another degree in psychology if I had known that meant hanging out with you all day. The reality actually seemed to be hanging out with rats. I still remember the mandatory rat lab I took at Brown and how our professor told me I couldn't name our rat because . . . well, because I'd see soon enough. (He died, Rachel. Fifle's DEAD. Fievel? Fyfull? He died and nobody even bothered to learn how to spell his name!) Sorry. You're fragile.

If it makes you feel better, I don't actually know what I'm doing with my life at all. My Mandarin isn't good enough to land me a fancy job. People keep saying there's so much opportunity in China . . . but for what? On principle, I don't want to teach English. It's a slippery slope. You agree to teach English and then suddenly you're forty-five, with a fanny pack and Teva sandals, still teaching English, except inexplicably you have become a white male and you have a hot Chinese girlfriend and everyone else thinks you're a creep.

But, I feel a strange connection with China. Astrid keeps telling me it's because *these are your people* and I think she's kind of right. I find myself thinking about that a lot here, even when I have trouble communicating with them.

Even so, I still don't know what I'm going to do here. Sometimes I wonder if I should be in New York with you like most of our graduating class. I still haven't given up on my aspirations of being a reporter, but New York has the most concentrated number of journalists and aspiring journalists than any other place in the world. Someone sneezes and within seconds, someone has already covered it. It feels like there isn't any room for another one.

Also, it feels strange telling this to you, but I was always so terrified of moving to New York after graduation and just becoming a small cog in a wheel for the rest of my life. But don't think about that too much, okay?

Maybe you'd like to hear that I shower over a toilet. Perhaps I glossed over that in my other e-mails. It seems totally normal to me now. It's strange how quickly one adapts.

More importantly, things finally came to a head with the Maxwell and Astrid situation. I've taken to avoiding them when they're together, but our problems go so much deeper than our mutual adoration of Maxwell. When Maxwell's not around, Astrid and I go everywhere together. Every single person I've met, Astrid has also met. No one has met just me as me. I'm always in addition to her.

Last night we had a huge fight in a small alley while Maxwell waited in a bar for us. I wanted to go home to catch some much-needed sleep, but she demanded that I come with them to another bar. She told me that sometimes conversation falls flat between her and Maxwell and that I balance it out. I told her she was selfish and that I wasn't going to play the supporting role in her life forever. It was one of the most honest moments of my life. Somehow, and I really don't know how, we made up after this, but there's palpable tension. It feels like I'm stuck in a bad marriage. How do you break up with your best friend? You can't. Do you ever feel this way about Rosabelle or is it just me?

I'm also pretty sure we scared off the elderly Chinese people who live on that street. They wear their pajamas around town once the sun has set, but when they heard the first screech of an angry Norwegian, they scattered.

I'm planning to fly to Shanghai to crash on Jon's couch for a week to escape the tension. He's teaching there, and I'd love to see his face. Apparently, he's catnip to all the gay men in Shanghai as well as to every guy at Brown.

Missing you. Are you feeling better?

Love,

Jess

## Rachel to Jess

I think that what you're going through with Astrid is totally normal, especially when you've been living together so long. Does Maxwell even know that he's being fought over? And say hi to Jon for me.

Meanwhile, I may have solved my work problems!

1. Take a Xanax.

2. Arrive at work before Vince and make sure everything is perfect before he comes.

3. Hide from Vince, in the bathroom if necessary, until he has left.

4. Take care of everything else from the day.

Perfect solution.

Claudia says I need to get out more. And so I've been trying to go out at least one night a week. She might be onto something, because last week I met someone. Or *re*met someone.

I ran into Bill Broadwick at a gallery opening. I think you met him just once or twice—he was in my fiction class in college. He wrote really dense, obtuse prose that was so brilliant no one understood it. He also has piercing green eyes and a deep voice. I hadn't seen him since graduation and was actually in the middle of taking off my work shoes and slipping on my high heels when he caught me, one shoe on, one shoe off. It's not the most graceful of poses, but he did offer his arm to help me keep my balance. Someday in the future he's going to make some Cinderella joke when he's down on one knee. I didn't just write that. Ignore that. That never happened.

We wandered around the gallery together, me mostly following behind him, because I prefer to view paintings with his wavy blond hair obfuscating most of the artwork. We eventually got separated when more people arrived, but I want to see him again. It was strange to be in New York together and not sitting in a classroom. I almost felt grown-up, but the whole shoe-changing scene canceled the feeling out. As I was leaving, he caught me on the way out to say good-bye. I wanted to make a joke to lighten the mood, because my heart was racing, but instead I managed to just smile demurely and nod. He left saying he'd call me later in the week.

Meanwhile, I feel like almost every guy I meet here plays in some terrible band, reads Rilke, drinks Brooklyn microbrews, and has a bad beard. Yet I still manage to convince myself I really like them! Lack of good options does this to you. Maybe I'm projecting and I'm trying to get them to solve my problems for me. It would definitely fit in with the passivity that's taken over my life so far . . . as in, I still haven't quit my job.

Rosabelle has so far interviewed at: Dior, Chanel, and now is going for *Vogue*. Who knows. I bet thirty years ago she would have gotten all of those jobs, but these days they're like the Holy Grail. I eat her baking chocolate. She yells at me. It's like college, but without you and Astrid.

I remember when the four of us were inseparable senior year. How is it that you took half of our group to China? Come back, you guys! We've got really good cupcakes over here (another New York pro I've come up with). Also, remember how much we liked lying in Sheep Meadow in Central Park? What else . . . We also have a canal in Brooklyn that will literally strip the flesh from your hands!

Claudia is still my best friend next to Rosabelle. Today I told her about how hard it is to meet anybody and that most of the time, I just don't have the energy to make an effort. I know in your mind, therapists are Austrian men with beards, but you are mistaken: Claudia is a German woman with a slight mustache. She is probably about forty, with a black mane and lots of frumpy clothes. You must now imagine this woman scolding me: "Your future husband does not know where you live! He does not have your address!"

I go to too much therapy.

Love,

Lady-in-Waiting

## Jess to Rachel

I remember Bill Broadwick. He had all the makings of a great guy, but he seemed a bit robotic to me. Like the male version of a Stepford wife. I won't say that in my wedding speech, though, so don't worry.

It's colder now, so I've seen the first real glimmer of blue sky since I've been here, because usually it is a gray, smoggy haze. I've been to Shanghai to visit Jon since I last wrote—I flew down there for four days and he came back with me for three. He left yesterday and now I really miss him.

Jon took me around Shanghai, which is glitzier than Beijing, with fancier high-rises and more fashionistas walking the streets. We ate dinner in the French Concession, which you would have loved because it has leafy streets and '30s architecture and French people. Everywhere we went, skinny Chinese guys batted their eyelashes at Jon, because apparently the curly haired, blue-eyed look is very sought after in the gay community here, and he is totally living it up.

It was strange meeting the people in Jon's teaching program—those would have been my friends if I had taught English with him in Shanghai like I'd originally planned, and it's rare to get to see your alternate life up close. I still think I prefer Beijing, which has a big art scene and live music venues and a soul. Overall, Shanghai has more bankers and bubble-tea stands. Jon thinks it's better than Beijing, but he's wrong, just like he was wrong when he thought I was a lesbian freshman year.

Anyway, I don't know what's wrong with the men in your life. Are we entirely sure they are straight? I ask because Jon and I went to a lot of gay clubs together in Shanghai. Why did Astrid, Rosabelle, you, and I ever think this was fun? It is not fun. The guys there just kind of wonder if you are lost.

Jon thinks he'll only be in China for one year, but I'm still open to staying longer. I'm back in Beijing and realizing that my only skill now seems to be speaking English. Even if you have zero other skills, a native English speaker with a pulse can find work teaching English or even just speaking it. And so producers from the cartoon job called me up to see if I could do some English-language voice recording. I'm paid the equivalent of $70 per hour to tape an English lesson for kids. I'm currently recording the Christmas lesson. I wish I were making this up, but I'm really not—I had to pretend to be Santa.

When I met the producers at the recording studio, they handed me enormous headphones and led me into a booth. For a moment I felt like I was about to record a pop album. The experience was unnerving because the mic amplified everything—I could hear myself swallow through the headphones.

And then the dream ended. I had to put on the only voice I can do (angry old man) and talk about Christmas trees and snowflakes. The producers' only complaint was that I didn't sound happy enough. Do you know what it's like to have three Chinese women yell at you, "BE HAPPIER!"? I want to shout back, "I'M A JEW! WE AREN'T HAPPY AND WE DON'T HAVE SANTA CLAUS!"

I've been told this is going to be distributed to at least fifty thousand children, which I try not to think about.

Astrid and I went to a Yeah Yeah Yeahs outdoor concert this week and it poured the entire time. Incredibly muddy. We pushed our way to the front. It's easier to be rude when you can't understand what people are yelling at you. I just kept saying, in Mandarin, "My friend is up there, my friend!" Then I saw a British guy trying to get in front of me, so I pointed to him and yelled, "Foreigner!" in Mandarin to rile up the crowd, but it turns out he knew Mandarin better than I did. Oops.

Anyway, two hours later with hair completely soaking wet, we danced around and screamed to "Maps." Obviously it reminded me of all the long drives we'd take in Rosabelle's car blasting that song. It was one of those moments when I really loved Astrid and was so happy that we were on this China adventure together. I almost forgot about her and Maxwell. I just don't let myself entertain thoughts of actually dating him, and I shove him far into the friend corner. Also, we never ever touch, which is fundamental to this arrangement. Maybe this will all blow over.

I am also trying to apply for real jobs, and the advice everyone always gives is to network. Network! Network! Not sure what this means, because apparently my version of networking comes off as flirting. I can't seem to master the vital, final step of the networking process in which you say, "No, but really. Enough about your trip to Japan and your new apartment. Hire me."

Honestly, I'd love to be back at school now that the weather is finally turning cold. Astrid doesn't understand my nostalgia. I guess Norwegians aren't really known for their nostalgia.

I want to walk to a café after class and see you sitting there with your copper-tinted hair and dark blue eyes buried in a book. . . . I wonder who's sitting in our usual places there now.

I want to hear more about your life in New York. If you want to imagine mine, imagine a lot of Chinese people. Also, crowded streets, delicious street food, misty mornings, and something called "split pants." It's what toddlers wear here. Instead of diapers, their pants are split open in the back. The streets are dirty. You do the math.

Okay.

Karen O from the Yeah Yeah Yeahs wanted me to tell you:

They don't love you like I love you.

Ai*,

Chinese Santa

*Mandarin for love

OCTOBER 20

## Rachel to Jess

Dear Jess,

If you ever mention split pants again, I'm going to immediately delete your e-mail before finishing it. You're making me miss Jon too, because nobody else can make me laugh so hard I fall off beds. Also, you know he'd stop calling you a lesbian if you just threw out that biker jacket.

I'm also searching for a new job. The more I think about the opportunities that this city actually has, the more I realize that the art world I'm in right now is cold and more about money than the actual art itself. And I've come to realize that I don't love art the way I love writing, or even film. I know about art, and I appreciate it, but it is not worth putting up with somebody who behaves as badly as my boss, Vince, does. I wake up early and sit in the park to work on cover letters and my résumé, thinking, "Didn't I just do this?"

Because, yes! I have decided to quit! This is with a lot of encouragement from Claudia and the rest of my "support network" (therapist talk). I can't wait to do it, but I'm holding off until I'm a little bit more stable (financially and emotionally).

Also, I am totally terrified of any confrontation whatsoever. There's also that.

I'm supposed to be researching hotels in Rome for Vince's next trip, but screw work. Instead, I'm going to tell you about the date I had with Bill Broadwick!

When I last left Bill Broadwick at the art gallery, I was Cinderella to his . . . oh, I can't even say it. You know. I recently remembered that at Brown he was dating a girl named Tara who every boy ever always fell in love with, even though (because?) she had a mullet and wore only plaid. Every outfit she wore always had a bird somewhere on it. Bird print, bird pin on her bag, bird charm bracelet. (Does this attract men or hungry cats?) Anyway, that was a long time ago and I think I remember hearing that they broke up recently.

Instead of waiting for him to call me—he does not know where I live—I called Bill yesterday and we decided to meet for a coffee today.

I wanted to look casual, but I couldn't resist curling my hair. I did not curl my mullet, because, let me remind you, I don't have one.

He walked over to Fort Greene, and we went to a café called Bittersweet (I don't think I've taken you there, but I will someday). It was crowded, so we took our coffee and went for a walk around Fort Greene Park, which for the record is not that big, so we had to circle it several times. It was twilight, and beautiful, but I was cold to my bones.

We fell into easy conversation about our daily lives, but now I feel strange because I barely know anything about who he is. Maybe it's his slightly aloof demeanor and his opaque writing, but I guess I just wanted to hear stories about playing down by the creek with his brothers when he was a child or how he spent his high school prom night (if he even has brothers or went to prom—because I still don't know). I think this really is a problem with me, because on dates, I either make small talk, or I want to delve into childhood trauma, unfulfilled dreams, hopes, etc. I no longer know what the middle ground consists of.

I turned into some weird, saccharine, muted version of myself to compensate. So nice. Way too nice.

Me: So are you still writing? Your story about the yurt was so amazing last year. You're so talented. If you ever wanted me to proofread your stories, I would totally do it for you.

BB: Yeah, maybe. I submitted that to a bunch of contests, but I haven't heard back yet. Mostly I'm working on my art writing right now.

He is just as beautiful as I remember and so insightful and intelligent. In case you were wondering if green eyes, blond hair, and rosy cheeks look radiant against a black peacoat, the answer is yes.

Eventually conversation died, so I walked him to the corner. His good-bye: "Well, I'll see you around the neighborhood." And I went in for the hug. Yes, I did. I tucked myself under his arms and squeezed (in case you don't know what a hug is). He hugged back but in, like, a limp way with a sad pat on my shoulder.

I just texted him a minute ago with the name of a film we couldn't remember and he has not written back.

Q) WHAT DOES TARA HAVE THAT I DON'T HAVE?

A) Nothing. Girl mullet.

Anyway, I have some semibig gossip about Ted. Aren't you impressed that I haven't written about him since we graduated? It's so strange that a guy I loved so much (even though we never dated) suddenly doesn't hold any power over me anymore. Or so I thought.

The other night Rosabelle and I were out at this party (all people from Brown, again—meh) and left at around 4 A.M. to go home. We were hungry and so we stopped by an all-night diner. I walk in and it hits me: It's the exact same diner that Ted and Jon and I went to freshman year. We'd driven up to the city for the first time and it was snowing when we went to Brooklyn so I made snowballs and threw them at Ted, and then he put snow down my shirt, and my fingers were so cold that he had to hold them until we got back to his apartment. The memory made me nostalgic and so I called Ted like four times, thinking it's only 1 A.M. in LA. Voice mail. Rosabelle stopped me and told me that Ted had moved to Toronto for a job and his phone number doesn't work anymore. I couldn't believe that she knew this and I didn't.

This made me tear up, maybe too much for the occasion. That's what I'm figuring out about depression; it's two steps forward and one step back.

Granted, it was 4 A.M. and bitterly cold, but I had this moment— remember when we were all so young—again, I know we're young now (but not *as* young)—and being in New York seemed so glamorous? At least it did to me.

Sometimes I wish I were in China too. And that is saying something, because I *really* don't want to live in China. It'd be easier if you were here in New York with me. Come back at some point in the next few years—it would make me really sad never to see you again except in passing.

To tempt you, let me remind you that New York has amazing movie theaters—I'm being sucked into spending all of my money and free time at Film Forum discovering a love for bleak Swedish films. And the MoMA! That is something I *know* China doesn't have, because I walked past it yesterday and it's still here.

Does it frighten you that Santa is relying on YOU to teach fifty thousand children about being naughty or nice? That's a lot of pressure.

Are you still in love with Maxwell?

Loooooooooooooove,

Rachel

P.S. I've started writing fiction again. What do you think about a story about a girl who works at a gallery but then falls into the Gowanus Canal and dies. . . . No, wait, I lost it. Too real. More later.

**OCTOBER 24**

## Jess to Rachel

Although I think you'd look great with a mullet (you really have the bone structure for it), I just don't think Bill Broadwick is the right guy for you. You definitely need someone who has an emotional range that goes beyond neutral. He is a cold, beautiful statue, and he's not the kind of guy who is going to comfort you or listen to your feelings. However, he is such a hot statue and I know that if I had been on a date with him, I would have said all the wrong things and just blurted out weird opinions that aren't even mine to fill the silence. Hot and smart men are unnerving. I would have wrapped my arms around him and squeezed, like, wayyyy too early and made it awkward for everyone. I probably would have also shouted something weird like, "Hug time!" to try to stop the oncoming awkwardness.

Something I keep remembering: Isn't he also pretentious? He would go to the "naked parties" the hippies would throw on campus but keep all of his clothes on and just write about what the naked people were doing. (Comparing penises? To his own? I don't know. I've never been. To the naked parties, or Bill Broadwick's penis. But if I did, it would be awkward. "Penis time!") But in any case, I do approve of your proactive approach to life and hugging.

A French hairstylist named Jerome told me it was time for bangs.

I don't know how he knew this, but I trusted him. Yes, I have full-blown bangs now. So there you go. Long, blunt, and in my eyes.

I didn't tell Astrid about it beforehand, and her reaction when she saw me was that I look like a haughty Chinese girl, which, incidentally, might have been the look I was going for. With these bangs, I now look nearly 75 percent Chinese, not just half like I actually am.

So I was feeling okay about my bangs, when I walked into my favorite hole-in-the-wall serving steaming-hot noodle soup (this stuff is amazing. I could and do eat it every day) and I saw my doppelgänger. Same bangs. Same black coat. Same black jeans. She was even a halfie like me, except she had a nose ring. She looked exactly like me but only if I had an amazing magazine job and a boyfriend who sings in a band. She just looked like she had her shit together. The kind of girl who doesn't give a fuck about what anyone thinks about her. It was like walking in on a cooler version of me.

Then I saw her flirting with the noodle guy that *I* always flirt with. No! It was actually really awkward. I'm sure she noticed the bangs and the coat likeness. I had to leave. I backed out slowly. So she won.

But I was fatter, so HA—got her there! (I seem to only eat noodles, buns, and rice here. I don't know how Chinese women are so thin. It's one of the greatest mysteries of the universe.)

I had dinner with Maxwell after my haircut. He told me he hates bangs. That's okay. I'm okay with that now. To answer your question: No, I no longer love him. I'm realizing that he's one of those rare characters who enchants everyone he meets. Every time he steps out, he draws in new friends and he literally cannot accommodate everyone who wants to hang out with him. I just made the mistake of thinking that our connection was special, when in fact, everyone feels connected to Maxwell.

So, yes, he's charming and if you met him, you would briefly love Beard Brother too. Astrid's grown tired of sharing him with all of his fans, and he seems to have moved on to pursuing someone else a little less intense. I used to care about his love life, but I no longer do. I'm just glad I don't feel like I'm competing with Astrid anymore, although we still haven't acknowledged that we both liked him.

I still feel like we're changing, though. As you know, she and I have always had such an intense friendship—I've probably said more words to Astrid than I have to anyone else in my entire life (and not just because we are both incredibly fast talkers). Four years of sleeping in the same dorm room, of traveling together, of having all the same friends. I'm thinking about moving out of our apartment. I hinted at it a few times, but Astrid hasn't taken the bait.

I want to branch out. I only just got here, so why have I spent so much of my time fixating on these two people, who are distracting me from things like my future career and the other 1.3 billion people who live in China?

I'm finally realizing that I'm so glad I came here. I'll wander along to the fruit market downstairs and haggle in Mandarin with the market stall owners, observe the old ladies sitting in a row fanning their faces, wave hello to my noodle-shop boy, and buy a green-bean-flavored popsicle (sounds gross but is very refreshing). Then I'll hop on my bike—a used one Jason gave me—and cycle to class singing at the top of my lungs because no one can hear me over the deafening roar of the construction sites and traffic horns.

These beautiful moments are a nice distraction from the stagnation of my career. (Is it stagnation if it hasn't begun?) For some reason, I thought it would all fall into place as soon as I got here. Astrid got a job, and it's freaking me out. First of all, it's a great job. She's working for some Chinese advertising agency that needed a German copywriter. You know how Astrid is fluent in about ten different languages. When both of us were just hanging out all the time, it felt like a totally normal and acceptable lifestyle. Now while she leaves the apartment so early every morning, I lie in bed and just have this sense of overwhelming, urgent panic before I have to get ready for class.

I need to stop going out all the time, but it's so hard to focus here with the constant traffic of new and exciting people at the party. But I can't continue to wait for the perfect job to fall into my lap.

I haven't been able to find journalism jobs that don't require fluent Mandarin, so I've arranged two interviews at PR agencies (one of them Ogilvy) and they are both for positions editing PR documents. I met a guy who had one of these jobs a few months ago. He said it's pretty thankless and I would learn nothing and never move up. I don't know what to do. How do I go into an interview already hating the job? Plus, I hate wearing blazers. Bulky, ugly. Dilemma. I think I'm being cornered into editing Chinglish and I don't know how I'm going to escape this.

Important question about interview attire:

I know it's cold, but do you think it is okay to wear a long skirt (hits calves) with bare legs instead of wearing opaque stockings that look weird with heels? Or would bare legs look slutty?

And, if the skirt is black, can I wear a blazer that is black with gray stripes, or should it all match perfectly? Please respond soon—my interview is at 10 A.M. tomorrow!

OH GOD, WHAT AM I DOING WITH MY LIFE?

Love,

No-One-Told-Me-What-Blazer-to-Wear Jess

P.S. You better write back. At least two lines.

**OCTOBER 25**

---

## Rachel to Jess

JUST WEAR THE STRIPED BLAZER *AND* THE TIGHTS.
This is my two-line e-mail. I write three cover letters a night.

## Rachel to Jess

Jess—I did it. I quit my art gallery job.

My mom once told me that you know you're an adult when you can stick your hand down the garbage disposal and deal with all of the shit that's down there. I am maybe not enough of an adult for this, but the idea's the same—it really is the first time that I've had to do something really unpleasant on my own. Well, with you on the other end of the . . . what, the Internet? The ethernet cable? The other side of my computer screen? I feel all comfortable and calm when I read your e-mails, and then I shut the computer and I gradually start to get fearful and anxious again—until eventually my arms and legs are numb.

I was so terrified about how Vince would react. I got to work an hour early and sat in Central Park listening to Madonna's "The Power of Good-Bye" on repeat to feel empowered. So . . . that happened. And I took some Xanax. But these are not the same thing as courage.

And then I went in and had to be all, "Vince? Can I talk to you . . . alone?" It's like breaking up with somebody. The second you say it, you both know what's going to happen, but then you're caught in this script that you have to play out.

We went into his office and I shut the door behind me. I was trembling. Had to stick my hands in my pockets. Now, normally, you know how I am about quitting things. When I quit the job at the library that summer, I just stopped going. It scares me.

So I told him why I'm leaving. The nice version, that doesn't involve him punching walls. I mumbled something about his temper. He just stared at me, told me I was neurotic and that they needed me for two more weeks. It wasn't as bad as Madonna and I thought it would be. It never is, I guess.

I don't know if my next job will save me from the kind of despair

I've been feeling, but I know I want to work somewhere more pleasant and relaxed. Prestige is so much less important than I ever thought.

I can't believe I'm turning twenty-three this month. One year closer to death. This is the novel year. I have to write it. My therapist says that this is not a healthy attitude toward either my career or death; we shall see.

I'm so glad I'm almost done with this job.

I want to call you, but you gave your American phone to your mom. And what would I say to her?

Love,

Rachel, Who Is No Longer a Slave to the Gallerist from Hell

**NOVEMBER 17**

## Jess to Rachel

Congratulations! Did you punch him in the face? Did you swipe all of his mail onto the floor? Did you slide a piece of paper across the table that said, "This is all your fault"?

By your mother's definition, I will also never be an adult.

You'll have to tell me all the devastating details, and you *can* call my American phone—because I'm home in Amarillo for Thanksgiving. I flew in last night. I'm in America, land of drip coffee and reality TV!

I'm trying to distract myself here, because I'm still unemployed. I did not get the PR jobs. I blame the blazer. My bank account is still slowly dwindling.

I've realized since I've been home that I like being away from Astrid. It's a relief not having to invite her everywhere I go or having to plan my day around her. This isn't healthy. I'm going to have to move out of our joint apartment, and I just have to figure out how I'm going to tell her.

So I've been secretly perusing the ads for new apartments. I think I'm going to try to break the news to her as soon as I'm back in China. She's the longest relationship I've ever had. Advice? You're the only person who knows her like I do.

Anyway, it feels like I never left—Amarillo is still full of white people, flat plain lands, and mom jeans. In Beijing, I'm usually the whitest person on the street. In Amarillo, I'm the Chinese girl. In high school, whenever I would go into department stores with my mom, the saleswomen always thought I was a random Asian girl asking a white lady for things.

Maybe you'll go through this strange feeling as well when you go home for the holidays. You will wake up in your childhood bedroom and think, "Was it all a dream? When am I going back to Brown? Or am I still in high school? Omigod—did I even get into college yet?" And then you'll blink a few times, reach for your glasses (because you're old), and realize the truth.

I always regress to my seventeen-year-old self when I visit home. My childhood best friend, Paige, is back in town as well, and we're doing the same nonsense we always did: driving around aimlessly, staking out various coffee shops for old acquaintances to see who is balding and who got fat and who has babies, and raiding our parents' refrigerators just because we can. Whenever I run into my old boyfriends, they are inevitably still driving the same pickup trucks that I made out with them in six years ago. (Forget this information, immediately.)

I'm back to living with my parents, which feels strange. For example: In Beijing I cycle home alone at 3 A.M. I eat almost exclusively street food from vendors who have no qualms about spitting on the ground as they hand me my food, in a country where food safety standards are shoddy at best. On the other hand, here, my mother is telling me to please be extra careful when driving to Paige's house (which is three blocks away) and to hold a hot baking sheet with *both hands*.

Little does she know that I drank three shots of questionable alcohol the night before I flew here from a country that doesn't seem to know about the seat belt.

My dad is testing my Mandarin to see if it's as good as his yet. He left China when he was eight, so he has perfect pronunciation, but is stuck with the vocabulary of an eight-year-old. I'm still hovering at the vocabulary of a five-year-old, so maybe in three years I'll catch up. Once he tried to tell my Chinese grandmother we were going skiing, and all he could say was, "We're going down a big hill with two sticks. There will be snow."

He keeps reminding me, "It's never too late for Caribbean medical school." Caribbean medical school is where you go when you can't get into medical school in the States, and he says this to me every time I leave (for the record, I never applied to medical school in the States, but I'm ignoring the implication that if I did, I wouldn't get in. However, I would definitely not get in).

With that nugget of confidence, I will board the plane back to Beijing in a week.

Love,

Jess

P.S. I ate a whole box of Pop-Tarts this week. But it's okay. That's okay, right?

**NOVEMBER 22**

## Rachel to Jess

Wait. You used to make out with guys in the backs of PICKUP trucks? And you never told me? Friends tell friends when they make out with hillbillies!

You, my friend, are dead to me.

Fine. I'll take you back, but honestly.

When your number showed up on my phone the other day, my heart leapt. I miss talking to you every day.

Since you called, I've had two real job interviews and about six billion meetings with people who can in no way, shape, or form help me find a job. It's harder to choose now that I know how temperamental employers can be, even if they seem nice at first (in order to lure you into working for them). I still don't know whether Vince is the exception or the rule to the art world. I'm looking now at less traditional art jobs and nonprofit work—those people seem like they have more potential to be friendly and welcoming. I'm still applying for assistant jobs, but at least now I know how to be an assistant.

The first interview, at this very fancy performance space, did not go well. When I arrived, the door was locked, and I could see through the frosted glass that there were a bunch of big objects in crates—they were doing some kind of installation. I knocked. I knocked again. Finally, a janitor let me in, and I asked for Bettina.

He did not reply, but just left me there. In this big white room full of strange objects. I just had to wander around, timidly crying out, "Bettina? Um . . . Bettina?"

Finally she emerges. I am dressed entirely in Brooks Brothers clothing and look like a banker. She is wearing a short Marc Jacobs dress and huge pearls, long red hair teased up in a bouffant. We sit down *on a crate* and I pull out my résumé to give to her, but she shakes her hands like, "Don't give me your filthy résumé!"

The hardest questions she asked were these:

"What were your three favorite performance pieces of this past year?" and "How much money do you think you could make here?"

The first one was the worst, because I could not say, "I find performance art ABSURD." The only pieces I could remember were from my feminist art class, and all took place in the 1970s. The more the interview went on, the worse I knew I was doing.

Finally, she slaps her hands down on the crate. "Look, I'll tell you right now. You're not getting this job."

Punch in the gut.

"Do you want to know why you're not getting this job?"

NO! I never want to know shit like this—you know this about me. Don't tell me why we're breaking up! Don't tell me what's really wrong with my outfit! DO NOT CONFRONT ME IN ANY WAY, SHAPE, OR FORM.

"Um . . . yes?"

"You come off as very shy. You shouldn't have your previous job on your CV at all, because you were only there for three months. Your salary expectations are absolutely ludicrous."

I had given $25–$30k as my salary range.

"You would be lucky to be earning twenty thousand in this environment, and the fact that you don't know that tells me that you don't know this world well enough."

I know she probably meant the performance-art world, but it kind of felt like she was talking about the world in general. I slunk away with my tail between my legs.

I have now been trying to network (I know) with tenuous connections, and so far, everyone says pretty much the same thing, that it sucks to work in any kind of creative industry because you always have to start at the bottom as a PA or settle for something that only marginally represents what you actually want to be doing, like an entertainment lawyer, or a guy who writes jingles, or a medical illustrator.

On the plus side, I've gotten a lot of free coffee. And I've met a lot of interesting people, but I hate being in a position where I'm asking for favors I haven't earned. But it's finally paid off.

I interviewed at a nonprofit art gallery, which I loved. The two women, Joan and Sally, who interviewed me were nice and laid-back. The job was "office administrator," and as long as I don't have to be somebody's personal assistant, I think it will be better than my last job with Vince. Besides, I still get to be around art. Still, one week later, and I hadn't heard back. So I called them . . . and e-mailed them . . . and basically had to act aggressive, which Bettina could tell you I am not, just to get another meeting with the codirector, Sally, who told me that they are hiring an assistant next month—me!

So that is my biggest news—I am employed! It's over in Chelsea. So far, my boss is kind and encouraging. There are also interns and artists coming in and out all day.

Best thing? I can wear jeans to work. And I get a real lunch break! What could be better than this?

I cannot convey what a big deal this is for me (job, not jeans).

In the meantime, I still have not heard from Bill about meeting up again, but he e-mailed me to tell me he's going back to Providence today to figure out what he wants to do with his life. I'm fine with that, as long as it involves staying in New York and dating me. But maybe you're right about this one. I always give guys so much credit for things they haven't even remotely demonstrated, such as empathy or kindness or . . . liking me. But I really don't know.

As part of my "new things" initiative, I applied to a writing group that meets in Park Slope once every two weeks. It seemed like it would be a good way to make friends who didn't go to Brown and who don't work with me. However, I submitted my story and made it up to an interview with the leader of the group—it's a "free" group (as in, open to all, though it costs twenty dollars a session), but it's competitive. It was definitely insane to be applying to a writing group like a job.

The first thing he does is describe the group to me.

"We've been going for ten years; I have three different groups a week meeting at my apartment."

Let's do the math. Three groups, ten people per group, twenty dollars a time = six hundred dollars a week. More than my salary—to work three hours a week. Out of his apartment. What does that job description look like? "Serve wannabe writers Trader Joe's wine in plastic cups"?

Am I just bitter that I didn't invent this job first?

In any case, it didn't feel right for me. I guess that's what I get for trying to make friends on Craigslist.

Meanwhile, Rosabelle took a job as a copy editor for a free newspaper here, which is better than making soy lattes for yuppies. She's also baking a lot of pumpkin treats that I try to get to before Buster devours them. I do have the advantage, though, because he gets scolded when he doesn't use a plate, and I don't give a shit if Rosabelle scolds me.

Also, they pulled down the shower curtain bar while having an erotic shower the other day. I walked in to find the shower curtain folded neatly over the shower drain. Rosabelle's like the Martha Stewart of breaking things. They may not work, but they definitely look nice when she's done with them.

I can't believe Rosabelle's shower curtain drama took precedence over this, but are you really leaving Astrid? Well, at the end of the day, it's your life and you have to do what's best for you, not her, as long as you don't overtly go out of your way to hurt her. I am thinking about this the way I approached leaving my job—as much as it was terrible and hard and horrible, you have to just have faith that something better will come along and it will.

Living with Rosabelle has also been so different post-college—Buster's so much more important to her now, and with her real job, she's so unavailable. Time is just more precious now . . . or maybe we're all just changing.

My advice: Don't live with a couple. Especially a couple of assholes.

Love love love,

Rachel

## Jess to Rachel

I thought performance art was miming. Maybe you didn't get the first job because you spoke at all. But congrats on the second one! That's great news!

I'm back in Beijing and arrived still looking for a job. I think it's depressing that most people our age want exactly what I want: to be journalists. They really need to stop making TV shows and movies about the thrills of being a reporter—it's setting up entire generations for extreme disappointment. A friend put me in touch with someone who graduated from Columbia Journalism School two years ago. She wrote me a really nice e-mail about how she was taught by Pulitzer Prize–winning reporters and how she landed great unpaid internships at magazines and how she started her own pie business because she couldn't find a paying journalism job in New York.

I wish everyone would stop telling me to start a blog. Meanwhile, I can't just sit around doing nothing.

I applied for another job that seemed vaguely related to public relations. I put on a boxy blazer and stupid work pants that swish when you walk and went to the interview.

The job was at a small, private Chinese PR firm run by a really aggressive woman, Blair. For the interview, she left me inside a boardroom and asked me to write five hundred words on what it means to be effective at public relations.

Um, what?

I know nothing about PR except that it involves pointy shoes and pearls, so I had printed out a lot of information on successful PR campaigns so that I could review them on the ride over. I made sure the door was closed and used my cheat sheets on my surprise essay. It felt like a teacher was going to walk in and suspend me. Afterward, Blair glanced over it, looked me and my blazer up and down, made sure I was fluent in English, and hired me on the spot. Then she ushered me over to some Chinese girls in the office, named Candy and Coco (these are the kinds of English names cutesy Chinese girls pick for themselves).

Blair sat me down and told me that her firm was making a pitch to represent the biggest music and arts festival in China and that I would be responsible for editing the Chinglish for every document in the office. She gestured to a mountain of paper. And I would be paid by the document, which, if I worked extra hard, would end up being the equivalent of six hundred dollars a month.

My first reaction, inside my head, was, "Hmm, no, thank you." But I've been unable to find a job for so long that I decided to go with it.

Instead, I said, "Sure!" and then had a silent, secret heart attack (I clutched at my blazer but no one noticed).

I turned to Candy and Coco and asked them how long they'd worked here. They started last week. I remembered seeing ads for a vacancy at this PR firm nearly every month, so I'd figured that they had a lot of employees, but from what I can tell, it just has three people. Three different people every week.

I thought about your old boss Vince.

Blair informed me that she had a woman cook lunch for all of us every day, so there was no reason to leave the office, ever. Then I *really* thought about Vince.

Then, Blair had me edit bad Chinglish for nine hours and said I could go home at 7 P.M. I did not come to China to do this. I saw my life if I stayed at the PR firm, and the dread and fear of that life. That same day, an editor at an expat magazine contacted me about an interview for a job I'd applied for weeks ago. The magazine is distributed all over Beijing, and I stayed up all night prepping for the interview because I couldn't bear the thought of spending the rest of my days editing Chinglish for Blair.

The next afternoon, I snuck out of the PR office for my magazine interview. If it sounds like I'm going crazy, that's because I am—the pace of life in Beijing is absurd. Even I can barely keep up with what I'm doing from one day to the next.

When I showed up at the office of the expat magazine, everyone was young and wearing jeans. I was asked to write and edit a few articles and interviewed with the director of the company and an editor. I felt so much more competent at these tasks than faking public relations skills. I thought I had a decent shot at the job, but I needed to make sure I was the clear choice. The editor asked me to e-mail some ideas to pitch for the magazine and so I sent her two hundred.

I got the job!

You are now reading the words of a deputy managing editor. I'm responsible for editing each article, coming up with headlines, arranging photo shoots, and basically helping out with everything else because we have a small staff.

My boss, Victoria, is a sassy Chinese-American from New York who also writes for *Slate* and the *Wall Street Journal.* I want to be her when I grow up, although she scares the shit out of me.

And so, I'm fully employed for the first time ever—finally. No one ever tells you how strange it is to actually get paid for your labor. After having so many internships, the money just feels disconnected from the actual work. I'm finally getting paid for my editing, writing, and ideas.

And, just like that, my life is completely unrecognizable from what it was last week. I wake up (always late) in the mornings and I have somewhere to be. I pick up a vegetable bun and hop into a cab, where I apply smeared eyeliner during the bumpy ride before I enter a buzzing office, where I have a desk.

It's not perfect, though. Did I mention that I am the deputy managing editor for an expat FAMILY lifestyle magazine? Yes, yes, I am. It's not cutesy or annoying—the layouts are glossy and beautiful, with travel features, recipes, restaurant reviews, and some really great articles. But still, there is a lot of focus on kids, which is not exactly where I saw my career starting. It's strange that I'll be writing about children when the only one I know is my four-year-old nephew, whose favorite thing is to play with my makeup and who once asked for a purse for his birthday. I'm not sure if this case study can be applied to the general kid population.

The office publishes four magazines, so I'm also writing features and music and book reviews for the other expat magazines, which keeps me sane. The editorial staff at the office is young (most of us seem to be under thirty), gossipy, and full of Brits, Americans, and a handful of Australians, which means entire afternoons are wasted on arguing about the correct word for swimwear (swimsuit, bathers, swimming costume, *budgie smugglers?*) while each nationality declares superiority. Office dress code seems to be anything goes besides budgie smugglers.

The managing director sometimes brings his dog Xiao Xiong (Little Bear), who is currently sitting at my feet.

When I told my editor, Victoria, that this was my first real job, she said, "*This* is your first *real* job? You're kidding me. This isn't a job. This is summer camp." Which makes her my strict, intimidating camp counselor, especially when she edits my copy with a red pen, or circles a phrase and writes "NO" or "WHY?" or "SOUNDS LIKE CHINGLISH."

We have a very strange relationship, because we laugh together, but we aren't particularly close. And sometimes her remarks are slightly offensive, or she turns her back to walk away when I'm still in the middle of a sentence. I imagine that this is what it would be like to have an older sister.

Together we plan the content for the entire magazine, edit the columns, and organize the layouts. However, I don't have my work visa yet, and that makes me panic because I feel that I could be deported at any moment. My current Chinese visa expires in a few months. Minor detail.

Meanwhile, I'm still trying to figure out how to navigate the co-worker/friend territory. My entire office often gets drunk together after work, and there's many a handsome enough expat at each gathering. Getting drunk with coworkers is unnerving, especially when most of you are single and of similar ages. You start getting totally trashed, everyone is a little too touchy, and then the next day you're back in the office, passive-aggressively asking them for page forty-three's layout. This, more than anything, is the reason you shouldn't ever date anybody at work. The sexual tension is fun, but then page forty-three gets really fucked up.

Anyway, the new job means I'm going to tell Astrid I'm moving out soon.

I'm off.

Love,

The Worst Aunt Ever

**DECEMBER 5**

## Rachel to Jess

Oh my God, does this mean that we're officially adults now? I still feel like I'm just playing at being employed, but now that Astrid, Rosabelle, and you all have jobs, I think we just might be on the verge. CONGRATULATIONS, by the way! I'm so glad you ran like hell from the badly paid PR job. The magazine sounds like what you've always wanted: no blazers, no swishy pants, puppies in the office. Oh, and writing, of course.

However, you are wrong about Victoria acting like an older sister. An older sister does not make subtly offensive comments—she makes directly offensive comments, sees you crying, and then backpedals and tells you that you are perfect. Also, she never lets you use the phone. It's obvious you grew up with older brothers. Mostly because you never share clothing.

And I agree about being paid for working. It must have to do with direct deposit. If we were paid in gold coins at the end of every shift, I think we would feel the connection more.

I think that we can both agree that our new jobs are exponentially better compared to what we almost/did have. I listen to Ryan Adams and Joni Mitchell and Nico (all singing about Chelsea, where my beautiful loft office space is located) on my commute to work and on my much-loved lunch hour. It is so great. TELL NO ONE.

Chelsea is gritty but full of glamorous people and so . . . fake-gritty. There are a lot of homeless people and a lot of art galleries in buildings that look like factories and usually were (mine was) and no trees. Cracked sidewalks and women with huge bouffant hair and gay men walking dogs and lots of girls like me in leggings and tall boots and scarves smoking and carrying coffee to our art jobs. I'm beginning to feel like I fit in.

However, there's a strange guy who mans the elevator at work, and he's taken to calling me Dimples. I stare at the ceiling and count the floors.

I had blocked Bill Broadwick from my mind since he disappeared (frustrating to know that he could actually be back, just a few blocks away, not calling me). I don't think I told you, but I've been meeting up with Platonic Nick from Brown a lot lately. Why can't I fall in love with him? He'd cook me pasta and watch old movies with me every night. Also, he gives great massages and always texts back. But you know how it is, I just see him as a friend and vice versa. Maybe this is because of his name, Platonic Nick—he is cursed in this sense. I think we're both kind of lonely, so we turn to each other for distraction—of the nonsexual kind.

I am actually beginning to like New York again. Now that I'm not on the Upper East Side and am dividing my time between Brooklyn and Chelsea instead, it's gorgeous and all the things people always say it is. I spent yesterday afternoon at the New York Public Library, which made me think of Joan Didion, and which really struck a chord with me—it really is set up like a cathedral for books. It was beautiful, and I got a lot of good writing done.

Point being, though, I was in Midtown during the holiday season and it didn't make me hate the city.

I've been staying in a lot lately, and not just because it's been bitterly cold. My new resolution is to save money, and so I've stopped going out. I don't want to be in a position where I can't afford to leave this job or even this city. So I've been spending my time running a lot—as much as I can out in the cold (scary because no health insurance for the first three months—so if I break a leg getting hit by a bus, it's just going to have to stay that way) and writing as much as I can. It's hard. Working all day takes it out of me.

I still can't help thinking: Is this the best life I could have? I miss having the time to mull over ideas for stories and to actually write. Tomorrow, the plan is to get up early to go to Café Angelique (the good one at 49 Grove, NOT the bad one at 68 Bleecker) and write before I go to work.

In only a few weeks I'll be in Wisconsin for Christmas, riding horses with my sister and pretending that we are the girls from *Sense and Sensibility* (don't you dare judge me, hillbilly kisser).

I'm glad it's almost Christmas break. I'm going to keep running when I get home to Wisconsin. Right now, I'm going to read *O* magazine, which my mother sent me, because apparently I am forty.

WRITE BACK.

I LOVE YOU. And capital letters.

Love,

Dimples

P.S. What does a four-year-old carry in a purse? Crayons? Lipstick?

## Jess to Rachel

I can't move my knees. I just Googled "delayed-onset ski paralysis," but it turns out this is not a thing. Sometimes Google is blocked here, sometimes not. YOU NEVER KNOW. One time I urgently needed to know how to kill a spider without looking at it and the Internet refused to tell me. I still don't know!

Last night I returned from a skiing trip with Astrid and some of her coworkers. We drove a few hours away from Beijing, but the snow is artificial (it's not naturally very snowy near Beijing, but why let a good mountain go to waste?).

Learn from my mistakes: Do not ever give into snow sports peer pressure OR take your first snowboarding lesson in Mandarin without *first* taking a Mandarin lesson in snowboarding vocabulary. All I remember is being near tears halfway down the mountain with my Chinese instructor (the only word she could say in English was "No"), looking down, and picking out which pile of fake snow I would prefer to die in because anything was better than continuing to try to snowboard. Luckily, I made it down the mountain alive, but I never went back up again.

Invigorated by near-death, telling Astrid I wanted to move out didn't seem like such a big deal. I think she had been sensing my growing unhappiness, and at dinner that night I finally just told her how I felt and that it will be better for our friendship in the long run if we lived separately. And actually, she didn't freak the fuck out. She agreed, and seemed to take it really well, until a few glasses of wine later, when her eyes filled with tears.

"You're abandoning me. We came here together, we spend all of our time together, and you're abandoning me. You're my family, and you're abandoning me."

I felt like a terrible person, but she and I can't keep going around in circles like this. I tried to explain how I needed to focus on my life and that when she and I are together, entire days go by where we don't leave the couch or we just sit in a café and talk all day. I didn't come to China to spend my days with Astrid, but I didn't know how to say this. Finally, I explained another point that has been on my mind lately: Eventually, one of us will get a boyfriend who would probably spend most nights at our place, and neither of us wants to live with the other one's boyfriend. When I said that, something seemed to click. She got it.

The name Maxwell was not mentioned once.

Anyway. I've already found a new roommate and place to live.

Before I even told Astrid I was moving out, I responded to an online ad from a twenty-one-year-old guy from New Zealand named Chris, and no, I'm not attracted to him because he has huge muscles and blond hair. He has a beach house in New Zealand that his twin brother is currently living in. I'm not going to lie; half the reason I wanted to live with him is because I was imagining myself at this beach house.

I asked him if he's the type of guy to sleep with a different Chinese girl every night and Chris said, "No. Sometimes the same one." Yeah, I asked this during the roommate interview, and I still got accepted.

He seems friendly and fun, and he said he wants a roommate to actually be his friend. He laughed a lot. However, the place reeks of boy. It's covered in popcorn and beer . . . but it would be nice to have someone to visit in New Zealand?

I move in two days!

After our first meeting, Chris invited me out to have a beer at a bar downstairs. I don't entirely understand his accent. At times, it was harder to understand his English than to interpret Mandarin with locals. He had to repeat himself three or four times before I got what he was saying.

From what I can tell, Chris says *cunt* a lot. But he says it in his accent, so it's not as jarring as it would be in ours. "He's such a stupid cunt." The first few times, I didn't even notice it because I thought he was saying, "He's such a stupid cat," or "He's such a stupid cad." I found myself laughing or agreeing before I realized what he was saying. And then I thought, am I encouraging the usage of *cunt*? He only refers to males as cunts, which is even more confusing. I never call girls dicks. He's definitely brasher than I'm used to.

I have never had someone call me soft before, but Chris does all the time. As in, "You don't like looking at my scars? Or talking about cunts? You're fawking [NZ accent] soft." I'm also cheeky. Cheeky and soft. Which sounds like really nice toilet paper.

The lease expires when Chris goes back to New Zealand in a few months, so it's not long-term, but it was available immediately. I hope this is a good idea.

Love,

Jess

P.S. Why do you read O magazine? Are you looking for advice on how to get your twenty-two-year-old son to move out of your house? You wear colorful knitted sweaters and you drink hot water in the morning because it's cleansing and you make time for yourself, because you deserve it? That's okay. Just tell me what Oprah would tell me to do.

**DECEMBER 22**

## Jess to Rachel

drunky drunk drink

my new kiwi flatemaste came hone and he smoked on my winsow sill. it was actually nice. then he climbed in my bed. but i kicked him out. no worries.

danced like crazzy at a chinese club.

miss you heapssssssssssssssssssssssssssssssssssssssssssssssssssssssssssssssssssssssssss
sssssssssssssssssssssssssssssssssssssssssssssssssssssssssss

### Later that day

## Rachel to Jess

Don't sleep with your roommate!!! You never had this problem when you lived with Astrid. . . .

## Jess to Rachel

Rachel! Rachel! Wake up! Wake the fuck up! I met a boy! All because I live with Chris, and apparently boys are like Russian dolls—if you find one, he leads to other ones (who are inside of him???). Or boys beget boys who beget boys or something. (I don't know, Rachel! Old Testament? WHAT DOES IT EVEN MEAN?)

Sorry for the yelling. I don't know where to begin. There. Is. A. Brazilian. Boy. Asleep. In. My. Bed. THERE IS A BRAZILIAN BOY ASLEEP IN MY BED! I think he is a belated Christmas present.

He plays on Chris's rugby team, and I met him at a terrible, terrible trashy Chinese nightclub when I was out with Chris. I wish I had some witty story about how we started talking, but we were mostly SHOUTING into each other's ears to be heard above the music. It was dark, there were strobe lights, and I was holding a gin and tonic in a plastic cup. I think the conversation went something like:

Me: WHERE ARE YOU FROM?

Him: NEW ZEALAND.

Me: OH! Like Chris! NEW ZEALANDERS UNITE!

Him: NO! BRAZIL.

I said it wasn't a good story.

The rest of the rugby team attempted to sit down in a crowded booth and I ended up on top of him. Bruno. His name is Bruno, and it turns out he is half-Chinese, half-Brazilian. He has a heavy accent and he is a male god. Dark beautiful skin, thick lips, broad shoulders. Somehow, sitting on his lap turned into full-blown making out, and I just didn't care that I was in public. At all. This is growth, right? I'm growing. Since we're both part-Asian, we compared our Asian glows. Do you remember this phenomenon? It's when I (and most other Asians) drink alcohol, and our skin turns bright red, our eyes become bloodshot, and our skin becomes hot? Well, Bruno has it too (as will our children).

At 4 A.M., he came home with Chris and me, because he lives outside the city, and now he's fast asleep in my bed. I can't sleep when boys are in my bed! One person tells you that you snore and you're doomed for life (Damn you, Astrid!). Besides, there is a Brazilian god in my bed—who can sleep at a time like this?!

How do I make him stay there . . . forever? He was a really good kisser.

He is completely naked. Nothing happened besides making out, but in his drunken tiredness, he flung off all of his clothes.

What do you say to a naked Brazilian god when they wake up in your bed? I would try to Google this, but currently Google is blocked in Beijing AGAIN.

Text me your reply. I don't care if it costs three dollars to text China.

AHHHH,

Jess

*Later that day*

## Rachel to Jess

Look, are you even sure he speaks English? I have no advice for you! In movie scenes like yours, the girl often brings back a bag of bagels and coffee and then they walk around Central Park, and the guy sort of brushes the girl's hair out of her eyes, squints, and says, "Let's do this again," and he gets into a yellow cab. So . . . do that.

I am at home and just finished a juice fast. I will never drink juice again. I did lose four pounds (all back now, in case you were wondering—WORTHLESS). I would not recommend.

Even back home and faint with hunger, I've gotten more writing done than I have in the six months since graduation. My dad and I just sit up in his office with our backs to each other and type, type, type.

It's such a peaceful life.

It hasn't snowed here yet, so everything is brown and muddy and gray, with bare tree branches and huge flocks of blackbirds, and in this world, New York City does not exist.

Back there, I still have really low periods maybe once or twice a week, where it's impossible to see anyone. Here, though, I feel steady and calm and peaceful, and I start to wonder: Even though I love my work environment, do I really love my job? Is that what I want to be doing for the next twenty years? And why am I even in New York, other than the fact that it was the default graduation plan?

To my older sister, who traveled around forever and then moved to Madison after graduation, these questions seem so stupid. "Rachel, nobody is making you stay! Can't you just leave?" she asks.

I hadn't even considered that. When you want to work in the art/publishing/creative universe, New York seems like the only place to be. But when you hear it said out loud like that, it seems so obvious that there are other great places.

I've been going back and forth with my future plans. I always thought I'd go to creative writing grad school at a certain point, but I feel like that's just following too closely in my father's footsteps. Also, I really only want to go to one school, and the deadline for the Iowa Writers' Workshop is in just a few days. On the other hand, I just read a book of short stories from the Workshop's alumni, and so many people just write about being middle-aged professors who hate their spouses and have affairs with their students, or who have to run their English departments. It's hardly fiction, and I feel like I haven't lived enough to really focus on my writing. I don't think I'm ready.

When I really let myself dream big, in my fantasy I get to study film and live in Paris, the city I love the most. The six months I spent there during college made me so happy, and I've always vowed to find a way to return.

And so I've applied for a Fulbright fellowship. I just want to see if I'll get it. No, that's a lie. I applied for it because I want one SO BADLY. Instant ticket to a new life. Rosabelle also applied for one, to Argentina. I think being at home makes adventures seem both more exciting and more possible, but also somehow more imaginary (like, I don't think about how to sign up for French health insurance, only planning my outfits for wandering along the Seine).

Also, you don't deserve this, because you were far too flippant toward Oprah and her wisdom, but she had some advice that I think you should know about.

You can make your own potpourri and turn it into sachets!

Just kidding.

ACTUALLY, her advice was: Stop looking for The One, but before you do, think hard about what you really want. You're supposed to write a list of everything you want in someone, and you should be very specific, even down to eye color, height, weight, etc., and then you just let it go. So of course I did it. Thinking, I'll never be able to let it go.

Okay, and yes, this might be embarrassing, but here is the list (you make one too):

1. Must be very sensitive and yet strong and decisive about everyday life

2. Hilarious but in the throw-off sort of way (not trying to make everyone laugh all of the time)

3. Must kind of sort of want children but be willing to wait a very long time

4. Pretty eyes

5. Foreign is ideal. I like making fun of accents.

6. Medium build, slim but fit

7. Athletic but not obnoxiously so

8. Interested in the arts, especially books

9. Must think that I am delightful and endearing, always

10. Must never fight with me, or be very satisfying to fight with (as in, I can always convince him that I am right)

11. Loves dogs

12. Speaks more than one language

13. Has interesting family, so we are not bored over the holidays and I am reassured about our children's genetics

14. Charm too is most important but must not flirt with other women

15. Between five ten and six feet

16. Interesting career, must not work too much (no more than ten hours a day *usually*)

17. Love to travel, desire to live abroad

18. Calm, deep, pensive

19. Should smoke some of the time, socially, but not too much; be willing to quit eventually

20. Have interesting group of friends, much like mine: very smart but also charming

21. Must be intelligent about obscure topics

22. Should appreciate my writing

23. Should always over-respond to my text messages and e-mails and initiate contact much of the time

24. Should be adept at hunting, playing polo, and other terribly aristocratic activities

25. Should be wonderful in bed

STOP JUDGING ME.

Oh: The point of that list being (and this is important) that you write it, you let it go, and then you get him! The universe just sends him your way. Like custom-ordering stationery or a monogrammed pillowcase. That is the magic of it. And apparently it totally happened to all of these women in O magazine.

You have to remember, though: You can't go out looking for it. And you can't live your life eliminating guys off your list because you think they don't have these qualities. You just do this exercise once, give it to the universe, and then completely forget about it.

Okay. There's your daily dose of my self-absorption. Now, yours.

Love!

Rach

---

**DECEMBER 30**

*Two hours later*

## Jess to Rachel

"Wonderful in bed" is a little vague to me. I imagine him performing magic tricks for you while you sit up in bed wearing a silk robe, clapping your hands, delighted. "It's just wonderful!" Also, hunting and polo? Seriously? Well, at least someone will love those guys.

For mine, I had to remember everyone I have ever dated or tried but failed to get.

I took this pretty seriously with the mantra "Be careful what you wish for!" running through my head. What if I met the perfect guy who fit everything on my list, except he was a Scientologist who likes talking about motorcycles? What then? The universe would just reply, "Look, you gave me a list and I delivered. I gave you a man who has *no body odor* who likes *Fleetwood Mac* and now you want me to tweak him? Deal with it."

This is what I came up with:

1. Very funny in my particular taste

2. Adores me and only me

3. Dark hair

4. Beautiful hands

5. Gorgeous smile

6. Has close friends he confides in (If a guy doesn't share his feelings with anyone, he doesn't have any. Friends or feelings. Period. I'm not going to be the one to fix him.)

7. I must find him very sexy. (Don't care if the world thinks he's gross as long as I don't.)

8. Secure enough to dance in public and be silly with me

9. Will carry a conversation when I am being too awkward

10. Intuitive

11. Open-minded and intelligent, but never condescending

12. Nonreligious

13. Taste in music is 80 percent like mine—I couldn't bear to resign myself to long drives listening to heavy metal or classic rock for the rest of my life.

14. Gets excited about life and new experiences

15. Polite to strangers

16. Ambitious but not so much that he neglects me, finds me very lazy

17. His presence must emanate safety, fun, and sexiness (like a firefighter).

18. Capacity for deep feelings

19. My singing, irrational habits, and snoring are endearing to him (this is a wish list, right?)

20. Healthy

21. Must not be a father yet

22. Can be serious

23. Loyal

24. Provokes a racing heart

25. Reads fiction and history

26. Unpretentious

27. Must have been looking for someone exactly like me, give or take fifteen pounds and a social smoking habit

28. Deep voice

29. Not too hairy

30. Never smells bad (Unless stranded without access to soap—then it is forgiven. I'm not a monster.)

31. Spontaneous but not in the "Look at the new face tattoo I just got!" way

32. Does not easily sunburn

33. Really good at sex and acts that precede it

34. Infinitely interesting, but not so much so that I feel infinitely boring in comparison

35. Not self-righteous

36. Excellent memory (I feel like I've met so many guys who just can't remember shit. What's the point if they can't remember?)

37. Willing to live in a different country but also willing to settle down somewhere in America

**DECEMBER 30**

*Ten minutes later*

## Jess to Rachel

38. cuddly
THE END

P.S. *Cuddly* is not code for *fat.*

*One minute later*

## Jess to Rachel

Shit. I forgot SUCH an important one:

39. Asks questions and listens to the answers

THE END!!! I GIVE YOU THIS LIST, UNIVERSE!

P.S. As I write this, Bruno is still snoring and taking up the entire bed. He fits nothing on the list except that he is brunette and sexy. That's like going to a grocery store to shop for Thanksgiving dinner and coming back with a frozen turkey and a bottle of Diet Coke. Good enough for now.

## Rachel to Jess

Well, it's the New Year, and I'm back in New York. On my final night at home, I was packing and found a bunch of empty Southern Comfort bottles under my bed—in high school, my friend Emily asked me to take them home after a party at her house. Years ago, I had shoved them behind my sleeping bag and forgotten about them entirely until I was searching for a backpack and found them ten minutes before leaving for the airport.

So guess where they still are? My parents are planning on redoing my old room, and I'm hoping they don't find them and think I've taken to drinking an entire bottle of SoCo . . . alone . . . in bed . . . every night for the past week. Little do they know, after they went to bed I was actually smoking a half a pack of cigarettes behind the garage in a parka and fingerless gloves.

Now that I'm back at the nonprofit and assuming my adult persona again, I am surreptitiously writing this e-mail while supposedly writing board minutes. Bored minutes—ha. Gets me every time.

Being at work is such a harsh shift. At home, I was curling up in front of the fire, I'm in a city full of dirty snow, getting up at dawn (this is always the hardest part for me), and walking through the cold to the office, where there are about two hundred irate messages from artists all somehow pissed that we took two weeks off at Christmas.

The other big difference about being back in New York is seeing my therapist again. It was freeing, in a way, not to have to "report back" to Claudia during my Christmas break about self-destructive behavior (smoking behind the house, sleeping eleven hours a night). She always asks the questions I don't want to answer. I know that she'll just want to talk about whether my dream of Paris will be any different from the realities of New York, once I'm there. I don't know that it will be, but I do know that Paris is more beautiful. It's so hard to make myself go to our appointments. I guess it's kind of like going to a dentist: You *know* it's beneficial for you, but in the moment you're paying so much money for someone to poke painfully at your gums.

This was Claudia's favorite topic for my first session back: "Did you apply to creative writing grad school?" No. "Why not?" I felt like I wasn't ready, and I'm not sure I want to teach creative writing. "What does this have to do with your self-esteem?" Okay, Claudia, you got me! I am terrified of being exposed as a fraud. Also, I have a fear of an imagined group of tweed-jacket-wearing assholes pointing at sentences I've written, reading them out loud to one another, and laughing hysterically. Claudia thinks that I have a tendency to dramatically catastrophize things, but I think she just SECRETLY HATES ME.

I'm getting so antsy thinking about all of the many, many possible futures that could still happen. I'm still waiting to hear back from the Fulbright. It's all about waiting.

My back-up was the master's program in Cinematographic Studies at the Sorbonne. I just want to be in Paris. It costs almost nothing in tuition, and health care is included! It is, however, taught in French. The application included a six-hour-long French test last week and a two-hour-long conversation with a French professor. These things are so strange, because you end up having conversations about things you would never talk about in your native language.

Professor: So, what is the national origin of your name?

Me: German and English.

Professor: Okay . . .

Me: Oh, did you mean *Rachel*? I think it's Jewish.

*Pause.*

Me: But I'm not Jewish.

[I remember the Vichy government and the complicated French history with the Jews.]

Me: But they have a wonderful culture! Such a rich . . . cultural . . . history.

*Pause.*

Me: *Au revoir les enfants* was such a sad movie.

Professor: Yes.

Me: Very, VERY sad.

I blame this total catastrophe on my faulty preparation. The only thing I did was watch the French news every day, but I kind of hate watching the news. Probably because this is what it sounds like to me: asdjkhf FIRE asdkjfhkj DEAD askdjh THE SOMETHING asdkhjfkj EITHER IRAN OR IRAQ.

Rosabelle's Fulbright application also made it to the next stage for Argentina and I am relieved that we both made it. Selfishly, because it is less awkward around the apartment; nonselfishly, because I really love her and think that she deserves it. There have been so many nights when I've come home distraught and she drops everything, sends Buster into their room, and pours me a glass of wine. And as much as he drives me crazy by eating all of my food and accidentally using my toothbrush, Buster has brought out a lot of the best parts of Rosabelle, while also proving that people are really strange. Once, as a joke, Buster wore Rosabelle's pink pajama bottoms that have a cupcake pattern. But now, he has taken to wearing them all the time and it's just getting weird.

For the moment, I shall have to settle for hugs from a hilarious man. That's right. Saul's back in my life; he called on New Year's Eve. The last time I actually saw him was on a Monday after work and we were both in our office clothes and beaten down and bland compared to our upbeat college selves.

This is my trip down memory lane—one in which it feels like I can go back and take care of unfinished business for the years he and I flirted in college and never even kissed. Off to dinner with him soon. I will report back.

Love,

Rachel

P.S. What's going on with the Brazilian sex god in China??

**JANUARY 20**

## Jess to Rachel

FACT OF THE DAY: *Gatinha* is Brazilian Portuguese for "foxy lady."

I know because Bruno calls me this. I know that my brain has turned to absolute jelly as well, because I fucking love it when he calls me this.

Where to begin, Rachel? Honestly. Honestly.

Well, *honestly*? Bruno doesn't speak the best English, which means that I can't be sarcastic with him or even attempt to be funny with words—he just doesn't get it. After marathon conversations with Maxwell that amounted to nothing, I take this as a good sign.

Most nights with Bruno are spent in bars, shouting to be heard, not being understood even when heard, drinking alcohol, and wasting time until we can leave at a respectable hour and go back to my apartment and I get to have wild rainforest sex with my Brazilian lover.

At college there was so much talking, talking, talking, but Bruno doesn't talk—he pulls me toward him and kisses me. Even though he remains mostly a mystery to me, we share little things, like our forays into Chinese grocery stores to pick up noodles or haggling together as we buy pirated DVDs from hidden shops (which he has to watch with English subtitles). But when he hands me my coat, pulls up my hood, and takes my hand, I feel happy even though our deepest conversations are limited to postsex basics that fade into him falling asleep and snoring softly.

And because we can't talk, I feel uninhibited. I like that he knows what he is doing, because God knows I don't. It's different from sleeping with American guys, at least the ones at Brown, where it always seemed to feel like there was a GOAL that must be met. With Bruno, it feels natural. I also feel uninhibited because he's only in Beijing for a few more weeks. I'm not really sure where this is going, but I'm having fun, and it's been a long time since I've felt this way.

The biggest thing that I don't like is his utter and complete lack of ambition. As in: He dropped out of his university Chinese class months ago, but didn't tell his family, so he has been doing nothing for the past three months. Why should this matter? He's not my boyfriend. And he's moving back to Brazil in two weeks. But it bothers me.

Anyway, we actually lost a little bit of time together because I got sick. It's bitterly cold in Beijing, the air is dry, and I had a sore throat I couldn't shake. My dad told me to go see a real doctor, but I've always wanted to try Traditional Chinese Medicine. Astrid came with me to a TCM clinic, where she asked for a massage and they suggested a "cupping" treatment to cure my ailments.

Okay, I know you don't know what this means, and neither did I. Cupping is like a massage, but instead of someone massaging you, they take empty glass cups, place a lit match in them to heat the air inside, then place the cups facedown on your back so that it forms a tight, painful suction. Then they drag the cups across your skin as they pull out toxins and leave you with circular purple bruises the size of tennis balls. It will also cause you to continually yelp the only Chinese word you will remember: *Teng.* Translation: *Pain.* Teng! Teng! TENG!

Meanwhile, Astrid was in the next room, getting a relaxing massage.

Cupping is supposed to cure anything but cholera. Apparently I had cholera.

I felt awful, maybe even *more* awful, after the treatment. But Chris, who was also sick and loves an excuse to get new drugs, went to a doctor who prescribed antibiotics, and was healed.

He offered me some pills as I was heading over to Bruno's. "Take two!" he yelled from the couch, as I put a sachet of pills in my purse and headed out.

Later that night, as Bruno and I got ready for bed, I took the medicine. While we were lying in the darkness, talking softly ("What do you call this body part in Portuguese?"), I began to see the most beautiful images of things that don't exist—colors melding together, cars that drive on their sides, birds with feathers and fur, and it was all so beautiful. I wasn't frightened at all, but completely in awe. I stared up at these incredible creatures and objects that appeared above us as I kept asking Bruno what he thought of them and if he liked them too.

That's pretty much the last thing I remember. And then—a big blank.

Ten hours later, I stirred slightly and I thought I was at home in

Amarillo because I could sense the light on my face and it felt so much like the light from my childhood bedroom. I felt content to be at home. And then I rolled over onto a Brazilian. I froze BECAUSE THERE WAS A MAN NEXT TO ME IN MY BED. Thank God I figured out where I was and who he was before he woke up.

Turns out I accidentally took two of Chris's sleeping pills, which can cause hallucinations and slight amnesia. This is why I don't do drugs. Bruno mentioned a movie we watched last night, and I remember nothing. Nothing but the fantastic images that appeared before me.

Then I asked Bruno if I sounded insane when I was describing my hallucinations, and he didn't know what I was talking about. He said I sounded like I always do.

RACHEL. HE DOESN'T SPEAK ENGLISH WELL ENOUGH TO KNOW IF I AM HALLUCINATING.

Fjdaklfjdsaklfjdkasljfdakslfjdaklfjdsalkfdsjferssjfkdjaljfdkjiwreirue-iawojakfjdskl!

Okay, I go die now.
    Love,
    The Girl Who Rufied Herself

## Rachel to Jess

Jessica. You roofied yourself? YOU ROOFIED YOURSELF?
Also, you don't know how to spell *roofie*.
Your hallucinations sound amazing. Do you think that sleeping pills work that way for everyone?
Just . . . kidding?

Stay away from anything stronger than vitamin C! You probably wore yourself out from having too much sex. But Bruno sounds like the ideal man to hibernate with for winter. I feel like I want to give you a sexual blessing. Mazel tov!

I haven't been "blessed" for about a year now—the only thing even vaguely romantic in my life is Saul.

Before our date, I showed my friend Sally from work Saul's online pictures of him filling a suitcase with Jell-O (to take to a picnic). She said he looked borderline insane. I can see that. He's the guy who will wear any hat at any time, even when it is not a hat but a poinsettia, and also he is at an Orthodox Jewish wedding. And he's holding a baby squirrel. And he's an investment banker. He is less like a man, and more like the incarnation of Mad Libs, where his whole personality is composed of randomly chosen words.

So naturally, I am still smitten with him.

I know that right now you are also remembering the countless conversations you and I had about why he never made a move, to my complete and utter confusion. But when he told me that he'll be in town for a few weeks, I really wanted to see him.

I met Saul at a restaurant around the corner from my house. He was very easy to find, because he was wearing a tie that was covered in bottle caps. He cried, "KAPELKE-ELF!" from across the restaurant and gave me a big hug. I ordered us a bottle of white wine, and he kept making sure my glass was full. I even liked him after he dusted off and kissed a wayward French fry that had fallen astray. He is way too nice to everyone and everything, but I could use some nice in my life.

He still resembles Larry David, whom I've always had a thing for (they are the only two men in the world who are so funny that you forget they look like Larry David).

Even though I hadn't seen him in months, we sat close and he reminded me about a bunch of happy memories at Brown. But I had work in the morning, so after lingering over our wine, I walked him to the subway to point him in the direction of the friend's house where he is staying.

And here I am: going to bed alone.

But now, at home, why am I thinking about Saul and a future with him? He doesn't even live in New York! He lives in Boston! And focusing energy on him when I spend all of my time trying to find a way to move to Paris is completely beyond me. If he came to Paris, he'd wear a baguette on his head and try to eat a beret.

I've finally adjusted to waking up at normal hours and not feeling dead all day. I've started leaving early for work to get coffee around the corner before I get on the train. I sit in the window seat of the café and watch all the harried commuters scramble to work. I think about the French Fulbright committee and how I really hope they pick me. And I think about you, all the way in China, probably having sex with Bruno for the fourth time that day.

Love,

Kapelke-Elf

**FEBRUARY 1**

## Jess to Rachel

Fuuuuuuuuuck.

Fuck.

This morning the condom broke.

I don't know what to do. I don't know what to do. I don't know what to do.

PICK UP YOUR PHONE. WHO SLEEPS AT 3 A.M.??????????? WHO DOES THAT?!?!?!?!??!

I don't know how this happened. Just, like, that in one moment, everything was fine, and the act was over, and then . . .

I panicked. I just fucking panicked. I sat straight up and as soon as I saw what happened, I went crazy. I asked him if he had STDs over and over again. I yelled: DO YOU HAVE ANY STDS? HOW MANY GIRLS HAVE YOU SLEPT WITH? EVER? DID YOU ALWAYS WEAR A CONDOM? WHY DID THE CONDOM BREAK? WHY DID IT BREAK? WHY? WHY? WHY?

He was speechless and then began answering in fragments—he had an HIV test before he was given his Chinese visa. He's slept with three Chinese girls since he's been in China.

WHAT KINDS OF GIRLS? WHAT KINDS OF GIRLS?????? NICE GIRLS OR SLUTTY GIRLS? WHAT KINDS OF GIRLS, BRUNO??????????????????????????

I threw my clothes on and ran outside to catch a cab back to my apartment. It had snowed the night before, but I didn't even register the snowfall until I was already inside the taxi. I shouted my address to the driver and slumped against the seat as I tried frantically to recall every single *Seventeen* magazine article I had ever read.

But all I could remember were the fucking dumb theories girls would ask about that turned out to be NOT be true. Like girls who write in asking if after they have unprotected sex, can they hop backward and not get pregnant? Or rinse with vinegar to prevent STDs. I COULDN'T REMEMBER ANY OF THE ADVICE OR FACTS!

I can't believe how stupid I am. I can't believe how blissful I was, how delighted I was to be sleeping with a beautiful Brazilian, becoming empowered, being a woman who feels SEXY for once, having an adventure, when ALL I WAS ACTUALLY DOING WAS FUCKING A STRANGER WHO COULD HAVE AIDS AND NOW MAYBE I FUCKING DO TOO.

As soon as I got home I ran into a hot shower to try to scrub my entire body clean. I was in there so long that the hot water ran cold and I just leaned against the toilet (because I still shower over a fucking toilet) and I cried. I don't know what to do. I don't know Bruno's past. I don't even know Bruno. Why didn't I listen to the fervent religious people of the Bible Belt who preached no sex before marriage? Why did I think none of that applied to me? Is this my punishment? What if I have HIV? What if I have herpes? What if I have thrown my life away just to feel sexy and exotic?

I got out of the shower and went to an expat hospital clinic where I had to tell a stern Australian-Chinese female doctor that I need the morning-after pill. Then when I told her I also wanted to be tested for STDs (ALL OF THEM), she was visibly shocked.

"Did you even know this person?"

NO.

She told me to take two pills immediately. I did. Then I reread the instructions which say, "Take one pill. Twelve hours later, take second pill." What?? I read this moments after I had swallowed both.

Also, I am supposed to be SICK right now and I don't feel ANYTHING. I would like to be writhing in pain just so I know they are working.

I hate sex now. I am so over sex.

Can you PLEASE call this number:

1-800-330-1271 (toll-free)

Because I can't figure out how to call it from China.

I need to know if I fucked up the effectiveness of this pill by taking BOTH pills at the same time. I took them five hours after I had sex. Plan B pills.

I didn't want half-Asian babies THIS BADLY, Universe. Never making a joke again.

Please, please, please call the number for me.

Jess

*Later that day*

## Rachel to Jess

Calm down and don't worry! This happens to people all the time!!!!

You are doing everything right, you really are. You will be okay, I know you will, but we will make sure of it nevertheless. I'm so sorry my phone was off—I hope that you could reach Astrid. Practicalities: I just spoke with that number and they said that some places, like Planned Parenthood, actually tell you to take them both at once. They also said that some people don't have any side effects at all and that you may get your period a week early or a week late, but if it's more than a week late you should take a pregnancy test.

I am going to call my sister (the nurse one, not the college student one) to confirm (I will not tell her who it is).

You will be okay.

More soon when I get home from work.

Love,

R

*Later that day*

## Jess to Rachel

thank you thank you thank you
love you love you love you

## Rachel to Jess

Are you okay? Did you ever get side effects? I conferred with my sister and she said that the only reason to take them twelve hours apart is because most people get bad cramps and both at once will make it worse. But if you didn't have any side effects, it doesn't mean it's not working. Your period should come normally. She also confirmed this with a doctor she works with.

This might lighten the mood for you. When I called the Plan B hotline, I was at work (they were only open during normal business hours—this is not when most of us have baby emergencies, people!). I waited until Joan and Sally were in a meeting outside the building, but we have an intern who I just couldn't shake. I went down the hall, but it still echoes. I refused to say on the call that it was for "my friend" because who am I—one of those girls who writes into *Seventeen*? No.

The intern comes out of the office to go to the bathroom and I turn around to see her just as I'm screeching at the Plan B people: "I'm not going to get pregnant, RIGHT?" She scuttled back into the office. When I came back in, she just looked up at me with big eyes.

"IT'S FOR MY FRIEND!"

Whatever, she leaves in a month.

You will like sex again.

You don't have an STD. I promise. Promise, promise.

If you are really worried, go back and talk to your doctor. But everybody I talked to seems convinced that you'll be fine.

Now might not be the time to ask, but what's going to happen between you and Bruno?

And let me know how you are.

Love love love love,

Rachel

## Jess to Rachel

Relief.

My doctor called and I do not have HIV. I do not have any STDs. I am not pregnant.

There are fireworks exploding all over the city for Chinese New Year and everyone is out on the streets celebrating and I'm celebrating my news too.

As you can expect, I'm feeling so much better than before, but I'm also trying to distract myself from thinking about Bruno because he flew to São Paulo this morning. The next time I saw him after the debacle, he was really sweet, but careful around me. We still slept together, tentatively, and then he left this morning. When I crawled back into my empty bed, my room seemed so quiet and lonely. I never imagined sharing so many intimate moments with someone and then having him disappear from my life forever. I'll never call him, I'll never write him, I'll never look him up. All we had rested on the physical. I kissed him knowing it was going to be the last time.

And this coincides with my two months with Chris ending. He's heading back to New Zealand forever tomorrow. Even Maxwell said that he's heading back to the United States soon. For so many people, Beijing is just a brief stopover. It feels like I just got here, but everyone I like is leaving.

At least I have Astrid, who is pulling me out of the gray bleakness. I don't have to be alone right now, because she'll always invite me over and stay up all night with me and offer to share her bed. Her love is so unconditional. I don't care about Maxwell anymore and I don't care that she and I spent our first few months in China fighting—at least she knows me and cares about me and I could really confide in her about everything that has happened. I don't know what I would have done without you two.

She lives alone now, and I'm going to as well. I looked at an apartment on the twentieth floor of a high-rise—it has a windowed wall and I can see all of eastern Beijing when I stand at the window and look out. I decided to move in next week and get serious about how I'm spending my time in this country.

Honestly, the STD thing has really scared the shit out of me. I've led a charmed life, a lucky life, and if I'm not careful, I'm going to waste it. Two years from now, I don't want to realize that I've squandered my time in Beijing by just messing around.

I'm trying to get up the nerve to send some pitches to other magazines to freelance, although it's a relief to be off work during this holiday. Before the break, Victoria and I sweated over a double issue of our magazine—twice as much work in the same amount of time. All you need to know about a double issue is: Fuck the double issue.

It sounds like a war zone here, with staccato explosions of firecrackers going off all night. They're thought to scare away evil spirits, so maybe we should both light a few.

I'm going to go eat dumplings with Astrid, because it's tradition. The more dumplings you eat during the New Year celebration, the more money you're supposed to make in the coming year. I am going to go eat thirty thousand dumplings.

Love,

Jess

P.S. Oh, and it's officially the Year of the Rat, which means it's your year to wear red underwear every day. Apparently it brings good luck.

## Rachel to Jess

Oh God, please send me a pair of red underwear from China! I need all the luck I can get! I think Year of the Rat is an understatement. . . .

That's my way of telling you that I slept with Saul.

Saul invited me to hang out with his friends at a bar in Park Slope, not far from where I live in Brooklyn. You might remember how sometimes he has great friends and sometimes he has bad friends, because he does not discriminate? They were all there. Also, he wore his bottle-cap tie again. How did this get invented? More importantly, how did this get worn, twice?

I had invited Rosabelle out with me, but she went back home for the weekend. I came alone. And so, for most of the night, I made small talk with his random friends in the corner, while Saul made his rounds. Or rather, held court. It's like he walks around with a permanent spotlight on him. People see that he's there and immediately head toward him to tell him about random news, like their refrigerator light bulbs burned out or how they took up beekeeping, and he actually cares about what they say.

Around 4 A.M., he tore himself away from his entourage and walked me home.

The fact that the walking was the best part of the entire night should tell you something. It was chilly and crisp outside and he swung my hand as we walked. It wasn't difficult to get him into my apartment, as this has been four years in the making. I just said, "Do you want to—" and before I'd even finished my sentence he said, very quickly, "Definitely." Before we even made it into the living room, he pulled my face to him. And kissed me.

Nineteen-year-old me rejoices.

It pains me to write about what happened because I know Jane Austen just wouldn't approve, but you know I'm going to anyway.

He was so romantic. And then . . . so awful.

I made him take off his bottle-cap tie. He kissed my neck a lot, but really quickly. It reminded me of the way I would kiss a hyperactive dog on the head. Or of a hyperactive dog itself.

I had to get up and get a condom from Buster. Buster gave me a wink. But Saul had followed me and so he, Buster, and I were all standing in the hallway for this weird condom pass-off. Which Jane Austen novel did this happen in again?

He lasted . . . and lasted and lasted, so long that at the end, he suggested that I just go down on him and get it over with.

Except I heard it as "let's get down on the floor and get this over with." So I did (because if that's what's going to make this end, then fine by me). He just stared at me. Then, as he looked at me on the floor while he was perched on the bed, I realized what he'd *actually* said, and the whole thing was completely ruined for me. The biggest thing Saul had going for him this whole time is how romantic he can be, and suddenly that whole persona felt like such a façade.

I wish it just ended there but it didn't. As soon as we were both done, he put his hand to my neck, in what I thought might be a caress. But when he kept it there, I realized: He was taking my pulse. To figure out whether I was faking or not.

From romance to disgust in fifteen minutes or less.

I don't understand how someone who can be so kind and caring can become so selfish during sex. I barely recognized Saul when we were in bed (or I was looking up at him from the floor). I thought being with him would make us feel closer, but I just feel exposed and semi-nauseated about the whole thing.

To tell the truth, I'm slightly scared that *I* did something wrong.

Why did he take so long? Do I not know how to have sex? It brought up all of these old insecurities. . . . Was he not that into me even though I'd worn a great dress and red lipstick?

I'm sad that he wasn't the guy for me. But thank God I realized this before I wasted much more time on him. I don't ever have to worry about screwing things up with him, because he has definitely lost any chance with me. He invited me to a party at his place on Friday, but . . . I don't think so.

Sometimes I think I really don't know what's best for me. Getting what you want can be the worst sometimes.

Saul hits exactly zero points on my list, by the way. But is it kind of my fault? I forgot to add "Will not be too vulgar or bossy in bed." I didn't realize how specific that list had to be.

Do you think that Frenchmen will be this way? I don't know, but I do foresee a lot of mistranslations and misunderstandings like "get down on the floor" occurring. As in, "Uh-oh. SORRY. *Where* did you say to touch you?"

Lots of love,

Rachel

P.S. Did you see that Bill Broadwick was published in *The Atlantic*? Hate. Life.

FEBRUARY 20

## Jess to Rachel

The last time I saw Saul, he jumped out of a closet and shouted, "PAN-demonium!" as he tackled me to the ground. Then he tried to put a hookah on my head.

You should have slapped Saul when he took your pulse to see how "excited" you were during sex. This is exactly what I mean about some guys having a goal—this isn't going on your résumé, Saul! And what's with the specific demands to finish him off? I feel like that's only okay once you've been with someone awhile—not the first time. You aren't a hooker!

Also, can I send you a picture of me and can you please honestly tell me if I look fat?

There's a café near work that I go to every day except I might stop doing this, because the employees have become very familiar with me. Too familiar. Nearly every day I walk in, they chime my order, "Small mocha!" and then a large Chinese man behind the counter says one of two things:

"Today, you look so fat!" and then he uses his palms to mime chubby cheeks. OR he greets me with, "Today, your face is so thin!" and then he gestures with his hands in a way that I take to mean, "I can see your cheekbones."

There doesn't seem to be any rhyme or reason to it, because my weight doesn't fluctuate (maybe the fat just moves around or something?)! I tried to see if I could figure out the system by taking note of how I wore my hair, but I just can't crack it. Yet he always seems certain. I think the worst part (or maybe the second-worst part after being called fat) is that he then yells it at the girl who makes the coffee and she always turns to look at me and emphatically agrees. "So fat today!" or "So thin today!"

Anyway, today is a fat day.

Last week, I went to a Chinese wedding for two of my Chinese coworkers, who no one even knew were dating. They announced their engagement to us last week and invited the entire office. They rented out a bus that took us to a huge banquet on the outskirts of Beijing. The bride wore a red, floor-length, high-necked dress called a *qipao* and then later changed into a white wedding dress. During the ceremony, the groom cried. It's tradition for the couple to come around and have a shot of alcohol at each table, and there were fifty tables. My coworkers and I were very drunk by the end and on the bus back to the city, a Singaporean photographer from the magazine told me, "Americans have too much fluoride in their water. Your smile is so . . . smiley."

What am I supposed to do with that information?

When I was watching the groom toast the bride, a Chinese coworker leaned over to tell me that the bride and I were the same age. How can this be when I feel nowhere near ready for that kind of commitment? I'm not sure I ever will.

Did I tell you that Maxwell left Beijing for good? Romantic feelings for him fizzled out long ago and Astrid and I went to his goodbye party together. Although we all agreed to stay in touch, we knew that we probably wouldn't.

A lot of my friendships here feel similar. Recently, I've been going out a lot, meeting a lot of different expats at house parties and bars around town, but it's not very fulfilling. I'm meeting more people than I ever have in my entire life, but after about ten minutes of banter, I start to feel very flat and want to move on. I end up leaving feeling lonelier than before I came out.

In addition, I feel really young compared to my boss, Victoria. She seems to have her life together and I do not. I need direction or a new goal or something, because I feel really unsatisfied right now. Even though I'm busy during work hours, I'm too idle on the weekends and I think this is bad for me.

When I first got to Beijing, I felt strong and brash and fearless, but when I get too comfortable and fall into a routine of not speaking Mandarin to strangers or going around my problems rather than confronting them, I soon revert back to being timid. Do you find that this is a struggle for you as well? I'm learning that I always have to fight to stay confident and strong—it's not something I can take for granted. I need to keep challenging myself to keep it up, now that I feel relaxed in my life here.

I don't know. Why do I feel so low right now? I'm trying to figure it out. It could just be that I woke up from a three-hour nap.

Love,

Jess

P.S. Actually, forget what I just said. When's Oprah's mail-order groom supposed to arrive? Is there someone I can contact in case he got lost?

**MARCH 3**

## Rachel to Jess

Yesterday Rosabelle and I opened the mailbox and there were two letters, both from the Fulbright commission: one fat and one thin.

But the fat one wasn't for me.

We've both been checking the mailbox every day looking for our Fulbright responses that went out last week. Even in this day and age, they send the acceptances and rejections by mail. MAIL.

I hugged Rosabelle. I'm happy for her. During the whole application process, she was practicing her Spanish around the house while she cooked dinner, as I practiced my French while I ate her dinner. She also pulled out volume after volume of contemporary Argentinian poetry, which she read in a soft melodic voice—sometimes to herself (borderline acceptable) and sometimes to Buster (gross). And she's been completely miserable at her job. Each night, she comes home with glossy magazines and her free newspaper that she copy edits. This isn't the way she imagined it, but now she has a way out.

Rosabelle and Buster quietly opened champagne when she told him her news. She hesitated when she asked me if I wanted a glass, but of course I wanted to toast her. I remembered the first time the three of us drank champagne here, on our first night in this apartment last

June. We climbed the fire escape to the roof and sat drinking out of plastic cups and now they're both moving to Argentina in a few months.

Focusing on their happiness actually helps mute some of my disappointment. I thought getting in was a done deal for both of us. To be honest, fresh rejections just bring up the memory of college rejections. How they hurt but also had no rhyme or reason. "How could you do this to me, Georgetown? Brown was twice as competitive as you!" (Rips pink ribbons out of her hair and stomps on North Face fleece.) "I didn't want to go to Dartmouth *anyway*, thankyouverymuch." (Throws away preppy pastel shirts.) Also, yes, I realize that I applied to a lot of schools where it is compulsory to wear polo shirts and pearls.

Of course, Claudia and I talked about the Fulbright rejection. We decided that not getting things is a necessary step in appreciating the things you do get (even I already knew this) and that there is more than one path to happiness (sometimes it doesn't feel like it).

My parents are sympathetic about the Fulbright, but my dad is being strangely conservative about my other dream to study film in Paris. He does make a lot of good points—namely, that I'd be giving up a good job to get a degree that will only qualify me to do exactly this same job two years from now in a different field.

However, my mother made the only point that matters to me right now. She said, kind of sadly, "You won't be able to do this ten years from now—just leave everything behind and go."

So much advice from so many different people. At the end of the day, I still feel like everything's riding on these Sorbonne applications. With each application, I feel like I'm determining my fate. If I don't get in, I feel like I'm going to be totally stuck here forever. I'll know everything by next week.

It's weird to think that by summer, Rosabelle, Buster, and, I hope, I will be abroad. There will be three completely new people living in this apartment. Or, if you go by fire codes/our rental contract, one completely new person.

Love,

Rachel

## Jess to Rachel

Rachel! What are you talking about? If you don't get into your Sorbonne program, you're stuck in your New York life forever? Come on!

Don't rest all of your life expectations on one outcome. When you have *no* expectations, you don't lose all that money on wasted ribbons and polo shirts. I flew to Beijing without knowing a thing about what to expect or what to bring. Granted, I also had to live without deodorant and the correct prescription of contact lenses for two months, but I survived. And so will you! Even if you don't get into your program, there will always be other ways to get to Paris and other ways to change your life.

I'm learning that we can't predict anything. At the magazine, I feel like Victoria is warming to me, although she still remains wary when I get too excited (she has a steely gaze, which goes with her stick-straight black hair). When I told her I was waiting until I was in my thirties to start saving money, she sat me down and said she felt morally obligated to tell me about something called "compound interest." Then she dismissed me. Do older sisters do *this*?

In my effort to do more things that challenge me, I've asked for a few writing assignments from our company's cooler, hipper magazine, which is aimed at twentysomethings. One of the perks about writing for a publication is that you get to do things you've always wanted to do but would never have the nerve to otherwise by declaring, "It's for my job, so I am completely justified in interviewing extremely handsome men/backpacking alone through Thailand/asking a jilted wife about her ex-husband's new wife."

Under the guise of writing an article is how I ended up at a speeddating event, clutching a notecard, and trying to come up with my answer to the question: What's your deal breaker? The organizers insisted we all write this down and that way we can use it in case conversation falls flat with any of the ten dates we'd meet that night.

As soon as I walked in, I knew it was a mistake, which was totally confirmed when I sat down with my first candidate. His name was Andrew, and he was an American who is twenty-six. He was almost cute, and he had a deep voice . . . for a woman. This canceled out any cuteness whatsoever. He said that all he does is study Chinese and lead a monk's life and he did not laugh at any of my jokes about how it seems weird for a celibate monk to speed-date. I asked him what his deal breaker was.

"People who don't take life seriously enough. People who make a joke out of everything."

I looked down at my own notecard, on which I had scrawled, "Deal breaker: people who take life too seriously. And mouth breathers."

Every other date seemed to have a similar trajectory.

Until finally, a familiar toothy-grinned man with green eyes and floppy black hair threw himself down on the chair in front of me, buried his face into his arm before looking up at me from the table, and declared that he just had to tell me about all the crazies he'd just met. He read my name tag and said, "Pan Jessi. Come with me. I need a pint, but beware that once I have had a few, my gentlemanly British manners will disappear. I'll become crude and I'll look like a fat red baby."

George. I'd met him briefly at my magazine when he was quitting at the same time I was being hired, and he remembered me. Before I could reply to his proposition, George whispered that we should ditch the speed-dating event to get "the spiciest chicken wings you didn't know had been missing from your life." I struggled to find my jacket and he grabbed my hand and said, "Hurry! It's going to shut soon and if I don't get chicken wings out of this abysmal night, I'm going to blame you." I followed him because he was charming and I had nothing to lose. (Also, I don't take life too seriously.)

He coaxed me down an alleyway before pulling me into what is best described as a cave that serves food. The hidden diner was loud and crowded, packed with tattooed Chinese punks. The walls were scrawled with colorful graffiti, and waitresses were running around delivering batches of hot chicken wings on skewers.

In bad Mandarin with British intonations, he ordered us a few plates of chicken wings and two pints of beer. George claimed he only attended the speed-dating event because he lost a bet about cricket in his office and was forced to accept the dating assignment for work. He began eating as he told me he worked for another expat magazine.

He seems to know everything and everyone in Beijing, including all of my coworkers. He had opinions on everyone at my office. The art director? Oxygen thievery of the highest order. The tech editor? Gets stoned all the time. The marketing director? Such a penis.

Do you now see how small the expat circle can feel? I'm in a city of seventeen million, but I run into the same hundred people everywhere I go.

And on and on the conversation flew off our tongues. We got into a heated debate about what kind of English accent I would have if I were from the United Kingdom, in which he passionately argued that if I were English I would definitely be too high-class, and also too lovely, to sound like Lily Allen.

Well, shit.

I'm a huge sucker for any man who can successfully pull off using the word *lovely* without talking about a garden party. And he did. (No

American man can do this. A refined Australian just might be able to, but it's pretty much limited to English men.)

After devouring our wings, I told him the spicy food had permanently burnt my taste buds and that I would kill for ice cream. Then he got up and said he needed to make a phone call, and when he came back, he handed me a packaged ice-cream cone from the corner shop. Then he snapped his fingers to get the bill.

When we parted ways after dinner, he put me into a cab and said, "Before anything happens, I want to be clear about something. You do know I'm not Hugh Grant, right?"

He's been the leading man in my life ever since.

We e-mail each other one hundred e-mails a day and send twenty texts every hour, and he sends me music that he insists I must listen to RIGHT NOW. I burst into laughter all the time as we type to each other while we're at our respective jobs. Or, as Victoria puts it, I "make love to my computer." But I'm still making deadline, so she puts up with it for now.

The last time I laughed this much was with Maxwell, but even he pales in comparison to George, who makes me laugh until I can't breathe. And Maxwell was always too busy mooning over Astrid— which isn't funny to me at all. For some reason, I seem to have fallen into George's favor. He's everyone's favorite person, but all of his attention is on me.

Suddenly my world has color. I want to tell George everything— everything that has ever happened to me, every observation I have had, ever, and I want to share every book, song, or movie I have ever loved. Spring finally arrived in Beijing, and I walk around in the warm air, perpetually heavy with the threat of rain, with a permanent grin on my face. Today, I walked into a construction site because I was giggling at something he had written to me earlier.

I love his voice and his hearty laugh and his smooth accent and the way he tells stories with his hands. He confessed to me in one breath that when he was fifteen he loved the Marx Brothers so much, and he wanted so desperately to be Jewish like them, that he would tell people that his uncle was a rabbi and that, no, he likes me for other reasons besides my lineage.

But despite all this constant correspondence, I keep turning down his invitations to dinner or to meet up with him at night—I only agree to meet up with our mutual friends from work or during the day. There's something stopping me from giving in to romance, even though our messages are rife with flirtation.

On the night we first met, when he came back and handed me an ice cream, I looked into his eyes and saw Will, my old boyfriend who went to Boston University. I think you met briefly in our freshman dorm hall right before I dumped him. The funniest, most intelligent, wonderful guy who adored me—whom I wanted to spend every waking minute with, whom I loved so much, and yet whom I never wanted to kiss.

There. I said it. Sort of. I think you get it.

Maybe, because nothing has happened yet, I just can't imagine kissing him. But I'm basking in my George-filled life, and I'm afraid I'm going to mess this up somehow. I don't want to lose my colorful world, but I can tell that he is smitten. I wake up to text messages about how nice my hair smells. I don't reply to them.

He's too smart not to realize what's going on and is trying to persuade me to have just one romantic dinner with him, where he is utterly convinced he will successfully woo me.

"You'll be nervous. I'll be awkward and speak too much. I'll say something inappropriate whilst trying to be funny. You'll get offended. You'll shake your head. I'll make you laugh accidentally. You'll slowly fall in love with me. You'll realize that what's missing from your life is a crude Englishman."

I'm in deep. How do I handle this situation?

I keep waiting to fall in love with him.

Love,

Jess Pan(ts)

P.S. He calls me Jessi Trousers. And when we're arguing, he calls me "Jessica the Bestica." And when he gets drunk, he calls me Jessibelle.

P.P.S. Oh, maybe I do love him so much.

**MARCH 9**

## Rachel to Jess

Jess! I am so excited you've met your witty future British husband! When you two move to London, you'll only be a train ride away from me BECAUSE I GOT INTO MY PROGRAM IN PARIS!

Yes, I know you told me that there are many other ways to happiness, but I felt such relief and excitement when this time I opened the mailbox and found out that I got into my dream program at the Sorbonne. Cinematographic Studies with a brilliant professor: light, aesthetics, narrative, Fellini and Godard and a whole bunch of stuff you probably don't care about! The Cinémathèque and a million movie theaters, midnight showings of Charlie Chaplin, strange French farces involving slapping people in the face with fish!

Do you know what this really means? Obviously you do. Cobblestones! Croissants! Ballerina flats! Rodin Museum! PARIS! I keep thinking: It will be such a beautiful life.

Also, Eurostar straight to London, which is why you must make George take you there. This is all in a kaleidoscope cluster of images inside my head, by the way.

Amélie! Bicycles and red lipstick and negligees!

Okay. Focus, Rach. The countdown now commences.

I'm writing to you from my Fort Greene café. The waitress is actually a French girl who is totally incompetent, but has a lopsided smile and likes to argue with me in French about why New York is better than Paris. Her reason today: because New York is new and exciting, whereas Paris is old-fashioned, stuck in the nineteenth century, and full of romantics.

Thank God for that.

More soon, *ma chérie*,

Rachelle le French

## Rachel to Jess

got hit by car. harrowing night. hard to type on tiny phone. my body is broken.

## Rachel to Jess

Oh God. If you couldn't tell from our phone call, Vicodin goes very well with antidepressants. Almost, you might say . . . *too* well. I wasn't hallucinating, but I had an overwhelming sense of peace in the emergency room. *So what if my head is bleeding and my body is broken? My spirit lives on!* This feeling lasted all through last night and into this morning, until I woke up, reached for a glass of water, and ended up knocking it off the table with my cast. Then everything came back to me. Including pain, because my meds were wearing off.

By the time Platonic Nick had taken me to the hospital, I knew I was all right—hence my loopy responses to you on the phone involving proclamations of love to you and whoever that British boy you were with was. Please clarify because the pain pills confuse things. For a second last night I thought he was Jude Law. Up until the hospital, though, it was anyone's game. I keep going over the events in my head because I can hardly believe them.

Everything felt so routine. Sally and I had to work late that evening, so I ran out the door at 8 P.M. because Nick was having a dinner party. I was really looking forward to it because I hadn't seen him in a while and haven't been social at all lately.

It was drizzling and dark out when I left, with all of the streetlights reflected in the pavement. I climbed out of the subway at the Lorimer stop and pulled out my umbrella. I delighted in my bright yellow umbrella against the black and gold of the Brooklyn night. I was wearing a light blue silk dress that billowed out with all the wind. I felt like I was in *Funny Face*, after Audrey Hepburn gets her makeover and starts to jaunt around New York. Cross street, look both ways, nobody coming. Left leg extends out, right arm swings with it.

BOOM. Body soars and head hits the pavement. All I think is: "So this is what it feels like to die." Because I am an exceptionally overdramatic person, and I have no idea what just happened to me, and for the first time in my life, my thoughts have paused.

And then: "This is so interesting, so foreign from everyday life."

But then the stillness abruptly ended as the sound of car horns surrounded me. What happened was that I was crossing at the entrance to the freeway and someone in a pickup truck had made a blind left turn just before their light changed. Clipping me in the process.

Because pedestrians kept going on with their lives as if nothing had happened, I assumed getting hit by a car was not a big deal—even though I couldn't get up for a few moments and cars swerved around me. The contents of my purse were strewn all over the street, and for a moment, I couldn't move my lungs, or my legs, and my arms were trembling uncontrollably.

*This is really happening.*

A man jumped out of the truck while I managed to stand up.

Guy: Holy shit. Holy shit. I am so sorry. Should I call an ambulance?

I wobbled to my feet.

Me: No, I'm fine! Really, I'm fine. Look, I can walk. I have to get to a dinner party. If something's wrong, I'll go to the doctor tomorrow.

Rosabelle was incredulous when I told her this part, but it makes sense to me. I was absolutely blind to anything that would distract me from my number one priority: getting to this dinner party on time. Apparently when you have a blunt blow to the head, your brain plays tricks on you. I just couldn't seem to shake the thought that everyone at the dinner party was waiting for me! Going to the hospital did not even seem like an option at the time.

Guy: Um, you're bleeding pretty badly. Fuck. FUCK ME!

Me: Where am I bleeding? (I had lost all sensation in my entire body. It felt like when your leg goes to sleep.)

Guy: Your forehead. Also your hands . . . maybe your legs?

Me: What are you talking about? I can't feel anything!

Guy: Should I . . . call an ambulance?

Me: Ahahaha, I can't feel my face!

Guy: —

Me: Don't worry! I am so late! Tell you what, I'll give you a call if I have to go to the hospital.

Nobody understands how I just left without calling an ambulance. Not the police, not my parents, nobody. The thing I'm piecing together is that when traumatic things actually happen to you, you react in ways you never would have expected. If I had been watching this on any kind of TV show, I would have been screaming at the TV, "GO TO THE HOSPITAL, YOU IDIOT!"

Instead, I just walked away from the scene of my own car accident. I did manage to get the driver's name and number, as well as his license plate, before I ran off. Then (this part's a secret, because in hindsight it makes me sound crazy) I walked into a bodega to buy a bottle of wine, still thinking I could make it to Nick's dinner party on time. It wasn't until I saw the frightened expression on the cashier's face that I reached up to touch my head and felt blood. The guy motioned for me to look at myself in the security camera mirror and that's when I saw what he saw: girl walks into bodega caked in dirt and blood, forehead slit open, hands shaking wildly, crazed look in her eyes. Needs wine. He handed me a paper towel to put on my forehead.

With wine in tow, I kept going and buzzed Nick's door. I climbed the stairs to his loft and as he opened the door, I immediately dropped the bottle, which broke as it shattered down four flights of stairs.

Me: Sorry I'm late! There was—

Nick: What happened to you?! Is your face bleeding? Your legs are all scratched up. And your face is *bleeding*.

He took me to the hospital, but he had fifteen people at his apartment waiting for his return. He stayed with me as I called my parents and Rosabelle. She came running to sit in the waiting room for three hours. I have never been so glad to see someone in my entire life. She and I sat there for hours with a guy in a wheelchair who was vomiting into a bowl.

A Spanish soap opera played on the TV above us and it seemed to be on a continuous loop. I think. It's all a bit fuzzy. I also feel like Jude Law was in it.

Rosabelle kicked into high gear. You remember how she sees herself as den mother to everyone. She went up to the night nurse and gesticulated a lot before stomping back to me. From then until the time I was treated, Rosabelle would look up at intervals and yell, "She's bleeding from her HEAD."

Finally a nurse called my name.

Once I was back in the examining area, the doctors examined me and finally they gave me painkillers. That's when I called you. In the postcrash haze, I was scolded by various members of the hospital staff for using my cell phone in the ER. But talking to you was so worth it.

So, physically this is my condition: bruised ribs, ripped ligament in my hand, eight stitches on my face. I got lucky. That's what the nurses at the hospital kept saying: "You are so lucky."

It's hard to feel lucky after you've been hit by a car. My first reaction was wondering why the universe did this to me.

Here is what Claudia says (I have a week off of work, so I am seeing her every other day): "Stop talking about the universe." This is embarrassing, but she actually pulled out a photo of the Milky Way and pointed at it. "You think the universe cares if you move to Paris or not? You think the universe put those stitches on your face?"

Come on, Claudia! I don't know! Probably not? And she counters, "Sometimes bad things happen and there isn't anything we can do about it in that moment. But we can't blame things on the universe."

This has been a recurrent theme with us—that I blame bad

things on my circumstances rather than on my decisions or passive behavior. Being in charge of my own fate (and it being my fault) frightens me.

But since the accident, I've been having trouble sleeping. I turn off the light at night and climb into bed and lie still, blinking in the darkness. The same thoughts resonate in my mind: "I could have been killed in that car accident and all I would have to show for my life is being a shitty assistant and a pile of unpublished novels and no meaningful romantic relationships."

I don't want to live like this anymore: aimlessly going to the same dead-end job every day, only hanging out with Rosabelle and Buster, constantly imagining myself somewhere else yet always following my current trajectory along passively.

I'm not going to let myself make these mistakes in Paris.

But on to the aftermath of the accident. Here's a tip if you ever get hit by a car while running late to a dinner party: Skip the dinner party. Call the police instead, or else they will think you are just a crazy Frankenstein-faced liar when you show up at their precinct the next day.

I need the driver to pay the hospital bills. New York is a no-fault state, meaning that the person who caused the accident has to pay the bills—my insurance won't cover it. I find it all incredibly confusing, and there's more to tell but it does hurt to type. I took off the cast myself today. My right thumb's all black-and-blue and I may have to have surgery next week.

Meanwhile, I'm so bored now that everyone's at work, and I can't turn the pages of a book without using my mouth. Entertain me! Tell me stories of deepest darkest China and witty Brits named George and what happens to him and an elusive halfie. Tell me about what you are writing for the magazine, and who you see, and what you do. I will be here, not crossing streets.

Okay. I love you. Wish you were here so that there would be

somebody else to wear pajamas all day with me and tell me how bad my face actually looks.

More soon.

Love,

Rach

## Jess to Rachel

You're still alive! Frankenstein stitches and all! When we spoke on the phone and you were on Vicodin and antidepressants, you kept giggling about how the universe didn't get you this time and then you would laugh maniacally.

I'm also glad the universe didn't get you—who else would pet all the horses? Who else has hair that curls while she sleeps? Who else but you is convinced that you are the reincarnation of Grace Kelly because you have the same astrological chart? See? The universe needs your brand of crazy. No, but seriously, I'm so glad you're going to be okay.

And I bet that dinner party sucked. What did you really think you would have missed? Official Dinner Parties tend to be awkward and forced. Although I'm sure you showing up covered in blood was a great conversation starter for the evening. Also, makes you seem very mysterious.

When George and I talked to you on the phone, he was supposed to be pretending to be Jude Law sending his well wishes, but he wasn't being slick enough to be Jude and we started arguing and then the whole thing deteriorated into shouting about what Jude would or would not say. Sorry that you had to listen to that in the emergency room.

But I guess it's indicative of my relationship with George, which teeters between friends and an old bickering married couple.

I would love to regale you with George stories like you asked. I
wish I could weave you a tantalizing tale of seduction about a British
man carrying me off into the sunset. But that is not the case.

The truth. I have to tell it to someone, because maybe it will force
me to stop what's happening. In groups, George is the center of attention, usually half hanging off a chandelier while telling a story about
the time he was so lonely he once befriended a sassy monkey who then
stole all of his food in Malaysia, as the entire room hangs on his every
word. And even at a distance, he maintains the same unwavering confidence and wit as he writes me e-mails on the hour and sends flurries
of text messages.

But when we're alone, he becomes nervous, unrecognizable from
the confident man I met the first night. He runs his hands through his
messy black hair and he swallows a lot and his green eyes dart between
my eyes and the floor. He says things like, "I've let my guard down
around you, and I never do that with anybody." I see a side of him he
doesn't show everyone—how he can be hurt and how concerned he is
with being more than the guy with a glossy, charming persona. Which
makes me feel even worse about my mixed feelings.

Inevitably, these introspective admissions conclude when he throws
back a few more pints. In a determined manner, he takes my hands
and looks at me with pleading eyes. He tries to lean in to kiss me, but
it feels more like he's thrusting his face forward and my lips are the
target. I'm hyperaware of his clammy hands. His nervous eyes are
begging me to love him back. And I know that my heart is racing for
a different reason from his: sheer fear.

I always break his gaze and then, embarrassed, he drops my hands,
drinks a few more pints, and eventually drapes an arm over me as he
tells me about how much his sister is going to love me, and how much
fun we'll have on our lovely drives (again, *lovely*) across the English
countryside, and with each pint, he becomes more and more confident that we are already together and that we have a future filled with

laughter and sunshine, and probably, I imagine, sexual romps on wild moors.

I am fine with sunshine and laughter, but my body seems ambivalent about the sex part. The truth is that I've started something that I'm not prepared to finish. I don't want someone to beg me to love him. I want the George who hangs off the chandelier, but I get the guy with pleading eyes and clammy hands. I can't be romantic with him because his insecurity turns me off and I don't feel attracted to him. And if I'm not his girlfriend, it's too late for me to just be his friend.

What's it called when you've suddenly found yourself with a boyfriend straight off your Master List, but with whom you have no intention of sleeping?

False advertising.

But, he lets me see him every day. This is such a simple thing, but I don't think I've ever had this with a man before. Men I've dated in the past were always elusive or busy or too scared to give away too much, but George gives me this.

Still, I can't dwell on this anymore right now. Astrid can't take much more of it either. She says I need to make up my mind and let George know, sooner rather than later. I know she's right.

But in the grand scheme of life, the important thing is you're *actually* alive and so am I! You survived a car crash! New York City almost took you out, and you survived! In time, you will cross streets like a pro again. You'll be able to give an all-star thumbs-up. You'll be left with a tiny silver scar across your forehead that will make a great story when you meet Parisians.

Let me know how you're doing now.

Love,

Jess

P.S. I'm glad you're alive.

## Jess to Rachel

Are you alive?? No reply all week? You're in danger of breaking our pact! I know you're having trouble typing. Just type back one letter so I know you're okay!

Love,

Jess

## Rachel to Jess

Q

## Jess to Rachel

Q is a dignified choice.

Are you still off work, lying in your pajamas, recovering? Sort of the best thing ever, if you take away the trauma, broken thumb, bruised ribs, and face scar, right? Am I right?

To distract you: Maybe you'll be seeing me sooner than expected and all this George nonsense will be moot. My days in Beijing could be numbered because of a recent crackdown on foreigners working illegally here. My work visa is supposedly being processed, but I had to get a temporary one for now.

In case you ever need to know, if you urgently need a visa to stay in Beijing, text a woman named Joy whom you meet at the McDonald's on Second Ring Road, because everyone knows where that is.

You'll hand her a wad of cash. She'll take your passport. Then a runner will head to Mongolia and get a new visa in your passport.

I just got back from the exchange and now I'm looking over my shoulder all the time, feeling like a criminal, although I actually have no idea if this is illegal or not. Better not to ask.

I hope you, your forehead, your rib, your thumb, and your scrapes are healing as if aided by a phoenix's teardrops.

Love,

Jess

**APRIL 10**

## Rachel to Jess

I just want you to know that I love you so much that against my doctor's orders, I have removed my ACE bandage and am now typing very slowly.

Before anything else, I just have to say: If you don't want to have sex with George, then his impression of Jude Law was definitely lacking and not worth the sexual frustration you are inflicting upon him.

Stitches on my face came out yesterday. It looks like I fell asleep with a spiral notebook under my eyebrow—it's raw but the doctor thinks that my scar will only be about an inch long from my eyebrow to my forehead.

Twice a week, I go to physical therapy for my hand, where I sit on a bench and twiddle my thumb. Literally. Just move it back and forth. Stretch it a little sideways. I can feel other people there questioning my presence out of the corners of their eyes. But still. My thumb does hurt. I never knew how important it was! Do you know how many times we use our thumbs each day? Like, say, try buttoning your jeans. Every morning, I visit Rosabelle's room and she fastens me up.

I've had a lot to think about during my time off to recover from my injuries. In a weird way, hitting the pavement somehow stifled my constant anxiety. I didn't realize this until I started going back to work and noticed that I care less about what the person next to me on the subway thinks of me, or if everyone at work loves me, or if I have to wait thirty minutes for the next bus. I don't care if Buster is taking too long in the shower (although I still don't want to think about what he's doing in there).

It's not like I've reached some higher plane. Even I'm not naive enough to believe that. But I am still here and, instead of anxious musings, I'm finally telling myself: "Wake up!" When Rosabelle and I walk through Central Park and the wind rushes through the trees, I think to myself, "You don't want to miss this."

This philosophizing may also be due to the fact that I keep skipping my sessions with Claudia. I imagine her sitting around drinking mint tea on her own and probably reading Freud or Jung or whoever is making her ask her opaque questions. I keep thinking that I don't want to create more anxieties or delve into old ones. I feel like I don't want opaque questions when, all of a sudden, everything seems so clear. I'm leaving my job soon and moving to Paris. It feels weird to quit a job I actually like, but it must be done.

For the first time in a long time, I feel okay, but it's such a delicate balance.

More soon,
Scarface

APRIL 18

## Jess to Rachel

I know the exact feeling you're talking about, when you step out of the incessant superficial chatter in your head and actually become aware of what's around you. I get it when I'm in the middle of a throng of motorists, cyclists, and cabs and look up and see an ancient temple looming over me.

As for George, you're right. He probably is sexually frustrated. Things progressed slightly. I'll say this much: I don't mind kissing him. But then again, that's the title of the least gripping romance novel in the world. Subtitle: He Was Just Okay.

I thought that if you get naked with someone, the attraction would just appear. But I was wrong. Once we start removing our clothes, I am completely detached. I tune out and it starts to feel like I'm just an observer rather than a participant. "So *that's* what a hand on my right boob looks like." So far, I've managed to escape actually having sex with him by always claiming to be late for an appointment I just re-membered I had. "I'm meeting Astrid and I have to leave NOW." It is a sign of George's politeness that he does not say, "But it only takes fifteen minutes!"

Other than you, Astrid took the brunt of my George angst. She tolerated session after session of my justifications for trying to talk myself into him: "We'd be such a great couple. Our children would be so funny. They would have the best accents ever. He says 'schedule' in the funny British way, and that will never get old." But you know Astrid can't take this kind of delusional shit.

Finally, she sat me down and said, "Look, George is great. I get it. He's funny and kind and it seems like he'll love you forever. I can see that, too. But if you don't want to have sex with him now, then you certainly aren't going to want to have sex with him in ten years. And eventually, he's going to hate your guts."

Flicks cigarette.

"So end it today and have him hate you now or drag this out for ten years and have him hate you later. Your choice. But either way, he will hate you."

Norwegian wisdom.

George came over to my apartment later that night. I let him in, trying to avoid his kiss hello, and he sat next to me on my couch with a smile as he reached over to pull me into him. But I stopped him and shook my head. He froze and we looked at each other for a few moments as I tried to get up the nerve to say something.

Only fragments ran through my head. The knowledge I would soon be ruining something special, the loss of someone that I genuinely liked, the fact that he really was one of the greatest guys I'd ever met. Instead of speaking, I started crying. I didn't say anything because I didn't have to. He put his arm around me and brushed my hair from my face. That's how great George is—considerate and understanding even when I'm breaking up with him. He said he understood, that he knew something was wrong but that he didn't want to face it.

Then he went from so nice to manic. He stood up and started pacing my apartment. After rambling for five minutes about how hard it was, how hard this was going to be, he abruptly announced that he was leaving.

At the doorway, he turned and said, "I thought we were going to be together for a really long time." Then he grabbed me and kissed me, hard. I let him.

And then I closed the door.

I still have my doubts, and have to go around wondering whether George is the last man who will ever truly appreciate me, afraid that I was being too picky.

I mope and Astrid tolerates it briefly. Every time I think about backsliding, she grabs me and says, "Think of his penis. Do you want to be with his penis?"

That's an old Norwegian saying grandmothers knit on throw pillows.

Why am I always writing about penises?? You don't even want to know what Google ads keep appearing in my sidebar.

Meanwhile, George told all of his friends that I have ruined his self-confidence, that I led him on, that I was cruel, and that he hates me. Astrid was also right about that.

Apparently, if you don't have sex with a guy you are dating, he will hate you forever. It doesn't matter how much fun you had together—all he will remember is that you refused to have sex with him. Nothing else. The rooftop conversations while overlooking a lake? The book you gave him that changed his life? The time you saved him from a burning building? No. For every photo he sees of you, his eyes will superimpose a red $X$ across your crotch and his heart will turn to stone.

Mutual friends wonder why I dated George at all if I'm not actually attracted to him. But friends become lovers all the time, don't they? Rosabelle and Buster! Harry and Sally! Luke and Lorelai! Only now do I see that this happens in real life when friends suddenly see amazing new things in each other for the first time, making them suddenly want to rip each other's clothes off. You can't work backward—"This person is amazing, therefore I will eventually want to sleep with him." It's saying something that I would rather attend six imaginary urgent meetings with Astrid than have sex with George even once.

His friends call me Nonstick. Nonstick Pan.

Rachel! Come to China and knock some sense into me (with the hand that's intact). How did I mess this up so badly?

Anyway, I have to finish editing and writing articles on breast-feeding and summer camps for Victoria (separate articles, thank God). I feel like I've been doing well at work—less heavy-handed editing by Victoria, and I've been given more responsibility, like ordering around the interns. However, the George drama did set me back a few days, and I turned in a book review to Victoria three days late. I think I've seen too many movies where the writer is depressed, incompetent, and lazy and their editor is patient and kind of a hard-ass who loves the writer anyway.

All lies, because Victoria's not speaking to me now. Via e-mail, she has assured me that she does not love me.

Love,

Sad Jessi Trousers

## Rachel to Jess

I feel sad for the demise of you and George, and not just because I had grown to love the idea of you two. I always thought that if someone was great enough, we would love them. That's the point of entire fairy tales. *The Frog Prince? Beauty and the Beast?* At least at the end, the frog and the beast turn into handsome men. In real life, you're stuck with unappealing bedfellows whom you then have to sleep with for the next fiftysomething years.

If attraction didn't matter, you and I would be married to each other!

I do think you are pretty, though.

Anyway, my hand is slowly getting better.

I quit my job last week. It was so different than when I quit with Vince, because I wasn't scared about my boss's reaction this time. My happiness is more important than inconveniencing two people for a short period of time. It also helps knowing I'm headed to Paris.

When I actually talked with my boss Joan, she just nodded sagely and said, "I knew you wouldn't stay long. You're meant for other things." This confused me. Why did you hire me, then? I mean, I'm glad you did . . . but then tell me what I'm meant for!

The feeling of having missed my calling again hit me after I posted my job description online to find my replacement. Responses started piling up after five minutes and by the end of the day, I had seventy-five. Each one made me question my decision to leave. "You are giving up a job people are lining up to take away from you. Most of these people are more qualified than you are in the first place! WHY ARE YOU LEAVING THIS JOB?"

I've made my decision, though, and I know that part of this fresh start has to be a refusal to dwell on things. So, moving on.

I'm heading to Wisconsin for a while to work on my French in a rent-free environment before flying to Paris. Rosabelle and Buster are both getting ready to move to Argentina for a year, so we're all moving out soon. We drank champagne for hours yesterday evening celebrating our impending departure. The highlight was Rosabelle lying faceup, spread-eagle on the floor. "I loved this apartment! Why do we have to let it go? We had to search *so hard* for you, little apartment!"

One month left to go here, but New York has already started to feel like a memory: walking in flip-flops down brownstone-lined streets, working in a white air-conditioned space with film images flickering on the Chelsea gallery walls, riding in a 1930s elevator at the nonprofit, smoking in the midday heat, sitting on rocks by the East River at sunset.

All my love,
Meant for Other Things

**MAY 8**

## Jess to Rachel

Last night Astrid and I stayed out really late and ended up at our favorite all-night duck restaurant, which we used to eat at all the time before we moved into separate apartments. While we were there, I was thinking about how great it was that finally we had our favorite go-to places when Astrid told me that she's ready to leave Beijing.

She said she wants to return to the United States for law school. She's tired of the language barrier, of not understanding most of what's going on around her, of feeling slightly adrift. She kept repeating that she's ready to return to real life. I don't feel any of these things. For me, this is real life. Life back in the States—that's what's imaginary to me now.

I can't fathom leaving Beijing after having worked so hard to begin a life here. Because Astrid and I came here together, it feels like if she leaves, I'm truly choosing Beijing, and this spur-of-the-moment decision suddenly becomes a real life choice. And as Astrid wraps up her life here, I'm finally realizing that this is a finite experience: At some point it will end for me too. I wonder what's going to eventually pull me away from China.

Since I'm now fully committed to staying, I have resumed Mandarin lessons during my lunch break with a girl about our age named Karen. She gave me my Chinese name: Jie Si Ke. (I know that this looks kind of like my American name, but actually, using Chinese tones two, four, and three, it sounds like *Gee-eh suh kaaaah.*) Karen is thrilled that I am attracted to Chinese men—so many Chinese-American women claim they aren't. I want to shake Chinese girls who say this and yell, "How can you say shit like that? If your mom had thought that, you would not have been born!"

Karen often invites me to dinner with her and her boyfriend, and each time there is a new bachelor waiting for me. Seriously. So far there's been an American, a German, and last week, a Chinese guy who is in the military. I haven't actually been on any dates with them, but sometimes the Chinese army guy and I text in rudimentary Mandarin. I don't think our exchanges about my favorite fruit are building the foundation of a romance, but even so, a Chinese coworker informed me that if I date him, we have to register our relationship with the government because he is in the army. Also, he's actually forbidden to marry a foreigner.

What? Sometimes I forget what a strange place China is and then I realize YouTube and Facebook are blocked on the Internet and the thought enters my mind that the Chinese government is reading these very e-mails.

I'm also beginning to really question how the skills I use on a regular basis will ever be applicable to any other job, even though I do enjoy working at the magazine. You know what I've learned so far this month? If you want to get into shape after pregnancy, don't torture yourself by Google image searching "Gwyneth Paltrow." Also, kids love pandas.

Sometimes on deadline I stay late, sitting with our non-English-speaking Chinese designer, Echo (self-named). She and I have reverted to pictographs to communicate, in which I draw elaborate layouts involving stick children and boxes for text. We argue heatedly about colors and fonts and then she gives me a big fake smile at the end of the conversation and says she'll take care of it.

Victoria and I have a running joke about how we are afraid that Echo is going to smother us in our sleep.

In an eerily uncanny coincidence, Victoria has just sent me an e-mail telling me she "wants to talk to me in private" after we put this issue to bed. This is terrifying. What does she want?

Maybe she wants me to stop spending work hours writing to you?

I can't believe you're really leaving New York. Everyone is on the move. I remember sleeping on your couch in that apartment before I flew to Beijing—and now as you leave, Astrid's headed back to the United States.

Love,

Jie Si Ke

P.S. My passport arrived with a new visa pasted inside. It says I got it in Mongolia. If anybody asks, that's where I was last month. I mean, that's where I was last month.

## Rachel to Jess

Big news. I never thought I'd be writing a sentence like this to you, but a few days ago I opened my mailbox and there was a check from an insurance company for ten thousand dollars.

I have to open mail now by kind of clawing at it while using my teeth, so it was all wrinkly and a little wet, but there it was. At first I thought it was one of those Publishers Clearing House–type things, like, in tiny type, "enter to win" and then, enormously, "$10,000!" But when I thought it over, I realized it was from the pickup truck guy's insurance company, and part of the check had already been signed over to my lawyer's firm.

But I was still so confused about why I had this check. At first I thought it was for my medical bills, but I looked through them and they were all paid in full. Then I thought maybe it was some kind of trap, like if I accepted this check, it would only turn out to be worth one cent because there was a decimal place error.

So I called my lawyer and asked him if it was hush money.

Long story short, he's been negotiating with them for "pain and suffering" money on my behalf, and this escaped me in my Vicodin haze. He has been e-mailing me ever since, but my e-mail filtered them into the spam folder.

So that's how I endorsed an insurance check today for ten thousand dollars. I keep looking at my bank balance and blinking hard. The legal fight, such as it was, was quick and painless, except for the scars on my face and legs and my hand brace.

It's kind of unbelievable that this is how things turned out. It seems like my time in New York was created to let me experience every possible human emotion, from the very worst to the very best. Depressive episodes on the subway, unrequited crushes in Fort Greene, bleeding on the street, healing in the springtime. Now I'm ready to move on.

Even though I'm starting something new, I'm glad that you'll still be in China. I like to imagine you waking up in Beijing, on your way to work in the busy, chaotic city as I start unpacking my belongings looking out over my new quiet courtyard in Paris.

Paris and a full bank account. I feel rich. Blessed. Broken. Zsa Zsa Gabor? Elizabeth Taylor?

Okay, okay—truthfully, I thanked the universe, but I did not tell Claudia this. She told me not to blame the universe—but can't I thank it for gifts?

Meanwhile, it's warm here today just as June finally approaches. I'm sitting in our living room full of boxes, writing this. It feels like you've been in New York with me. In case you were wondering, you live inside my computer, where you emerge with messages from time to time.

Tuesday was my last day at work. Sally and I spent the day secretly sipping a bottle of cheap white wine, and then went out to a diner. Sally's one of those New Yorkers who wasn't born here but will never ever leave. Like the guy who calls me Dimples, or the French girl who works at my coffee shop. For some reason, I find this very comforting.

Yesterday was also my last day with Claudia. I'll admit it: I cried. She was like, "You are ready! Go forth into the world! Go do amazing things, it is time!" And instead of my usual extended internal monologue, I just thought: "Well, maybe it is."

I'm going to miss Rosabelle a lot, but not her insane cleanliness standards. I know that the second I live somewhere without her, I will immediately get mice. I'm okay with that, as long as I don't have to clean the stovetop fourteen times a day.

But it's going to be weird to be without her. I'm going to leave my best friend in New York, who sat with me in the emergency room and in tiki bars, baked countless cookies, and walked with me in Fort Greene Park. Rosabelle will always be New York for me.

Buster went back to Chicago before meeting Rosabelle in Argentina next week. Here is what our good-bye looked like:

Me: So, uh, see you later, Buster.

Buster: Yeah, um. Bye.

That was my easiest good-bye. It's strange—I am suddenly sad to leave this great city, but then again, if someone said, "Oh, you love New York now? Here's an opportunity to stay here for two more years!" I would swim across the ocean to Paris rather than accept their offer.

Like so many of the other women here, I arrived thinking I was exceptional in that moderately precocious, moderately well-educated, moderately good-looking way, and was immediately swept under the rug. New York is full of girls like me, being ignored and full of rage and confusion about why.

But once you get over yourself, it is a place full of chance and surprise. You simply have to take your ego out of the equation.

I can't believe I won't be coming back here.

So now, ten thousand dollars richer and with all my belongings in boxes, I am ready for Paris and ready to immerse myself in film. Also, I'm starting to think that money is the first thing a writer needs. Maybe the *only* thing a writer needs.

Before I head to Paris, I'm reverting back to the college years and taking summer break in Milwaukee just like the old days.

And yet everything is starting now. . . . I can feel it.

Love,

Rach

**MAY 26**

---

## Jess to Rachel

First of all, writers are notoriously broke! Haven't you ever read Hemingway or George Orwell or Charles Bukowski or ANYTHING

EVER? And second of all, that money—Jesus Christ, that is a lot of money to suddenly get! Although if you go off of those writers' precedents, you are going to definitely spend all of that money on booze and women and possibly horse races.

That's really exciting, though! I know it's money for damages, but I feel like saying congratulations! So, congrats! Did you know that now you could buy six thousand bowls of Chinese noodles?

Well, you're leaving New York and it's Astrid's final week in Beijing. Last night she threw an over-the-top going-away party in a Chinese courtyard with an open piano where our friends played songs for her. She wore a long, flowing green dress and fluttered from group to group.

At around 3 A.M., we snuck off alone to revisit the old tables where we used to sit with Maxwell before he left. We laughed a lot, but it was also sad. I think in the past Astrid would have tried to make me come back to the United States with her, but she now understands that I need to stay in China. For the first time in our relationship, I don't know when I'm going to see her again.

All I know is that I'm definitely staying here for a little longer. Last week, I finally had my dreaded mystery meeting with Victoria. We went for dim sum, and she told me that she was quitting the magazine.

My first reaction was to feel sad, and then abandoned. As in, how could you do this to us? We were just getting to be good friends and we both cared about our little family magazine so much and now she's leaving it and me? I felt sad to lose her, although her decision has nothing to do with me. She wants to move back to New York—is there a rule that when one New Yorker leaves, another one has to take her place?

During our lunch, I was so distracted by all of the above feelings that it didn't even occur to me what this meant. She finally had to spell it out.

"So, do you want my job?"

I was surprised—but it's finally sinking in. Do I want to be the managing editor and have final say on every decision regarding the magazine? Do I want a pay raise? Do I want to drink coffee out of a mug that says "Boss"?

You know I do. She leaves in two weeks, and I'll be taking her job, if upper management allows.

Suddenly, without Astrid here and with the news of Victoria's departure, I really feel like I'm on this adventure alone now. It's exciting but it's also starting to feel increasingly lonely.

You'll be home by the time you read this. You better write me, because we have important things to cover before you leave for France. For instance, can you arrange a stopover in Beijing en route to Paris and perhaps during this stopover, bring me a bra from America that fits? Every single one here is so tight that it doubles as a corset.

Keep me posted.

All my love,

Jess

# YEAR TWO

*Three Months Later*

## Rachel to Jess

I'M IN PARIS!!!!!

I'm in Paris. I keep saying this to myself. Not out loud, though. It still feels like a strange dream. I'm writing this from a café around the corner from my house and am surrounded by retired men smoking heavy cigars. They are the only people around in the middle of an afternoon on a Tuesday.

In the cab from the airport to the city, I stared out the window: first at naked women on billboards, and then at the open-air markets, before reaching a grand boulevard with lots of identical white mansions. Finally, my driver pulled up to my building, on a street so narrow that cars park halfway up the sidewalk. My landlady had left a key for me under the mat, and I giddily sprinted through a courtyard to see my studio apartment. The floors are wooden and there's a bed on a loft upstairs. It's just beneath the eaves, so I have to duck to get into it. I flopped down on the bed and stared at the angled ceiling that was one foot from my face. Then, I immediately started sneezing, so I suspect a cat used to live here, but I don't care. I am in Paris. I am not in my nursery in New York anymore.

The downstairs has huge windows that open out onto the courtyard. Initially, I loved this, but actually it means that my neighbors can see directly into my apartment. Unless I'm sitting at the small desk in the tiny loft, everyone can see me eating cereal in my underwear. Yesterday, I was repeatedly trying to shove my giant suitcase into a small closest and eventually resorted to kicking it as hard as I could when I looked up to see a French couple peering in from the court-yard.

Even though, like New York, Paris has loud traffic and filthy streets, there are also little neighborhoods that are quiet and residential pock-ets tucked away down little streets right next to huge monuments like the Bastille. I can't hear any street noise from my apartment, just the footfalls of my neighbors and their light bickering (but since it is in French, they still seem charming). Every day, I walk by a little old lady in my courtyard who always seems to be pruning her tomato plant.

I live in the Marais, which is on the Right Bank of the Seine. The older buildings in the Marais are built with beige-gold brick, and have huge ancient windows. Down the main street near my house, there are cafés with awnings—it's true, just like the Parisian stereotypes—as well as bakeries. Oh my God, the bakeries! I'm trying to limit myself to one almond croissant per day, but resistance is futile.

Right now it just started drizzling and the Frenchmen at the café are glaring up at the sky and the waiter is glaring at me. My impres-sion that I could order one latte and stay at a café writing all day was disproven yesterday when, after half an hour, a waiter walked by and slipped the bill on my table. When I paid, he took away my coffee, my spoon, the sugar, and my tablecloth. So much for Hemingway, who made it seem in his stories like you could sit here forever and not be bothered.

Now everybody is darting around with their umbrellas and it re-minds me so much of an Impressionist painting. Are you rolling your eyes right now? But it does!

Soon, I'll be taking cinema classes with a group of about a hundred other students, mostly French students. You know the stereotype of French people being aloof? Now imagine French graduate students studying film. I'm a little anxious about it. I still have a few more Xanax left from my time in New York. I don't know yet if I will need them, but it's comforting to know I have them in case of a panic attack.

Today I went to an appointment with my new research advisor for my film program at the Sorbonne. Except I showed up forty-five minutes late; I'm still so confused about Paris's curvy streets and metro strikes. My supervisor, Pierre, has a very French manner: He keeps a totally stone-cold face even while listening to jokes, and laughs only after you are finished.

I haven't had a conversation in French in years, unless you count my French exam, and in front of Pierre, I rambled on and on in broken French, trying to get a read on him until I trailed off into a spiral of misconjugated verbs. Finally, he sits up and responds after I've managed to stop myself from talking.

"Rachelle, the first thing you have to know about French academia is that you are the only one worried about your thesis in August, more than a year before it's due.

"The second thing you need to know is that you are in France. Relax a little."

Then Pierre rather bluntly suggested that I work on my French. Agreed.

We then discussed the parameters of my project, which are not coincidentally also reflected in my life: the haunting of the younger self, or "the younger double." That is, when in a film a character comes face-to-face with him- or herself as a child.

If I came face-to-face with myself as a child, this is what I would say: "Rachel, start working on your French *now*. And a hard-on is not a kind of hammer, so stop pretending that you know what it is at slumber parties. Also, invent Facebook."

I thought about this on the walk home, among other things. My younger self did always love Paris. While walking past the ruins of a medieval church, I realized that I'd anticipated finally arriving in Paris for so long and, now that I'm here, I feel deliriously happy but also a little lonely. This city must be shared! Come and explore Paris with me! We will discover Chinese-French restaurants and I will show you where *Sabrina* took place, and we will drink sweet minty tea at Middle Eastern cafés.

I know so much is going to happen here, but I don't know how. It feels like Paris is full of so many adventures just waiting to be had.

For now, I'm waiting for the rain to stop before I venture out again.

Love,
Rachelle

SEPTEMBER 12

## Jess to Rachel

WHERE ARE YOU NOW

I THINK I AM DERHIKNKER THAN I HEVE EHVER BEEN

SPANSH BAR PARYT

I JUST KISSED A 41-YEAR-ODL. DANIEL CRAIG! DANEIL CRAG!

OH GOD. OH GOD. MY HEAD. ACHES. GOING TO GO THROW UP. SERIOUSLY GOING TO [PUKEKWJFS. I HEVER DRIVE THINK MUCH!

THIS IS WHAT I REMEMBER ABOUT PARIS:
SMELLS LIKE URINE
XOX

*Later that day*

## Rachel to Jess

JESS!
When he was our age, we were five. Hahaha.
More details, fewer capital letters, please.
R

## Jess to Rachel

Oh God. Oh God. Why? Why. So hungover.

My hangover is infinitely worse because I live in a country where you can't drink the tap water. Just lying in bed, thirsty, licking my parched lips, dreaming of water, trying to will water to appear in my bedroom. I finally dragged myself out of bed to run into a corner shop and bought three gallons of bottled water. And a box of cookies. And something called Pejoy, which are sweet, crunchy breadsticks covered in dark chocolate mousse.

Whatever, you'd like it.

I get drunk so rarely these days and this is why. THIS IS WHY.

And it was sangria. I got that drunk on sangria.

Here is what I remember.

I met this guy at a Spanish bar with Victoria because all of my other friends were at a party I was not invited to: George's housewarming. I remember talking to a Canadian expat who told me that I "spoke English surprisingly good for a Chinese girl." Then he asked how long had I been studying English. As I was replying, "I'm an American, *jackass*," a man, who'd overheard the exchange, interrupted. In an English accent he said, "No, but how *does* a Yankee speak English so well?"

And that's how I met Ray. I get to say he looks like Daniel Craig, because I secretly thought it while we were talking and then Victoria grabbed my arm and whispered into my ear, "What's with James Bond?" Vindicated.

I just remember finding out his age and being surprised. I've never dated outside my age group before and it confuses me to be attracted to somebody who was born when the Beatles were still together. He was born before the first moon landing. And he was *ten* when Post-its were invented. Of course, I only know this because I figured out what year he was born (1967) and have been trying to put that into context.

We continued arguing about inconsequential things. I remember feeling my face and body turn bright red from the alcohol and after a particularly heated debate about who spoke Chinese better, I remember shouting, "I'll call you when I'm forty!" as I went off in search of more sangria.

Remember how you once told a group of people we'd just met that you wished you could follow me around, apologizing for all the tactless things I say? I really wished you had been there to do that.

I pushed my luck and made another joke about Ray being old. Then he found out I worked for a family expat magazine.

Ray: "See, you're such a baby that you only report on babies." I couldn't come up with a good rebuttal. While lying in bed just now, I came up with a great one. Here it is:

"Go pick on someone your own age." Right? Right?

So there.

Anyway, he's English. Why do Englishmen have so much sway over me? It's not just the stupid accent . . . is it? I hope I am not this vapid. Evidence seems to support this theory, though, despite the huge differences in personality among them. Why do I have a feeling they have ruined me for all other men?

But Ray's the complete opposite of George. If George was a hilarious, sweet schoolboy who has a few more years of growing up to do, then Ray is a sexy man who smells like aftershave and is also kind of mean. He is probably also the guy who used to pick on the Georges of the world. He always seems to be sort of leaning back with a satisfied expression on his face.

At 2 A.M., the bar began to empty, and when I stepped into the bathroom I saw that my skin had become even more fiery red from the alcohol and my eyes were bloodshot. Not a good look.

I waved good-bye to Victoria, but when I headed out into the street to hail a cab, Ray appeared from nowhere, grabbed me back, pulled me toward him, and kissed me. Then he placed his card into my coat pocket and said, "I'll see you next weekend."

Only older men have the confidence to be this aggressive. I hate that it's working. But it's working.

After my physical ambivalence toward George, the electricity I felt with Ray was all the more potent.

Brad Pitt, Tom Cruise, and George Clooney are all older than forty.

Rach, what do I do, what do I do? Is this completely pointless?

But I must not think about this now. Tomorrow begins a busy week at the magazine before we go to print. It is also Victoria's last week and I need to hire my replacement since I am officially taking her job as managing editor. I sifted through a stack of applications, but it feels strange to be in charge of someone else's future. Especially when I'm nursing a hangover.

I just checked and right now, it's evening in Paris. I imagine tree-lined streets and accordion music. I imagine girls wearing scarves, sitting with their long legs crossed over each other, rows of high heels and red lipstick. They drink wine with pursed lips and say things like, "*Sacre bleu!*" I want to be sitting there with you! I want to visit you so much—I have a feeling that Beijing and Paris are complete opposites in many ways.

Right now, I can see flocks of Chinese women also carrying um-brellas, even though it's sunny and hot. Chinese women want their skin as white as possible. Whereas Westerners lie in any patch of sun-light they can find, Asian women run from it like vampires fleeing their imminent death.

Which is exactly what I did when I stepped into the bright light this morning.

Love,

Jess

P.S. Just remembered best part of Beijing. McDonald's delivers here. I could have gorged on a delicious mixture of fat and preserva-tives to restore my sad hungover body, rather than stale chocolate breadsticks. Does Paris have this wonderful service??

P.P.S. Oh God—the Big Mac was invented the year Ray was born.

**SEPTEMBER 18**

## Rachel to Jess

What, did you just Google "people in their early forties"? And then "things that were invented in 1967"? You don't need water. You need to close your computer and get out of your apartment!

First of all, it's very French to have an older lover (think of *Le Divorce*), so it's like you're actually being very Parisian in Beijing. No French maître d' ever makes the American mistake of asking, "And what will your daughter be having, sir?" They always err on the side of assuming that it is a May-December romance.

I know I can't stop you from pursuing something that's already begun in your mind, but my advice is to tread carefully. It's suspicious that a good-looking, witty, employed older man is single, isn't it? Or am I just being too cynical? What's happening with Ray now?

I've officially begun my film studies program here. But I did not get off to a very good start. The first class I went to was an exercise in humiliation. The professor looks around the room, crammed full of students.

Professor (in French) says, "No, no, no. No. Maximum of ten people in this class. There must be fifty of you here. I shall decide who belongs. Please state your name and what you think *the plasticity of cinema* means, and how it applies to your proposed thesis subject."

She turns to me, front and center. "Go on, mademoiselle."

At this point, I was still processing the sentence containing "maximum of ten people." What I said is untranslatable, but roughly, it went something like this:

"Me? Oh. Oh no, sorry, is hard. Plasticity . . . quality of plastic. Form. My thesis is un-in-determinable?" At this point, I was trying to think of the conjugation of "is" into "will be" and was totally stumped, as I felt fifty pairs of French eyes on me.

She cut me off with a slice of her hand through the air.

"If you're registered for the class, I can't stop you from taking it, but you will not do well with French like that. Next!"

I waited for break, which doesn't come until an hour later, and I glowed red with shame the whole time. Then I snuck out to the balcony for a cigarette. A girl who looks like a friendly elf (tiny, feathery blond hair) came up to me.

"It's so hard to talk in front of so many people," she said. "And everyone knows that professor's a bitch. Take the Tuesday section instead. I'm Marie, by the way."

And that is how I dropped my first French class—and made my first French friend. We go to the Tuesday section together and have coffee afterward. Because she is in her second year, she tells me gossip about all of the students in her year: who's an idiot, who is secretly smart, whom to avoid. And I mostly understand her: I'm much better one-on-one than in an enormous group.

I have to confess, though: She is my only friend in Paris. It's strange to walk around all day and then come home to an empty apartment. No respite from myself. How did you make friends in Beijing?

Your image of women in Paris is partially on target. I know you think Frenchwomen wear scarves everywhere, but only the old women do this. French girls our age wear close-fitting jeans with worn old beautiful sweaters or simple short dresses that flare at the thigh, with heels. They also put on very little makeup—maybe just a trace of eyeliner.

Taking a cue from them, I've started to wear heels everywhere, even in the face of treacherous cobblestones. It's a performance. I want to feel like I'm contributing *something* to the beauty of the city, rather than detracting from it in ugly old flip-flops.

Today, I went to the Tuileries Gardens to read and look out at the tourists, the couples walking hand-in-hand, and the groups of students sitting and laughing. The Tuileries are formal and manicured, but if you go down any side path, you reach squares of green grass surrounded by couples kissing on every other bench. I sit alone and when some sleazy man inevitably approaches me, this is what I do: just say *"non"* to whatever he asks and stare straight ahead until he goes away. Also, cover my purse.

Love,
Rach

## Jess to Rachel

Okay, the simplest way to make friends is to send out a mass e-mail to all of your friends back home titled, "You Can Stay in My Apartment in Paris If You Set Me Up with Friends Here." I guarantee everyone will reply and you'll get responses from people you haven't heard from in YEARS.

Well, I think I may be dating Ray, but I actually have no idea. He always keeps me guessing. A few days after our drunken encounter, we met up for dinner at a Japanese restaurant and it felt strange to sit across from each other completely sober. A silence fell over both of us after the waitress took our order and I could feel us both sizing each other up and thinking, "What are we doing here?"

At dinner, there were distinct differences between dating him and the other guys I've been with. He kept refilling my glass and he was very concerned that I liked the food. He kept asking if I was cold or not.

Boys just don't do this. All of this felt brand-new to me, but I kept wondering about how many first dates Ray has had. How many times has he told another woman about his past life as an unsatisfied lawyer? Is this empty Japanese restaurant his go-to place? That joke he just told—has he used the same exact one on other women? Or is he tailoring it to make it age-appropriate for me?

So in this relationship, I'm the incredibly insecure one. He's forty-one; I'm almost twenty-four. I moved here over a year ago and I already feel like I'm ten times smarter than I was when I first arrived. But he's nearly *twenty* years older than me, so what does *he* know? I won't know for another twenty years! I'm never going to catch up with him.

He paid for me, and I didn't protest because I'd ordered less than he had and I didn't know if that's just how he does things. And then, despite his being forty-one, we made out like high schoolers outside the bar. I guess some things don't change. I know if I could see myself from afar, I wouldn't understand the situation. What am I doing with him? I don't know, but of course he can charm me! Because he has been doing it since 1979.

I feel at once really young and really old. I leave work feeling secure and authoritative in my new role and then I revert into a shy version of myself with an older man who seems to want me to take on this role.

He casually dropped in how women lose their shit when it comes to him and that's why he's still single. Although older British men don't really say "lose their shit." It was probably "go mad about him." He offhandedly mentions that so many women become obsessed with him and he'd love to get married and settle down, if he could just find one with a stable head on her shoulders. If someone our age said something this outlandish, I would challenge them. But I didn't fight him on it. Because . . . I don't want to be one of those women.

Thoughts:

He might be too old for me.
George is funnier, but Ray is far sexier.
He must be damaged, right? A forty-one-year-old good-
    looking straight man who's never been married?
Or is he just a commitment-phobe?
Gray pubic hair?

We had a second date a few days later and conversation seemed to flow better because he got to talk about his work and I got to sit enraptured, both of us playing our roles perfectly. He's lived in Beijing for four years and he's one of the foreign correspondents for a UK national broadsheet. The last article he wrote was about the fight against AIDS in China and the importance of sex education in this country. I did not tell him that I just wrote about the fifty most kid-friendly restaurants in Beijing.

Ray goes to lots of fancy journalist parties and seems annoyed at the reporters who get more attention than him. I made some joke about how I imagine him trying to catch the eyes of passersby and they brush him aside to reach the *New York Times* correspondent instead. At this, he broke his charismatic demeanor and seemed irrationally mad. He breathed heavily through his nose and poured more sake. I reverted back to Shy Polite Amazed Girl and in a few minutes, he reassumed his preferred role of Worldly Seducer.

And even so, I still like him so much—he's intelligent and sharp and I feel like he keeps me sharp. And he's handsome. Intense gray eyes and black hair.

And because all we've done is kiss, I feel like I'm being courted.

Doubts still creep in, though. He feels unattainable, because he won't commit to plans more than a day in advance. It's beginning to make me feel insecure, just like all the other women who have loved Ray and then "gone mad."

Work, at least, is one place where I finally feel in control. I never knew how different it would be to be the boss of the magazine. I cared about my job before, but if things went wrong, I still felt like the blame always fell on Victoria. And now, I suddenly care so much about every single thing. I lie awake thinking about what would make this the best magazine ever and in the shower I find myself reeling off a hundred headlines for the cover feature and then fretting about the perfect one.

I ended up hiring our intern as my replacement. Isla is a really enthusiastic waif-thin Australian who is equal parts hyper and wise. She's tall with short white-blond hair and I'm short with long dark hair—I'm trying to ward off comparisons that she is a bowling pin and I am the bowling ball. Despite towering over me, she's younger than I am, so I feel free to have very outward freak-outs in front of her. Before leading my first editorial meeting, I confided, "Isla, I don't even know what I'm doing!" And she's like, "Nobody does! We're all bluffing!" Great advice.

We sit next to each other and the rest of the office calls us, collectively, "The Kids," because we are the youngest team in the office and we're also writing about children a lot. Sometimes when we are being too loud, we'll hear a cranky Scottish guy yelling across the room, "Shut up, Kids!"

Because I am adjusting to my new responsibilities and because we are understaffed, Isla and I spend nearly every waking minute together, sometimes coming in on weekends. She has a tendency to bang her head on the desk when we clash with our bosses, and I love her for this audacity. She's brave in a way that I aspire to be. But I'll never tell her that, especially because sometimes when we argue about our editorial vision, I want to shout, "I AM THE BOSS OF YOU!"

The power has gone to my head.

Ohhhhh God, Ray text. "I know it's improper to text the day after, but I'm looking forward to kissing you again. And again. I can't stop thinking about you."

You see? I am helpless in the face of this honed charisma. I wonder if this is an auto-reply to every woman he goes on a date with.

Love,

Boss

**OCTOBER 2**

---

## Rachel to Jess

To understand Ray, I think I should tell you about what my former colleague Sally told me about older men dating younger women. It's not just about sex. They like to feel superior. As in, "Why not be with someone hotter than you AND who looks up to you?"

I know that I would be so seduced by Ray as well, but he's had so much longer than you to practice his craft. The fact that he thinks girls go crazy on him is a big warning sign to me. This may be his veiled way of telling you, "I am going to make you crazy."

It feels like all of a sudden you are being expected to grow up really fast. You're running a magazine and dating a real man. Like, maybe you *should* be in your forties now. Which is weird, because usually *I* am the one you say is acting old for my age (I still read mystery novels and I just knitted a hat, so you might still have me there).

I do feel more adult now that I'm living alone. I love it so much that it makes me worry about getting married or moving in with somebody because I love waking up and not having to confront aggressive questions about how I slept (all questions seem aggressive to me in the morning). I love having the bathroom available whenever I want and not having to worry about what previously went on in the shower and what is still okay to touch.

However, living alone does have its problems. The neighbors next door played loud music until four in the morning and I had an 8 A.M. class (it was a Wednesday), and I found myself alone, banging on the wall with a broom. It's actually funny to go through this stuff with a friend, but alone, it's a little sad. Also, there's no Rosabelle to steal food from or remind me when my rent is due.

I've been seeing my friend from class, Marie, a lot. She knows all the good bars in my area, where she also lives. She's very direct and says the things I think about Paris but had no one to tell. When we were chatting, I felt tension release from my shoulders. I cannot explain how relieved I am to have met this kind of friend this early on. They're like gold dust.

And also, she helps me with my homework.

I still have downtime right now. French schoolwork isn't spread evenly over the year. Each class has either one final paper or one final exam. So while I'm coasting now, January and June are going to be a frantic effort to study and write. But for now, I'm devoting myself to writing in cafés (a secret pastime I hide from Marie, because it is so embarrassing to be an American writing in a Parisian café). My story has officially inflated into a novel, which is at once overwhelming and exciting.

I don't know if it's any good because I haven't shown it to anyone except my dad. I wrote to him asking him if he'd read it, but his feedback is so opaque and sometimes just frustrating. Last week, as a response to my chapter 3, he wrote: "Have you read *Shane*? Go read *Shane*. It's incredibly well plotted."

*Shane* is a 1950s Western.

He put me in contact with a good friend of his from the Iowa Writers' Workshop. He has a fancy literary agent and has been on Oprah discussing his book. I e-mailed him because, as Claudia loved to remind me, nothing was ever accomplished by someone who sits in their apartment alone waiting for life to begin.

I took your advice and sent out a mass e-mail to our friends seeking out their French connections. Platonic Nick wrote back, putting me in touch with his old roommate Jacques, a filmmaker. Finally—a night out with a real French person. I can't seem to force hot Frenchmen to have drinks with me any other way, it seems. I know that I live in the capital of Hot French Men, but it seems impossible to actually be a part of their world. Waiters who are expecting a tip and professors who grade your papers don't really count.

In the end, I stalked Jacques online (obviously) and he's drop-dead gorgeous, but the Internet told me that he also has a hot girlfriend. However, boys lead to boys who beget boys, as a wise roofied girl once told me.

Not to worry—a million Maries shall not replace you.

Love,

Rach

## Jess to Rachel

Oh, Rach, you are literally a little old lady now. "Eh, what's that? TURN YOUR MUSIC DOWN." Bangs broom on wall. "Fucking kids," you mutter as you kick off your slippers and slather on your night cream.

Anyway, beware of Jacques and all good-looking men—Ray just stood me up. HE STOOD ME UP. Second time this week. Stand me up once, shame on you. Stand me up twice, I fucking hate you. I canceled plans to meet Isla and her friends for karaoke and now I'm writing to you while wearing lipstick, which just feels wrong to me. I cleaned my entire apartment thinking tonight could be the night. And now what am I going to do with this clean apartment? Total waste.

I had two more semidates with Ray, dates that I had to completely bend over backward for and orchestrate on my own. It's like he hooked me and now I'm chasing him. I'm making all the effort: running out of work to catch him in time before he had a flight to Hong Kong, staying out late one night because he could only meet at 10 P.M. So far, there's still been nothing but kissing. Old-school rules?

Oh God, do you think this is how George justified my odd behavior?

Wait, that doesn't make sense. George and I are the same age. Discuss.

J

**OCTOBER 10**

---

## Rachel to Jess

Old-school rules? Jess. Ray was born in the 1960s. Not the 1800s. People have been having premarital sex this entire century and probably, in fact, for long before that. I think he's playing a game. I don't know how you can win it, though. What can you possibly win?

## Jess to Rachel

I win the sex with Daniel Craig? Except that I haven't. He always cancels. "I'm on deadline. Maybe we'll meet up later this week."

I can't live like this!!! The uncertainty is killing me!

Remember that Master List we supposedly sent the universe? The universe couldn't find everything in one man, so it sent me two. George had about 80 percent of the qualities and Ray has the remaining 20 percent (sexy, manly, fixes things, more worldly).

Telling detail: While George sent me one hundred e-mails a day, Ray will only send me one per day. Never more.

### *Later that day*

## Jess to Rachel

Oh! Oh! Ray text. He wants to meet up tomorrow. Feels serious. Romantic restaurant.

Do you think I have to get a bikini wax? I don't want to. . . . Do I have to? Don't want to.

Maybe he is used to old-fashioned ways.

Maybe, in fact, a bikini wax would freak him out and he'd be shocked by the lack of body hair?

*Later that day*

## Rachel to Jess

He's forty-one. He's seen porn. I think he knows about waxing.

## Jess to Rachel

He canceled again.

*Later that day*

## Rachel to Jess

I'm starting to think that he is the worst.
And you are the best, so something's not adding up.

## Jess to Rachel

I tried calling your Paris phone, but you aren't there. You're probably eating a baguette or discussing Foucault with French film students or being Parisian by showing up late somewhere. It's very comforting to think of you in the sunlight in Paris, when it is dark over in Beijing. Especially on a night like tonight.

How do I begin to explain what happened next with Ray? After the numerous cancellations, he called me up and told me how sorry he was and how much he wanted to see me. He made a joke about how he hadn't called earlier because he was trying to figure out the perfect place to take me. I knew this was a lie, but I wanted to believe it. It could have been true, right?

We met the next day at eight for dinner in a tiny Chinese restaurant. And we got along so well. The initial awkwardness and all of the doubts that I had before were gone. I wasn't worried about other women he's been with, about seeming young and shy, about teasing him. I felt totally at ease and he seemed to laugh at all my jokes. And at the end he told me how much he liked me.

We walked to a nearby bar, where we sat close together in a booth and he stared into my eyes. Again, he told me how much he likes me. He told me he was leaving for Hong Kong for two weeks, but I said, "Well, you have to see me Saturday, before you go." He said, "Of course. I have to see you before I go."

And I believed him.

We went back to his place, kissing as we walked. I tripped in his bathroom and broke his shower curtain. We laughed a lot about it, though. We laugh a lot.

We start making out on his bed. Clothes come off. (Note: There seem to be no discernible differences between a forty-one-year-old body and a twentysomething body. Maybe a tad softer.) Everything was going great. We're kissing, he's stroking my neck, and he's running his hands over my body.

This is the moment where one of us should have reached for a condom. I thought we'd continue kissing and at least discuss the next step, but instead Ray made the decision for us and just went for it, no condom.

WHAT? RAY! WHAT?

Suddenly, it was a flashback to my Bruno freak-out. Total shutdown of all of the sexual buildup as sirens start ringing in my mind. I am not having sex without a condom.

With Bruno, it was just a broken condom—his intentions were still good! I shoved Ray away from me but tried to play down my panic because I didn't want to completely lose the moment. I asked if he had a condom. He didn't seem to like this.

I reminded him I'm young (unlike him) and therefore fertile. He still didn't seem convinced. I had to finally firmly tell him NO—this was not going to happen without a condom, under any circumstances. And, as if on cue, he went completely, totally, limp.

He told me that condoms aren't sexy. What does he want? A condom with a naked woman painted on it? Would that be more effective than an *actual naked woman*? This coming from the guy who, *just last month*, wrote a column about the importance of preventing the spread of HIV through sex education in China.

I wasn't even freaking out at this point. I feel like I've seen movies where the guy loses his erection, and I always feel bad for the guy. I feel like it's ingrained in women that, around lost erections, we must talk in hushed voices so that we don't further scare the penis. We must protect the penis's feelings at the cost of all other feelings. And whatever we do, we must not comment on it and just have to pretend like it never happened.

And, Rachel, I was still thinking, "Maybe we can work through this." My mind kept coming up with solutions: Maybe we can both get tested for STDs and maybe I'll go on the pill and then we can have sex without the vile, off-putting condom? Maybe he'll change his mind. We'll figure this out.

So I was cool and levelheaded as we kept lying in bed talking. I try to change the subject and begin asking about his life in Beijing before he met me. I casually ask him about the last person he dated and slept with. He says it was a Chinese woman. Fair enough. Our hands are intertwined. I ask, "When was that?"

"Last week."

Last week! LAST WEEK! LAST FUCKING WEEK!

I met him a month ago. Three weeks ago we went out on our first date. Two weeks ago we were at a bar kissing while he ran his fingers through my hair! I thought he was crazy about me. I thought our waiting so long had built up sexual tension, and that he didn't want to rush things with me because he was considerate. But no—he was just off having sex with *someone else*.

And yet he wanted to have sex with me without a condom! He doesn't know any of my sexual history *and* he just assumed I would do this. He doesn't even *own* a condom, which means he's definitely not having protected sex with these other women.

I think my mouth actually dropped open. I felt the rage rising in me. Red-hot anger. My mind couldn't even compute all the information. It was like a domino effect of terrible revelations.

1. REFUSES CONDOM

2. LOSES ERECTION

3. SLEEPS WITH OTHER WOMEN

4. SLEEPS WITH OTHER WOMEN WITHOUT CONDOM

5. IF I STAY HERE, I WILL BECOME PREGNANT WITH STD-RIDDEN BABY BY PHILANDERING OLD NON-BOYFRIEND

I didn't know how to react outwardly, because I didn't know if I had the right to be angry. We never said we were exclusive. The worst part is, I felt embarrassed, like I wasn't good enough for him. This whole time, I'd been afraid I'd be one of those crazy girls he always bemoans who get so crazy and obsessed with him.

I totally get these girls now. They are not the problem. They are just like me.

I got up and got dressed. To my shock, this surprised him. He wanted to know when he could see me again. Despite my silence, he followed me out, because that's what older men do. He tried to kiss me good-bye as I hailed a cab at a busy intersection, but I just stood there, arms straight by my side, frozen.

What the fuck, what the fuck, what the fuck.

I hate him, and I'm angry, but I'm also hurt. Unbelievably hurt.

And embarrassed. What was I doing with him? I'm twenty-three! Why am I wasting my youth on this scumbag? Never again.

I think I'm particularly bewildered and bitter about Ray because I used to have George. George, who adored me and loved me and would never ever hurt me.

I never thought a lost erection would be a godsend, but it was. It was sent by my guardian angel, the Erection Angel, coming down and preventing me from sleeping with Ray. I'm counting my limp blessings.

Ray was a mistake I would erase in a heartbeat, and I really can't blame anyone but myself. I played an equal role in this and invited him into my life as I pretended to play some ingenue role that seemed interesting and fun.

I remember telling Victoria that I was young and I could make mistakes. And she said, "Make the wrong one and you'll regret it forever."

I'm going to try my best to never run into Ray, but the expat bubble in Beijing feels so small. We have so many people in common. I already feel like I know everybody here and so many of my good friends have already left. Maxwell's gone, Astrid's gone, Victoria's gone.

The saying here is that if you stay in Beijing for three years, you'll be here forever. I'm in year two.

I actually e-mailed a friend from my journalism class at Brown, asking him for advice about opportunities in New York, because I thought he might offer an escape route. He told me that he and a crew from our old class try to sneak into all the New York media parties and line up to pitch their ideas to editors. They have about a 2 percent success rate and most of them work in retail during the day. I guess I'm staying here for now.

I miss you.

Love,

Jess

## Rachel to Jess

I'm so disgusted by Ray. How many half-Ray babies do you think are wandering around China? It just seems like another one of his power games. . . . He's old, but he's not *that* old. It's not like condoms are a recent invention or something.

And WHAT THE FUCK? Last week?

I hate him. I wish there were something I could do to him from Paris that would totally fuck him up.

I think it is time to make the clean break with the past. This is the year we leave our Rays behind and put our plans into action.

My biggest news this week is that I had a response from my dad's author friend Lee about my first chapter in the novel I sent him:

> Rachel,
>> I am being pulled along by the language.
>> Please write and tell me what you dream for as a writer
> and a person
>>> What kind of life you want
>>> And send more
>>> —Lee

I stared at his reply for a while before writing back.

I think the absolute truth is this:

"I am almost twenty-four years old and beyond a few glimmering out-of-reach hopes, I still don't know what I want from life. I want to fall in love. I want to be happy, and while I'm still trying to figure out how, I know that it is contingent on writing."

I also considered adding, "I would also like to someday be so talented that my name gets turned into an adjective (as in Kafkaesque. "That mermaid scene was so Kapelke-Dale-esque."). Also, my book is translated into ALL the languages, and I get to be on the cover of *Vogue*, in which they Photoshop me to make me look fatter because I am too thin."

I'm trying to get the courage to send this to him (just the first part?). What I really want to say is, "I'm so happy now, and I want to figure out how to keep growing without ruining this balance."

All my love,

Rach

**NOVEMBER 3**

## Jess to Rachel

Send Lee the second part too, and see if he can have it arranged.

I also don't know how I would respond to his question about the kind of life we want. All I'm sure of right now is that I'm growing antsy. What would my name become if it were a literary device someday? Maybe it will refer to when a character relocates to another country on a whim. "She pulled a Pan and we heard from her six months later when she wrote from a boat off the coast of Ecuador."

I love Beijing but living here long-term isn't feasible. I'll never be completely fluent in the language. And there's so much pollution. A ridiculously fast pace of life. So far from home. I can't live here forever, but it doesn't feel right to go somewhere else without a purpose. I'm ready for a new adventure. I still feel too young to stop exploring.

My dad wants me to come home to America. Instead of saying, "You must come home this instant," he says, "I wish you'd come home. I miss you so much. You've been gone for so long."

I *have* been gone for some time now. It's hard to see my family only once or twice a year. I thought it would get easier as time passed, but it feels like as I get older, it makes me more sad. Sometimes I wake up in my apartment and really remember that most of my friends and family are more than six thousand miles away from me and I get a pang of loneliness.

It rarely lasts past noon, though. Work seems to help. I started a section in our magazine that gives free makeovers to moms. My plan to surreptitiously turn it into *Glamour* is slowly taking hold, although what do I do now that I can't be promoted any higher at my magazine?

My parents don't expect me to move back to Amarillo, but when they ask me to come to the United States for good, all I see is a vision of me ringing up customers at our local bookstore for the rest of my life. Whenever I'm back in Texas and someone finds out I live in China, they respond in one of two ways. Often, the person compliments me on the great missionary work I must be doing over here. Otherwise, they just ask, "But . . . why?" Lately, I'm beginning to ask myself the same thing.

The weather has turned very chilly in Beijing and they haven't turned the heat on yet. *They* is the Chinese government. The heat here is controlled by the government! They pick an arbitrary day to just flip the heat switch on, and it can't come soon enough. I'm sleeping in long underwear, sweatpants, a hoodie, and a beanie. I use a hair dryer to warm my frozen face in the morning.

Still, I might prefer this to senior year in our house, when you and Astrid waged shrill wars at 4 A.M. over the thermostat. It was so scary to lie in bed in the dark and hear voices in the hallway: "My sheets are colder than Norway right now!" followed by your shriek of, "It's so hot in my room that my hair is curling! Go back to Norway!"

I wish the horoscopes in *Glamour* really did work so I'd know what to do next. If only it were as easy as getting back in touch with nature or taking a bubble bath.

Love,

Jess

### Four Months Later

Four months followed, in which Jess toiled away at the magazine and Rachel watched a lot of bad French TV to master the language (and feel like she had friends in Paris). Many e-mails were exchanged, but mostly about our imaginary lives in Argentina, Spain, or Italy (Rachel) and India, Thailand, or Alaska (Jess).

**MARCH 6**

## Rachel to Jess

Help! Two problems! How the hell do you get glitter out of your eyelashes and how do you get the scent of a gallon of cheap perfume out of leather? Or maybe I should be more concerned that my feet are covered in grime and dirt and God knows what else. I also reek of the stench of a thousand cigarettes.

It's 3 P.M. and I just woke up like this.

Last night, I finally met up with Jacques, who used to live in New York with Platonic Nick. I met him in the eleventh district, where there are bars with red neon signs and students sitting drinking on steps. I was here once three years ago and remember this street as the place where Rosabelle threw up under a table and we were forcibly ejected from a bar.

When Jacques arrived at the bar, a blur of dark hair and cologne, he kissed me on both cheeks, with a big grin, and then ordered a glass of red wine for me and a pastis for him. Pastis is a disgusting licorice-flavored cloudy drink. Jacques and I spoke in French about how he used to live in New York, in Williamsburg. He loves New York, like every French person I meet does, but loves it in a totally overwhelming, "How could you think any place would be better?" kind of way. I think it is the way Americans think about Paris, and it's weird to hear it from the other side.

We were two drinks in when somebody tapped on the glass behind me. I looked to see a group of people grinning and waving at Jacques, who gestured for them to come inside.

I stood up to kiss each of them on the cheeks, but I'm still getting used to this. It's one kiss per cheek, but is it their left then their right, or no, my left, your right, or WHAT IS GOING ON? If you mess this ritual up, all hell breaks loose. And also, when there is a big group, you have to kiss everybody and it takes forever.

Finally, while I was pulling away from the last guy, Olivier, we locked eyes.

I know how this sounds, but I had never felt this sudden attraction for someone before. He has sandy-brown hair and light blue eyes, is about five ten, and has a dimple in his chin. I tried to look away, tried to distract myself, and tried not to have a look across my face that reads like my mind: "Hot Olivier, let's ditch this crowd and go make out on a bench."

We ordered a few more drinks and sat in the back, and I mostly listened and nodded. I ended up in a corner with a girl called Sasha, who is very tall and has dark flowing hair and a welcoming smile for everyone, even when she's telling someone to fuck off. She was very direct and asked me what kinds of French guys I liked, and I kept trying not to point at Olivier and say, "Him." Tall Sasha is dating Hipster Marc (this is the only way I can keep track of them), who has known Jacques and Olivier forever.

One of the girls invited us all back to her house, where her roommates were having a party. We left the bar and I fell into step with Olivier. He laughed hard when I tried to tell him that I missed my roommate in New York. Apparently, the expression I have been using for "roommate" has no real meaning in French, but roughly translates to "bedroom friend." I have been using my made-up expression for *years*. Finally, those strange looks are explained.

According to Olivier, my French is enunciated just fine but is formal, extremely polite, and slightly antiquated in a way that makes his friends laugh (with me? At me. With me?). Apparently, I use outdated expressions, such as "companion" for "boyfriend" or "moving picture" for "movie." Basically, in French, I am the little old lady who lives across from my courtyard.

By the time we arrived at the party, I'd had four drinks and was so overwhelmed by all the new French faces suddenly among me. Tall Sasha took my hands and pulled me over to the living room to dance, where thick smoke hovered over everything, and bubbles floated around randomly from a machine.

At one point, someone became too enthusiastic about a particular song and started spraying silly string and throwing handfuls of glitter. Some girl spilled an entire bottle of perfume on my purse, but I did not care. I was at my first party in six months.

At 5 A.M., the lights went on. Sasha and I were still halfheartedly jumping along to '80s music among the bubbles that were now puddles of foam. It was over.

The Metro wouldn't open for another half an hour, so we walked around the neighborhood just to kill time (I love that there is actually a French word for this walking with no purpose: *flâner*).

We all exchanged numbers, and when they all disappeared around a corner, I immediately double-checked that they were gone and took off my boots. My feet were killing me. They have four-inch heels, and I'd been dancing in them for hours.

I wandered home in my stocking feet as the sun rose and the alcohol was wearing off and my mind was clear. If you cycle down French boulevards or peer into bakeries at pyramids of macaroons or wander through the Rodin Gardens, but you cycle and you peer and you wander with no company but your own, were you ever in Paris at all?

I've been contemplating this for a while. I've been here long enough to watch autumn start to trail off into winter. I just kept going to my classes, taking my notes, and then walking across the bridge home and watching Notre Dame behind the veil of rain. There are days where I don't speak to anyone, and others where I speak only to the baker down the road.

But after last night, Paris feels completely different to me. I was in a different world. I wonder if I'll see Olivier again or if he will just disappear into oblivion for me. But Hipster Marc wants to meet me on Monday for a coffee break at the National Library, where we both have to do our research. I'm meeting Tall Sasha next week for a movie.

See? There is still life in me yet. I'm saying this as much to myself as to you. Last night, I was not an old grandmother, except when I took off my shoes, rubbed my feet, and thought, "Shit. Do I have bunions?"

I'm also still trying to write every day.

And I am, as always, waiting for my next dispatch from Beijing.

Love,

Rach

## Jess to Rachel

Hot Frenchmen? Fancy French cocktails? Dancing in bubbles?

Rachel! Quick! Let's trade lives! Why have we not done this earlier? Don't think too hard about it—just hop on a plane to China and you can ride in rickshaws and marvel at skyscrapers and eat duck pancakes with plum sauce. Meanwhile, I will pretend to be a film student in Paris, where I get to live in your loft apartment in Paris and chase around hot Frenchmen. You get to live in my Beijing apartment, where

I'll even let you shower over my toilet, and I'll bravely eat one croissant per day from your local bakery in Le Marais, so that they don't feel a sudden drop in croissant demand.

The only snag is that I don't want to learn French. I'm barely managing with Mandarin. My brain has reached a saturation point of Mandarin words and is currently rejecting all new information. I also don't have the heart to tell my Chinese teacher that I don't want to learn the vocabulary for tea services and gift giving.

Paris sounds amazing. I can so easily imagine you wandering around Paris with Jacques and his friends, not knowing where the night will take you and feeling that around the next corner could be a stranger who will change your life.

I remember when I used to walk around like this in Beijing, taking photos of Taiwanese ice cream, piled as high as the ceiling, or getting lost in a maze of Chinese alleyways for fun. You can always tell the new arrivals from the jaded expats: The new arrivals are the ones staring at the fried scorpions sold at the night markets (I remember it so well) and the weary expats are the ones yelling at Chinese waitresses for bringing out the wrong kind of eggplant dish.

I resemble the latter group more and more. I suddenly find myself growing impatient with daily life here. Before, when oncoming passengers would rush onto the subway before I could get off at my stop, I used to view it as a fun game ("Challenge accepted!"). Now I scowl and use sharp elbows. I don't want to stay here so long that I can't see the good parts anymore. Your adventures in Paris just made me realize how my experience in Beijing is already heavy with memories, not all of them nice.

In a cab on the way home from work one night last week, I turned to my right and saw Ray, next to the car window, cycling home. My first reaction was to roll down my window to get his attention, but before I could manage this, the light changed and my cab sped away from him. Watching him recede into the background is the most contact we've had since I walked out of his apartment.

I'd been trying to completely repress all thoughts or feelings about that whole situation. You're the only person I've told about Ray, because I feel so embarrassed about playing an ingenue to an older man. I shudder to think about how long the charade would have gone on had the Erection Angel not struck Ray down. I was never going to marry someone like Ray—cold, proud, and twenty years my senior. I could have wasted entire years on him.

Want to hear about my dream? Great! I'd love to tell you. Last night I dreamt that I opened the door to a doctor's office to find every guy I had ever dated sitting in the waiting room. They sat side by side in rows of chairs: high school boyfriends, flings from Brown, a few token Australians from my year studying abroad, and then Bruno, George, and Ray. They sat, absentmindedly flipping through golf magazines, and waiting for their names to be called for a checkup, unaware that their common link was me.

I don't need a psychology professor to tell me, "Your track record is not so hot!" I've fallen into so many flings because I've always felt that I must explore! I must have adventures! I only live once! But there were a lot of mistakes in that waiting room. Only a handful loved me, but those were the ones I never loved back.

I contemplated this briefly in bed before I realized I was already running ten minutes late for work. It doesn't help matters that another expat editor my age just got promoted and subsequently he's started wearing a suit to work every day. A three-piece suit. Why do some people have to go and ruin everything for everyone? He's breaking the code! Before his promotion, he wore tank tops, baggy jeans, and flip-flops.

Now I'm wondering if I was supposed to start dressing in a power suit when I got promoted. Also, perhaps I should not have come to work today with my hair pulled back in a bandanna, which I thought could be interpreted as vaguely "Chinese" instead of its real meaning, "I've lost complete control of my bangs."

I don't really care, though, because although I've loved working here, I think I'm over it. I've written hundreds of stories now about family relationships, been to dozens of tourist spots in Beijing, and finished fifteen full issues. I've fought with our designer, Echo, six thousand times.

But I still want to be a journalist—I'm just not sure how to get to that career from here. In Beijing, it's easy to brush up against journalists and foreign correspondents (or date them, i.e., Ray). I've met the foreign correspondents for *TIME*, the *New Yorker*, and the *Guardian*, but there's still such a strong distinction between their jobs and mine. Even if someone made me the correspondent for the *New York Times* today and told me, "Go report on the Chinese migrant community!" I'd just stand in one place holding my tape recorder. I don't have hard news skills, despite everything I've learned on the job here. I almost think that I do want to go to journalism school, but I'm still against doing this in New York, a city jam-packed with journalists and sky-high tuition fees. But where would I go? I'm scared to make a move, but I feel stuck.

Isla tells me that I've been sighing a lot lately, and so she's trying to drag me out of my funk. Why can't she just let me go home and order takeout and watch bad TV? This is my right as a person on the verge of giving up. She's sneaky, because she makes a big show of inviting me out in front of our entire office, which means I can't very well reply in front of my other colleagues, "Isla, I have a stack of pirated DVDs and a giant Toblerone waiting for me at home." This is social tyranny. She's insisting that we eat bad Mexican food at her favorite hole-in-the-wall and drink a pitcher of margaritas. Each. This is Australia's cure for sadness.

Isla also told our bosses that our workload is too much for two people, and she hired a new intern to help us out for a few weeks.

He has dark hair and nice hands. I tried not to notice this, but Isla sits between us, and it's the only part of him I can see from the corner of my left eye.

Do not worry! I'm not going to date my own intern.

Love,

Jess

P.S. He's English.

## Rachel to Jess

What is with you and English guys? I think you might have a problem. Not a big problem, though. What I really want to know is, how does a girl from Texas end up with a tendency to go after English guys? Wait. Isn't one of your brothers married to an English girl? Developmentally, what happened to you guys?

Right now, I'm at the National Library. Most days I come here to study with Jacques and Marc in the philosophy reading room and I cart my books over from film and media studies. The rooms are deathly silent. People frown at you when you sneeze. It is a VERY SERIOUS place, where Jacques and Marc pull out copies of Derrida and Foucault, and I pull out old movie magazines. Right now, they are sitting across from me with their noses stuck in their computers.

They're both a little older than me, and they love talking about movies and books and also my mistakes in French. It feels like what I imagine having older brothers is like. Do they make fun of your taste in movies and give you book recommendations and also sometimes get you drunk?

Sometimes Tall Sasha meets us outside and we stand on the steps shivering with Jacques and Marc, making conversation over our thick black vending-machine espressos.

Things changed so quickly—I remember attending a seminar here my first week of school and just thinking what a big, empty place the library was and how Paris was so lonely.

I see these guys all the time and Olivier comes out a lot with us too. I've figured out that he is not dating anyone, he is not gay, and he always tries to take the seat next to me. Because he's currently between jobs, we meet for coffee with Sasha about three times a week.

I can't help but feeling like Olivier's trying to get me alone.

"You like horses? Do you want to go to the races sometime?"

(Jacques cuts in.) "Yeah, let's all go to the races!"

Or

Me: I can't wait to see this movie.

Olivier: I've been looking forward to it too! We should go.

Marc: Great! How's Tuesday?

I know we're moving toward something, but at a painfully slow pace.

Most nights end like this: We're all standing around in a group, deciding where to go next, when Olivier takes my hand.

And kisses my cheek.

And waves good-bye.

Sasha brings him up and nods at me knowingly. I haven't confided in her, but she knows I love him. How do girls always know?

Also, the writer, Lee, wrote back to me again. He's now halfway through my novel and he sent me an honest e-mail about how important it is to write books that people will actually read. He told me about his early novels, and the books that made a big splash in the literary world, and the difference between them. He wrote that no matter how beautiful the language and the characters are, we read fiction for stories—which is what my book lacks. He added that the word *novel* means *new*, which is what mine needs to be.

Lee's leading a writer's colony in Canada over the next month but will get back to me on the second half as soon as he can. Meanwhile, I'm trying to interpret what his feedback means for my future writing. Writing a plot-based story is so not what I learned in any class. "Write characters," I've been told. "Write what you know."

He says, "All literature is longing."

To me this means every character is driven by desire, but I'm still mulling this over.

Sometimes I want to give up and just write a romance novel.

Love,

Rach

## Jess to Rachel

Um, I don't know how to tell you this, but I must do it quickly. I am typing furiously before Isla and our intern come back into the office from lunch.

I have a thriving online relationship with my intern. Oh God. I just turned twenty-four. I should know better. What am I doing? Oh God. Omigod.

There. It's out there. Now you know and now it cannot be stopped.

Cons: Could lose job? Least professional editor ever?

Pros: This could be great fodder for the plot of a romance novel you are going to write.

His name is Sam Singer. Through my company's online messaging system, we began discussing upcoming articles, which then broke off into questions about our own personal travels, and then escalated into making light jokes about our colleagues. Then, a thousand messages later, he's telling me he thinks the bandanna I wear in my hair is cute.

This is not standard boss/intern territory, right? The typical intern job description does not include calling the boss cute, does it? If it does, this definitely explains why all of my summer internships led nowhere.

Other than the intricacies of flirting via instant messenger, here's what I have learned:

Before Sam arrived in Beijing, he spent a month backpacking

through India and from there he flew to Nepal to climb Mt. Everest. I'm going to let that sink in for you. He climbed Mt. Everest!

He is from a specific part of Northern England that makes him a "Mackem." Whatever the hell that means. His accent sounds more Irish than English to me; it has a melody to it. His sentences dip low and then end high.

He has dark brown hair and light hazel eyes. He has a grin that makes him look just like a young, slightly crooked Tom Cruise. When he smiles at me with one eyebrow raised, I know I am not strong enough to ignore my attraction to him. Why must his eyebrows have the ability to do that?? What evolutionary purpose does this serve except to make women want to throw themselves at raised-eyebrowed men?

Okay, I guess that is actually a pretty good evolutionary purpose. I just figured out the answer to my own question while typing this. Well played, Evolution.

Unfortunately, I can't technically see him without blatantly turning my chair around to look at him. Why must Isla sit between us? She's already as thin as a rail, but since I can't directly stare at Sam throughout the entire workday, I need her to be entirely invisible as well. That way, I can see what Sam is doing, what the back of his neck looks like, and if he's looking at me. This is not too much to ask, is it?

While chatting online, we are the funnier, wittier versions of ourselves. In person, our conversations are stilted, hindered by the constraints of work etiquette. We ended up in the elevator together yesterday and it was very awkward—he rambled on about taking A-levels in French and then I blurted out something about you in Paris. We work on the twenty-eighth floor, and as the elevator slowly rose, I tried to salvage the conversation by asking to see what he was listening to on his iPod.

Rachel. This is what I saw. I saw Ryan Adams. Paul Simon. Damien Rice. Kings of Leon. Bright Eyes. Jeff Buckley. Carole King. Then, I saw Joni Mitchell's entire album *Blue*.

My immediate reaction was, "Oh, he is not straight." He often wears pink button-down shirts and his clothes always seem freshly ironed. But when he holds my gaze, it makes me suspect that he likes me.

My magazine held a launch party at a hotel last night, and I spotted Sam across the room. We kept our distance amongst our colleagues, but I noticed that he wore a T-shirt instead of his usual buttoned-up shirts. At the hotel bar, Isla leaned over to say, "Holy shit. Look at Intern Sam. He has muscles. I can *see his chest muscles*." I just blinked at her, trying to give off an aura of professionalism. She has no idea. Also, if she goes for him, I will kill her.

I thought the flirtation with Sam was all just in good fun, but when I stood in the elevator this morning, waiting for the doors to open into my office, I felt my heart racing. It's too late. I'm in deep. My heart has decided.

He's only in Beijing for another five weeks before he travels through Southeast Asia. Then he moves to Australia permanently.

What do I do, Rach? Go with my instincts and behave rashly? Have a fling with my intern? Act mature and end this before it has begun?

Am I going to make a huge mistake?

Here's a hint: probably.

Love,

Jess

P.S. According to Sam, I am twenty-six, instead of twenty-four. I wanted to retain some veneer of authority so I pretended to be older than him. This is how it begins. WEB OF LIES.

P.P.S. No, Jacques and Marc are not acting like older brothers. Brothers make you sit in the middle seat during road trips and they will always try to bribe you with chewing gum. Don't fall for it!!! Then they grow up, marry nice women, and suddenly start cooking dinner for you. This almost balances out all the false gum bribing and forced middle-seat sitting. Almost.

## Rachel to Jess

Jessica! You are really pushing the boundaries of being a boss. Obviously I am riveted, though, so I must know more! And are you going to have to write his reference?

Also, you keep saying he looks like a crooked Tom Cruise, and I don't even know what that means. His face is sideways?

I've been going out to lunch with Olivier because he doesn't work very far away, although the library boys tag along. I'm starting to really like him. Today, our thighs kept grazing each other's during lunch. However, I didn't understand the waiter at ALL. At all. Then the waiter asked if I spoke French and Olivier goes, "A little." I hit him on the thigh hard. And he laughed.

Wherever this is going, I wish it would hurry up and get there.

In other news, as I'm sure you've heard, Astrid just left after visiting for a weekend, while on her way to Norway. I took her to my favorite spots and on Saturday we ended up at Shakespeare and Company, the famous English bookstore on the Seine, for a book launch party. It was a book about mysticism, so they set up mini tents around the bookstore: a gypsy who tells fortunes, a woman who reads tarot cards, an I Ching demonstration, and so on.

Stunned-looking people kept emerging from the fortune-teller's tent exclaiming about his talents, so Astrid and I stood in the long line to have our palms read. Astrid went into the tent first and emerged half an hour later. She didn't even tell me much about what they talked about, but said he mentioned her having a lucrative career. Then I took my turn.

The fortune-teller wore a ruffled shirt and a gold earring. He didn't say anything to me, but just studied my palm. He stared at it silently for at least two or three minutes. Then he let it go and looked at me.

"Romance is vital to your life," he said.

"I did just meet someone," I told him.

He nodded. "All I know is that you will have one dominant love in your life, which will be very happy, and to which you'll devote yourself completely. But right before that, you will have met somebody who you think is the person for you. He is not."

"So is the guy I just met The One or the one before The One?" I asked.

He shrugged. "I have no idea."

"Does my hand say when I will meet The One?"

He looked back at me.

"It's not a calendar," he said. "I don't know."

Okay, so then I felt dumb, but wasn't he the one claiming he could read my future on my palm?

I mumbled thanks and pulled back the curtain to find Astrid. We went out next door for drinks and shivered together under a malfunctioning heat lamp as we drank red wine and watched the boats go along the river. I sat stunned for a while, while Astrid brought me back to earth by joking about the way the fortune-teller might have been mistaken for a pirate in other circumstances, given his costume. I looked at her handbag and told her his "lucrative career" tip-off about her might have been obvious by her designer purse.

I hadn't seen Astrid for two years and we talked about this a lot. She told me that it seems like I'm finally learning how to be more proactive and take things less personally and we discussed how you are starting to think long-term about your future. Of all of us, she feels the most scattered. While most people are narrowing their options and focusing on one thing, she still wants to be everything. She's in law school, but she wants to take acting classes and make documentaries, as well as start her own business. She talked at a million miles per hour.

Even though I know all of this stuff about her life, and it feels so far from mine, Astrid feels like the same person I knew at Brown, just amplified. She both is and isn't the Astrid I knew before, and though I love her just as much, I have these fleeting moments where I feel like I hardly know her at all. You want to become an actress? When did this happen?

I wish I'd had more time with the fortune-teller. In addition to his vague advice about The One, he also talked about my having a creative career. Does that mean I should keep going with film? Or that writing will eventually take over? Or some combination of both? I should have asked him when I had the chance.

Maybe it just means that he thought I looked "arty" and spoke accordingly.

Love,

I Paid Twenty Euros for a Man in a Ruffled Shirt to Tell Me Someone Loves Me

APRIL 22

## Jess to Rachel

Why are you guys doing things like visiting fortune-tellers? Did we ever do this before? Also, I want to come. I want to hang out under heat lamps with you and Astrid and discuss our destinies. But I know what you mean about Astrid changing—I think I saw glimmers of it when we were in Beijing together and she was working three completely different jobs at once. I love her but I can't keep up with her because she always has a new life plan and a new life philosophy that she wants me to embrace. This month the plan is buying a mountain chalet and the philosophy is Dostoyevsky-based.

Whatever *you* do, don't get drunk and ask Olivier if he thinks he's The One or the one before The One. Promise me.

However, do as I say, not as I do.

I couldn't stand the mixed signals from flirting anymore, so I invited Sam to a friend's going-away party, and he showed up at the bar at 2 A.M., completely drunk. At work, he is polite, almost *too* polite, responsible, and very buttoned-up, but tonight he became the online persona I've been flirting with for the past few weeks. When he showed up at the party, he was loose and carefree and greeted me with a big hug—the first time we've ever touched.

We sat alone in a corner talking and quietly making fun of everyone else at the party. If true love isn't sitting in the corner with someone and gossiping about everybody else while they press their leg against yours, then I don't know what is.

At one point, an acquaintance came over to say hello and Sam introduced himself as my favorite intern. I blamed my red face on the effect of the alcohol and then pretended to fire him again and again. Every time he brought me another drink, I rehired him.

We decided to leave around 4 A.M., but we had nowhere to go. This is where things became tricky. It was too soon to invite him over to my place, and yet we both didn't want the night to end so quickly. We shared a taxi to our respective homes. After all of our joking, he suddenly became serious as we entered my neighborhood. He said, "I'm glad we're finally talking in person. But you've got to remember that I'm leaving Beijing in two weeks." The cab driver arrived at my building. "But you also have to know that you're my favorite person in China."

Not sure how to take this. Why only in China? Does he have a girlfriend in the United Kingdom? In Australia? Oh God, the insecure doubts are upon me.

The night was late, my eyeliner had migrated down my cheeks, my apartment was in shambles, and I was exhausted. I got out of the cab alone, promising that we would continue this another night.

He called out from the window, "Hey, Boss!" I turned around and he grinned. "Good night!"

This interlude before anything begins is always my favorite moment. So much unknown, but everything is already set up and we both know something is going to happen—but we just don't know how or when yet.

Although it better happen soon, because he is leaving in two weeks.

Love,

Worst Boss Ever/Best Boss Ever

P.S. He did not climb Mt. Everest—he went to Mt. Everest base camp. Apparently, climbing Mt. Everest requires superhuman strength and dangling your life in front of death's jaws. From what I gather, in comparison, Mt. Everest base camp is like wandering through the hills in *The Sound of Music*, except you have altitude sickness.

**MAY 1**

## Rachel to Jess

I feel like I'm bad for encouraging your Sam affair, because his departure is imminent. He sounds great, but we need to listen to the warnings that guys give about themselves.

Oh, like what I say is going to make any difference anyway!

More important—do you have pictures? Send pictures.

You're lucky that you get to see him every day, for the moment at least. Don't take this for granted! I haven't seen Olivier in a couple weeks, although he invited me to a poker game they were having last Thursday night. Unfortunately, I had class that night. Also, Jon once told me that playing poker with me is like taking broccoli from a baby. Not candy, because taking candy from a baby is actually hard.

There's been another strange development in my life. A neighbor I used to see only in passing has started trying to strike up conversations with me; once I let that happen, he started showing up at my door with trays full of couscous and tagines around dinnertime. He reeks of cologne, uses way too much hair gel, wears lots of gold neck-laces, and is thirty-five and unemployed. And nearly every night I come home, he swoops up to my door (he can see the courtyard from his window) with a tray of food, and he says, "Eat dinner with me!"

I made the mistake of eating with him the first time, after which point he tried to kiss me and I ducked under his shoulder. He tried to kiss me again and I ducked under his shoulder again. Finally he laughed. "You seem so tense," he said.

"I am," I said. "Very tense. My back is . . . rocks." (He doesn't speak English and I don't know the French word for *knots*.)

He asked for my number to call me later.

I can literally hear you asking me, "*Why* did you give it to him?" Well, I panicked. And also, he knows where I live.

Now, three to four times a week, I get this message, more or less verbatim: "massage? i have the very good hands ;)"

These messages make me feel ☹.

I've been taking extra French classes at school, trying like hell to prepare for my exams. I've written the final papers for the classes that will let me, but I desperately need someone to correct them! I'm going to have to ask Jacques and Marc for a big favor.

With my own writing, when I have time, I'm trying to take Lee's advice and be more plot focused, but everything I come up with ends up sounding like a Lifetime movie. *Girl in car accident learns to love again. British Duke falls in love with sassy American girl. Famous painter gets Alzheimer's disease.*

There are so many unknowns right now. Maybe the fortune-teller is rubbing off on me, but I'm starting to think there are no wrong choices in life. I mean, meth is a bad choice. But with things as unclear as what to do with Sam, I think you should go with your instincts and just let it play out. You really like him. Start from there.

Love,
Rach

P.S. Get a French person to try to read the word *hodgepodge* out loud. They will say, "hogey-pogey," and it will be the best moment of your life. Olivier tried to use this word and it totally made up for the *bedroom friend* translation debacle.

**MAY 13**

## Jess to Rachel

First of all, I don't know what you want. A man is offering to cook for you every night! He's offering you free massages! This could be great material for your book: A French cabana boy waits for a nice American girl on her doorstep—and then kills her. This is your warning. Lock your doors.

You need to be here for a marathon session in the kitchen from senior year where we stay up all night talking and drinking and stealing Rosabelle's chocolate banana bread. Wish I could call you, but . . .

I just crept out of Sam Singer's bed!

So, you may have noticed that since I last wrote to you, things have changed. Like I have slept with my intern. I have slept with Sam Singer. Many times. Because I am accidentally dating Sam Singer, who is also my intern.

We finally ended up in bed after Sam finally asked me out for dinner and we had our first official date.

We met up after work, but were still wearing our work personas for the first hour at the restaurant. Even though I'm supposed to be his boss, he makes me so nervous because I like him so much. He's done so much that I've always wanted to do—he told me more about how he spent a month backpacking around India, and while I tried to pay attention, I was distracted by how much I liked his dark eyelashes and his hands.

At the restaurant, we overheard an Englishman with a very posh accent talking about his old Oxford buddies and as a joke, Sam transformed from his native lyrical Northern accent to a regal, upscale voice. When I attempted to imitate him, he told me I sounded like a Russian who had lived in India for the past twenty years. He doesn't know what he's talking about—I definitely sounded like Prince William.

Afterward, we went for a walk in a nearby park and Sam's phone rang. He leaned against a wall to answer it, so I milled about the park, not knowing what was going to happen next and watching Chinese people taking their dogs on evening walks. After Sam hung up, we stood there facing each other, rambling about nothing. And then finally—finally!—he pulled me toward him and kissed me. He put his arms around me and I could smell his shampoo. It was a great moment.

First kisses and their aftermath are almost always clumsy, but Sam has this ability to disperse awkwardness. I think it has something to do with being English and used to an abundance of awkward, fumbling encounters.

Also, I don't know how people kiss without one of the parties resting against a wall, because it allowed for my body to lean into his without knocking him to the ground.

From the first raised eyebrow, I think we both knew what was going to happen. Traditional dating rituals of waiting three dates before sleeping together are just ridiculous in our situation. We don't have time for this! Why would we bother with that when we're already moving at a million miles per hour? And we already like each other so much.

So Sam came home with me that night.

Since then, we've spent every free moment together. Every day after ignoring each other at work, he waits for me around the corner and greets me with a kiss after making sure no one is around to spot us. We always have grand ambitions of going to a museum or a different part of town, but inevitably we always end up at my place or his, because our time is so limited.

That first night with Sam, I had a brief moment when we were lying on my bed before anything heavy had happened and I thought, "What am I doing? Why am I sleeping with my intern?" But then Sam took off his shirt. He has a six-pack. I have never seen one of these in person before. I was convinced they were just myths, like unicorns. I am not only attracted to his abs, but fascinated. I had to immediately touch them, like examining an ancient scroll.

And I had forgotten what good sex is like. No, *great* sex. The kind where you don't care what you look like. The kind where you find yourself thinking about it and him and nothing else for the rest of the day.

He makes my heart race, but at the same time he's reassuring—I don't doubt his affection or feel insecure. He caught me taking a photo of him while sleeping (what? He looked great.) and while he made fun of me, he also laughed a lot about it. Sam studies me, noticing my chicken-pox scar over my right eye, or the way I always sleep on my right side. He holds me so closely and looks into my eyes.

I don't know where our relationship will stand after he flies out of Beijing in two days, and I'm just so confused and lost thinking about it. Sam doesn't say, "I've never felt this way about anyone before." He doesn't say, "Visit me in Australia." He doesn't say, "I don't want this to end. I need to see you again." I'm beginning to wonder if there's a girl in India and a girl in Nepal, just like me, who waited for Sam to say these things but he never did. A girl in every port.

Last night, he arrived at my apartment at midnight after being out with his friends. He was very drunk and when he came into my apartment, he pulled me close, and buried his face into my neck and mumbled, "I like you so much. Everyone else is rubbish compared to you."

When we woke up together this morning, we talked for a long

time in bed. I can't get over how I can actually fall asleep next to him (without roofie-ing myself) and how much I love his scent.

He asked me about living in Beijing and if it was permanent. I told him that I was used to my life here and that I was content with the way things were for now. And then he asked, "Content? I think you deserve more than that."

I like that he's someone who doesn't want to settle. I like the way he's led his life: by working hard to save money so that he can travel to exotic places for months at a time. But talking about the future just reminds me how every moment is shadowed by the dread that he is leaving. He is leaving. Sam is leaving Beijing forever in two days. Our relationship has been accelerating at 120 mph and now it's just going to drop off into an abyss.

I know it's early for me to say this, but I can't stop thinking about how I don't know if I will ever find someone like him again. He's fun and sexy and kind. He was also a really good intern.

There's something about him that stands out from everyone else I've been with. I feel like I might be losing something that I should try very hard to hold on to, but this is all going to end when he flies out in two days. I think I might be alone for a very long time after Sam.

I can't tell anyone about him because I'm always surrounded by my colleagues or people who are friends with my colleagues. I even considered asking a taxi driver here what he would do in my situation ("if your soulmate had to move to Australia but your taxi business was based in Beijing"), but I managed to rein in the crazy.

I save that for you.

Love,

Jess

P.S. I would totally read that "British Duke Falls in Love with Sassy American" book.

## Rachel to Jess

I think a six-pack is actually the opposite of a unicorn—you have to be *non*virgin to come across the perfect abs.

Is Sam gone? How are you doing? Remember that British men never know how to express their feelings. This is why Hugh Grant stutters so much in movies—you might have to be the first one to say the things you wish he'd say.

Love you,
Rach

## Jess to Rachel

He left this morning.

When I came home from work today, I went straight for my bed and just lay there, staring at the spot where Sam used to sleep. And I cried. I cried a lot. An embarrassing amount, but I don't care. I was so deeply unhappy and frustrated and devastated. I never knew this exact feeling before. Exhausted from the tears, I fell asleep before the sun had even set and then I awoke suddenly at midnight, confused about my whereabouts. There's always that delicate moment when my brain knows something bad has happened but still doesn't remember what it is until suddenly it all comes rushing back: Sam's gone. Forever.

In my mind, there exists a clear divide between before I met him and after and I don't know how to go back to the before. When he was here, he sent me twenty texts a day. I was excited to see him every night. Sitting next to him in my office every day. And now, nothing.

Beijing suddenly feels very loud to me—the people, the traffic, the construction, the bustle. In comparison, I feel so morose. Work isn't even an escape, because for the past five weeks, I would walk in and see him sitting at his desk every day. But he's gone. It was all I could do to not turn my head and stare wistfully at his empty seat next to Isla. Instead, I faced forward and looked at my computer, trying to make myself care about work again. Even now, nobody in my office knows that Sam and I dated.

He's in Hong Kong now, before he travels to Vietnam and Malaysia and then flies on a one-way ticket to Sydney.

In the days before he left, I tried to summon the courage to tell Sam how I really felt about him, but every time I came close, I couldn't. I needed him to say it first and he never did. He must have some idea of how I feel, though. I slipped a postcard into his backpack and I made him an incredibly mushy playlist for his plane ride, so if he's intuitive at all, there's no way he won't pick up on my feelings.

I've never been this scared to tell someone how I feel, but I don't think I could have handled it if Sam said he merely thought of us as a fun fling. On our last night together, when I once more looked at him and failed to articulate my feelings, I tried to will him to read my mind. "I like you. I am crazy about you. I am terrified that I will never find someone who makes me as happy as you do." Every time I tried to say something serious, my voice started to crack and I kept clearing my throat and making up some excuse about maybe getting a cold.

The closest thing to the truth I could say to him was that I had lived in Beijing for two years and that people had left me before, but that I had never felt as sad as I do now. I told him, "Whatever happens, if you still miss me in a few months, tell me. Let me know. And if you don't miss me, then don't tell me. That's okay too." I delivered this so casually, but it was incredibly hard to say.

What I meant was, "If you feel a crushing sadness and hole in your life the way I will in mine, please, please, please tell me." I don't want to be the one to make contact first. I want the next move to be his. It's so hard to be the one who's left behind, while he goes on to travel and have adventures alone before moving to Australia. I can't ask him to forgo that and stay behind for me.

He was silent. He didn't say anything in response to this, which I interpreted as rejection. We had drinks last night before going back to his place, and it seemed like he was not in love with me. I kept looking for signs or evidence and read too much into everything. I kissed him good-bye this morning still looking for answers, but I still don't have any.

Right now, I'm listening to the saddest Ryan Adams album in the world. Wallowing while listening to it is the only thing I'm remotely enjoying right now.

I can't imagine going out to a bar ever again. Flirting with someone else. No. I don't even *want* to get over him. Unless he gets over me, and then I want to get over him immediately.

It usually goes like this: They leave and I'm left, but then eventually I move on. The leaving always hurts, but the person actually being gone, I could accept. I always knew I'd meet someone new. But this one—this one feels different.

But why didn't he ask me to meet him in Australia? Why didn't he ask me to meet him in Southeast Asia? Why didn't he ask me to be his girlfriend? Why did he let me go? I guess I wasn't enough to love. I feel lonelier than I ever have in my entire life. I'm in Beijing, China. Astrid's gone. Victoria's gone. He's gone. You're so far away. My family is so far away.

It's so clear to me now how we are all alone. We die alone.

Oh no. The sad album is on repeat. nonononononono

Write me anything but please write me as soon as you can.

Love,

Jess

## Rachel to Jess

Jessica. You're enough to love. I can't formulate that in a way that makes it sound not crazy, but you are. I think Sam was probably preoccupied with his next adventure. Or just being typically British: reticent and not forthcoming. Haven't you read any Jane Austen? British men lock their feelings inside.

I felt that lonely when you left New York. It wasn't so bad when other people left, because you were still there. But when the last close person leaves—that is when the breakdown happens. I don't know what else to say because I didn't handle it so well (Xanax, Claudia, bad sex with Saul). I think you just have to make yourself get through it. You're going to have to leave the house and act interested in meeting people when all you want to do is stay in bed. That's the only answer. But it's going to be okay.

And remember that this feeling is temporary—no matter what happens.

I'm sorry. I wish I could distract you with stories about Paris, but not much is happening here. I feel on the verge of so many things. I feel like I'm so close to dating Olivier, figuring out my thesis, and reworking my book's final draft.

I've still been corresponding with Lee, who continues to say profound and encouraging things about my book's plot development. It's about a girl in London who has memory problems, but I can't figure out how to end it. Do I make her murder somebody and she doesn't know if it's real or not? Everything I've learned about plot just makes me more hesitant and confused, because I can't seem to fully understand my protagonist's desire. Lee thinks this comes with life experience and time.

In the meantime, I got Jacques and Marc to proofread the early parts of my thesis, which I've been laboring over for weeks. The thesis is almost like a story: tracing four films that show characters confronting themselves as children, in literal and metaphorical ways. Fellini, in *8½*, watching his younger self as though he were in a film he is directing. Bob Dylan, in *I'm Not There*, turning away from his younger self, denying that he was ever someone else.

There's something in this subject I find so moving. How do we deal with all the people we've been? What happens when we have to confront them? It's a poetic topic, but it becomes very prosaic when I write it in my French. And bad prose at that. Apparently, I am incapable of distinguishing street slang from antiquated expressions, and use both indiscriminately. Sometimes Jacques laughs out loud, circles a sentence, and hands my paper to Marc to enjoy. "Rachel, if you translate this into English, it literally means, 'She is a woman of ill repute who spends a lot of time with her gang.'"

However, I did not point out that last night Marc called a steep hill in English "so much, too much, too high. So much, too far."

In return for their editing my French essays, I'm correcting their applications for US exchange programs. They both want to go to Yale this fall. What, Brown isn't good enough for you? More than that, you want to trade in Paris for New Haven? Who are you people? They're both enchanted with being near New York, though. They find Paris "boring." However, *boring* is the same word as *annoying* in French (which actually explains a lot about how French people think). We're basically switching dreams, though I don't want them to leave. They're becoming such an integral part of my Paris dream, and not just because I'm still holding out for Olivier either.

Anyway, I know this talk of people leaving isn't helping. Just remember that no matter how dark everything seems now, you will get through this.

Have you heard from him since you last wrote?
Love,
Thinking of You
(Rach)

## Rachel to Jess

I'm waiting for my e-mail!!! Tried calling you but your phone is off!

Where are you?

*Five minutes later*

## Rachel to Jess

How do we feel about nude stockings for going out? It's not quite warm yet, but somehow I feel very Queen Mother when I put them on. Also, did you see the photos of Rosabelle and Buster in Argentina??? He grew a mustache and a potbelly!!! It does not look good.

And why you no write back?

Jessica, where ARE you????

Love,
Rachel

## Jess to Rachel

Um . . . Malaysia?

Malaysia!

I'm here in Malaysia with . . . SAM SINGER!!! Who is right now wearing flip-flops and my baseball cap and trolling the beach to find us banana smoothies!

I'm with Sam! We're about three thousand miles south of Beijing, on a tropical island that can only be reached by boat, right in the middle of the South China Sea.

After a week of coming home and wallowing in my apartment with Ryan Adams, I received a text message—it was Sam in Hong Kong asking me, "Has it been long enough for me to tell you that I miss you yet?"

I stared at the message for a long time.

How do I know if I'll ever feel this way again? I had to tell him because I had nothing to lose—I had already lost him.

I wrote him a very honest e-mail telling him that I was crazy about him, that I missed him, that my e-mail was by all means a love letter, that I thought about him all the time, and that when I looked at my life in Beijing without him, I found it severely lacking.

The next morning I awoke to an e-mail from him, in which he confessed, "I miss you so much. Your playlist has had countless run-throughs. I'm soppy and I know it. But I don't care. If my plans weren't so firmly set, and my flights bought and paid for, I would have stayed in Beijing instead of flying out to SE Asia. Australia just doesn't seem as appealing a prospect anymore, but I already have my ticket to Sydney. But I can't stop thinking about you."

Of course, the first thing I did was find cheap flights to Malaysia, his next destination. It's not peak season, and tickets cost about as much as five banana smoothies.

I wrote about my flight search to Sam, and he immediately replied: "Come as soon as you can!"

I wanted to write you earlier but I felt too low and then too frantic. I called Isla to see if she could close the magazine issue for me, because I needed to go to Malaysia (although I was vague and did not mention Sam at all), and she assured me that she could, although she was puzzled. Then I scrambled around frantically trying to finish two articles and buy a swimsuit.

Three days ago, I took a train to Tianjin, a city outside Beijing, where I spent the night and then woke up before dawn the next day to catch a six-hour flight to Kuala Lumpur. Then I spent five hours in the airport eating *laksa* and trying out all the lotions in The Body Shop before boarding another hour-long flight to the eastern coast. As soon as my final plane landed, I ran out of the airport and got into a cab. The air was balmy, the stars were out, and I immediately started sweating in the tropical heat.

When I stepped out of the cab, I sprinted to the door of the hostel, where Sam Singer, tan from his adventures and with a newly shaved crew cut, appeared. I jumped straight into his very tan arms.

Then we immediately got naked.

The next morning we took a boat together to the island from where I am now writing to you. Crystal-clear blue waters and hot white sand. It's sunny and hot all day, and then when we are lying together in our wooden bungalow, it pours and thunders all night. The only other people I've spotted are couples on their honeymoons. And while walking along the beach with Sam, I also have the eerie feeling that *we* are on our honeymoon. We are doing everything out of order.

We spend twenty-four hours a day together, which I'd never done with a guy before. In the hut where we are staying, our bathroom doesn't even have a door—just a flimsy curtain! Now it feels like we're *married*. There's no TV in our room. There are no distractions but the sun and the ocean, and in our abundant free time, we have sex three times a day.

It is literally the desert island test, and by default my five objects I can't live without are Sam, banana shakes, sunscreen, goggles, and this Internet café that has at least four resident cats. There is a white kitten sleeping on my foot as I write this, and right now my biggest problem is figuring out how to stand up without disturbing him.

Despite all the sex, right now I feel supremely unsexy. My face is bright red with sunburn. This morning, at breakfast, my skin was peeling off. I kept trying to shield my face from Sam, apologizing for how disgusting I was, even to myself. I was in the middle of saying something about how I was a molting snake, when finally Sam reached over and said, "Stop. Nothing you do can disgust me."

This contradicts everything I have ever read in a magazine, ever. It is also the most romantic thing I've ever been told.

It almost scares me to like him so much. We talk and talk about our families or how strange a place Beijing is or we make wild speculations about all of the people we've met during the day and he runs his hands through my hair until eventually we fall asleep. I can't think of when I've ever been happier in my entire life.

We nearly miss dinner every night because after being at the beach or snorkeling all day—we come back as the sun sets, shower, sleep together, and eventually end up sprinting to the only restaurant on the island as it closes. Last night we were informed that the kitchen had already closed, and we begged the woman to at least let us have milk shakes for dinner. Sam and I both chose Mars bar milk shakes. This felt like some sort of confirmation: We'll never live in a household without chocolate.

We leave in two days. I'm beginning to feel melancholy after all the giddiness of traveling to a new place and being reunited, but I feel so much more assured about his feelings for me and mine for him. If I'd shown up here, and he'd been inconsiderate and boring, at least I would have known what I wasn't missing.

I know that this is still an interlude from real life. I don't know what I'm doing, but whatever this is, it feels right to me.

Maybe in your book, Girl meets Boy, Girl goes to Malaysia with Boy, Girl loses Boy. Now give me a great ending.

Love,

Jess

P.S. I haven't met a single sassy monkey. Don't know what George was talking about. So disappointed.

JUNE 2

---

## Rachel to Jess

Okay. Um. Malaysia. Yes.

WHAT? I don't even know how to respond to that. WHAT? Malaysia? With no notice? You *would* be in Malaysia! How did you take total sorrow and devastation and turn it into utter bliss within a matter of days? And also, how can I write you an ending when I didn't write this story—I also want to know what happens next!

Everything sounds so far away it's almost hard to imagine. I am currently facing exams. They are three to four hours long, and professors provide the students with one question and a stack of Blue Books. Sometimes, if the students are lucky, we get a choice of three questions.

In my hardest class, the question was something the professor repeated during every class: "According to cinema theories, what are the XXXXXs in film?" I only knew one translation of the XXXXX: "1920s hat." So was he really asking, "What are the 1920s hats in films?"

I did not know the answer to this for months.

Finally, finally, I asked Jacques about it. XXXXX also means "existing problems." Oh.

So for the exam, I sat down and filled out four Blue Books full of all of the theories about what's wrong with cinema: the way we regard it, the way we react as spectators, the way it plays with the female gaze. I knew exactly what to write but was unsure of exactly how to put it in academic French. I ended up with what is very likely an ungrammatical, choppy French essay about hats.

Four hours later, one hundred of my fellow classmates and I emerged from the lecture hall, scrambling for the door with our collective severe nicotine withdrawal. I have been initiated.

After all our suffering together, I truly feel like a French student now.

I'm really hoping I pass. I did manage to string together pages and pages about why cinema sucks. But, if I fail, I lose my visa unless I repeat the academic year (which I don't have enough money to do). I can't imagine having to leave Paris after already laying down the foundation for a life here.

Olivier, meanwhile, invited me over for dinner the other night. I'm sorry, what I meant was, OLIVIER INVITED ME OVER FOR DINNER THE OTHER NIGHT! Here's the short version:

I'm in so deep I can't see the sky.

Anyway, I had shaved my legs. Although every girl knows this is the surest way to going home alone, I still did it. I arrived at his apartment after carefully picking out a bottle of red wine. Actually, I glanced at the rows of bottles and chose one based on the fact that the bottle was blue and beautiful, and had a picture of the ocean on it.

Olivier opened the door. Cheek kiss, cheek kiss. I handed him my wine and then offered to help with the salad, but Olivier wouldn't let me make anything. I stood at the sink, pretending to help wash vegetables, and when he tried to reach the dishes around me, he would place both his hands on my waist to move me over an inch or two. I hovered at the sink as often as possible.

It's been way too long since I had sex.

Everything he said, I found sexy. Parmesan cheese? Don't mind if I do. Olive oil on that salad? Oooh, yes, please.

We sat down and we talked about his brother's new baby and my nephews. This conversation made me think that he was sensitive beneath his casual exterior.

And then the doorbell rang. It was Sasha and Marc, who had decided that since they were in the neighborhood, they would drop by. I immediately felt disappointed. I was immensely gratified to see the strained welcome on Olivier's face.

Marc began to tease Olivier for the "shit" wine he had served, and I turned bright red. What, I'm not a French person! This knowledge is not inborn in me! I know nothing of your wine and your ways! Whatever. It tasted fine to me. Who cares that I can't pick out wine! So what if I can't understand French idioms!? So I can't write in perfect French!

Olivier threw some more pasta in the pot and we crowded around his little table. His knees kept touching mine. We stayed there, talking and drinking shit wine until about 3 A.M., when Sasha and Marc walked me home.

It was such a fun evening, but I couldn't help thinking that it could have been romantic. And now I'm still waiting on Olivier to make a move. I came home and wrote for a few hours in French, but immediately deleted the story. It was all about a girl who falls in love with a winemaker. But I didn't know any of the right words. For example, is *winemaker* the correct term? Even in English?

Oh, and I miss you. True story. Come back from Malaysia.

Love,

Rach

## Jess to Rachel

I like this new attitude of yours. So what if you think the problem with cinema is hats? Very innovative! So what if you write French like an eight-year-old? Who cares? So what if I ran away to Malaysia on a whim and told no one but you? Doesn't matter!

I just landed in Beijing a few hours ago. Malaysia already feels so far away. The only evidence of ever having been is how tanned my skin is and the forty e-mails from Isla in my inbox.

Very early this morning, I left Sam. It was rushed, but last night was when we really said our good-byes.

Although we didn't directly address anything, we grew more serious last night. He asked me about how much longer I wanted to stay in Beijing. I told him that I loved Beijing, but that I didn't know what more I could get out of living there and that I wanted to pursue serious journalism. I mentioned that I wanted to go to journalism school, but I didn't know where. The question just sat there, unanswered. I stood up to finish packing my bag. He stood up and said, "I think there are journalism schools in Australia," before he stepped into the bathroom, turned on the water, and got into the shower. WHAT KIND OF EXIT IS THAT?? I wanted to knock on the door and ask, "I'm sorry, what? What was that part about me being in Australia again? Just one more time, please."

We didn't discuss it again, although it was all I thought about for the rest of the night.

This morning, we took a boat back to the mainland and I kissed him good-bye while rows of taxi drivers looked on. I tried to linger, but I was sharing a cab with a Chinese couple who were also heading to the airport. I got into the car while Sam boarded a bus to Penang.

In the cab, the couple began speaking to me in Mandarin. The girl, who had witnessed our good-bye, asked about my "boyfriend." I tried to reply in Mandarin although my brain was emotionally fried.

"Oh, him? He's moving to Australia."

"So when are you moving to Australia?"

*Pause.*

"Oh . . . I'm not moving to Australia. I will live in Beijing and he will live in Australia. We will not be together."

Then the guy said something in Mandarin that I didn't understand, so I asked the girl what he meant. She leaned forward toward the front seat, where I was sitting by the driver. In English, she said, "He said that he feels sorry for you."

I nodded and then stared out the window at the lush green fields thinking about Sam onboard a bus, driving away in the opposite direction.

After boarding my plane in Kuala Lumpur, I stared at the back of the seat in front of me for a few hours. My mind was drifting off into random thoughts—the abyss of sadness that awaits me, my itchy sunburn, the new magazine issue to plan, the sand in my armpits, and Sam's soft kisses in the mornings—when I realized, suddenly, fully, absolutely:

Sam is everything on my Master List! He is sexy and kind and adventurous and smart and a good listener and he makes me laugh. He is it! He makes me feel safe. He makes me feel wanted. He has great hands. He even has dark hair. And he didn't sunburn once! He even appreciates girly folk music. My heart raced.

I almost looked around for someone on the plane to shake and tell the news! I found him! There was no one to tell, but no matter. I knew.

And I know that Sam isn't perfect. Sometimes he seems overly cautious or far too polite to everyone, even waiters who completely ignore us. Sometimes he thinks my never-ending questions to strangers border on intrusive and he tries to step in and apologize on my behalf, which I find really irritating. And the biggest thing is that he seems to lack direction in his life right now, as he moves to Australia without a job or a plan.

But when I think about how he always holds me tightly or the way his voice sounds when he says my name or his acute observations about everyone, I don't care about any of the above. And didn't I move to Beijing without a job or a plan? Even if there is someone better for me out there, I cannot imagine him. I do not even want him. I want Sam. I choose him.

And then, with that settled, I felt the exhaustion that follows five days of steady sun, sea, and sex. I fell asleep and woke up in China.

When I got home, I dropped my bags and looked at my empty apartment.

Rachel, I know what I'm going to do.

I'm going to move to Australia. I'm going to be with Sam.

Love,

Jess

JUNE 7

## Rachel to Jess

Australia! Malaysia? Australia? WHERE ARE THESE COUNTRIES?

Are you really going to move to Australia? Wait, I just had a flashback to senior year when you announced you were moving to China, and I kept saying, "You're not *really* moving to China . . . right?" I actually cannot believe that you are going to do this! What are you going to do there?

Also: AUSTRALIA? You're already so far away and you're choosing the one place that's even farther! Is part of this the fear of missing out on something really big? It's a huge decision, but you sound so sure. You better not stay there forever, though. I don't want your kids talking like that.

I still have actual letters you wrote me from when you were studying abroad in Melbourne your junior year and I was in Paris! (Is this progress or regression?)

But more important, I can't believe you actually found someone who ticks everything on the Master List. Do you think we should tell Oprah? The most ridiculous thing is that Sam applied for that position! You posted an internship vacancy, and Sam sent in his résumé for the job. I'm still trying to wrap my head around this. I'm thinking of posting my Master List to Craigslist.

I really can't figure out if Olivier is right for me. He doesn't seem to love my writing, because it would take him forever to read it; he's shorter than I requested; he doesn't want to live outside of France. But I do feel connected to him. Even now, when he's been visiting his parents and I haven't seen him in two weeks.

We do have really good banter, finally. He loves to tease and I have to respond quickly in French to keep up with him, although it's taken me a while to get to this point. And yet—all talk, no action.

I don't think I've ever humiliated myself as much working on anything as I have humiliated myself in the aims of improving my French these past few months. Today, I went into a bookstore and bought a Marguerite Duras book in French, which I started to read on the Metro, for pleasure—*and it was pleasurable*. The process of polishing this language is becoming less painful and starting to be fun. However, last week I made a fool of myself at the supermarket by labeling my oranges wrong even though it's the same word in French and English (*orange*). I had just made a mistake. Some things just don't change.

Okay, well, I'm off to study more French. If you learn a language, and you have no French lover to share it with, did you really learn it at all?

Australia?!?! Jess. Really?!?!?

Love,

A Dingo Ate My Baby

(Sorry, that's the only thing I know about Australia.)

JUNE 9

## Jess to Rachel

Why won't Olivier just make a move already? Do you want me to call him? Let him know that there is *no time* to mosey about?

I know this because I've been covertly researching journalism schools in Australia (yes, I'm really doing this!) and the next school year begins in six weeks (weird backward Australia system). Jesus Christ! When I found this out, I had a heart attack and then frantically called up the admissions officers, who assured me, in very strong Aussie accents, that I can still apply, but that I must get everything in before the end of the week. I've spent my nights writing essays for my application and cramming for the requisite news quiz everyone takes for admission. Really hoping China hasn't blocked a major news event from the Internet, or else I may fail. What if something huge happened in Japan or Taiwan and I just don't know because the nature of the event doesn't agree with China's official propaganda?!

On the other hand, if I fail the news quiz, I can just blame China's Internet censorship. Solution.

And so, I've told my landlord I'm leaving and I finally had to tell Isla everything because she will be replacing me at work. Also, she's from Australia and I knew she'd be full of wisdom about what journalism programs to apply to and where to live. We went to dinner and sat outside in a tranquil Chinese courtyard where she completely lost it when I confessed everything about (intern) Sam and me.

She sat in shock before loudly protesting, "This is all a big joke, isn't it? You're totally fucking with me, right?" People in the restaurant stared at us. Isla didn't believe me until I handed her my phone with a photo of tanned Sam and me sitting on a boat with the blue sea behind us. I tried to show her more, but she swatted me away as she studied the photo carefully, and then handed the phone back to me, proclaiming, "Well, then. You little minx."

She told me about the best places to go in Melbourne and she told me that she always thought Sam was a really good guy. I listened to her carefully, as if she were my own personal fortune-teller.

She also gets my job when I leave, so everyone wins.

In the meantime, I talk to Sam on the phone—there's a two-hour time difference between Sydney and Beijing, so after work every night, he calls me. I assume that most people in long-distance relationships already know each other really well before undertaking this kind of thing, but we're learning the basics about each other over the phone. I'm learning so much about him so quickly and yet I'm beginning to forget exactly what he looks like.

It makes me sad that we've spent so many of our intimate conversations on the phone instead of lying in bed together. Other new couples can spend time together watching movies or talking nonsense while comparing hands in bed—Sam and I don't have this luxury, although I feel like I know him so well.

I've decided that even though Sam lives in Sydney, I'm applying to the journalism program in Melbourne, which is an hour-long flight away. I loved living in Melbourne during my year abroad and have no desire to live in Sydney, and he understands this. Moving to Australia is such a big change that if I'm going to do it, I really want to choose the journalism program and the city that are best for me. Sam's found temp work in Sydney but is planning to find a way to move to Melbourne sometime after I start my master's program (if I get in). If I don't get in, then I have no idea what I'll do. Maybe move to the Chinese countryside to sell eggs, as I've always feared, because I'll have no other options.

I'm almost grateful for being forced to move this quickly with my life. If I had time to stand still, I might talk myself out of this, but it's hard to change your plans when you've burned your bridges and are sprinting full speed toward your next destination.

Yesterday, I was in a park and I saw a Chinese man out walking his birds. In each hand he held a birdcage as he strolled, showing the birds the park scenery before hanging the cages from a tree while he went to go socialize with his fellow bird-walkers.

I'm really going to miss this place.

Love,

Jess

JUNE 10

## Rachel to Jess

God, I can't believe how fast everything's moving. To be honest, I never knew when or if you would ever leave Beijing because you seemed so happy there. It's almost surreal how quickly everything is changing and that you'll be living on an entirely different continent soon if all goes as planned.

And so much unknown is waiting for you there—just this time last year, I was getting ready to go to France, and I had no idea that Sasha even existed, that French men are not all romantics who will immediately sweep you off your feet but also include a distinct subset of creepy men hitting on you in parks, that no matter how many times I proofread my French essays, I still make ten grammatical mistakes per page.

But it's over—my first year—and I have passed!

I just saw my exam results and I passed all of my classes, with an A-minus average! I am assuming some heavy pity-grading was involved but am nonetheless relieved.

To celebrate, a bunch of us went up north to Brittany the other day, to an old resort town on the coast where Jacques has a family house. That sounds grander than it was, but Sasha, Marc, Jacques, and I all stayed for the weekend. I was a little disappointed that Olivier had to work, but it was peaceful and calm without him—I didn't have to think about how I looked or if he was looking at me, or if he would try to get me alone.

We were one block from the ocean, but it's fall here and the temperature was already ridiculously cold. We couldn't go into the water. Sasha and I would take long walks up and down the beach while the guys kicked around a soccer ball. I don't know how guys, like toddlers or puppies, can be completely entertained just by giving them a ball to play with, but it seems like they always can.

Take one guy from every country in the world, throw them together, and inevitably, you'll find them playing soccer. Well, except for the token American guy, who will have to sit on the sidelines, cradling his football.

Sasha and I were wearing sweaters and freezing, so we sat on a terrace at a café overlooking the beach. The waitress gave us a blanket and we huddled together.

The little village was so quiet and all we could hear was the ocean (and the boys swearing) and I felt so far away from the life I had in New York almost a year ago.

Sasha asked me if I ever miss New York. I hadn't really opened up to anyone before about my life there. I started telling her about all the events from my time there that led to me being in France now. I hadn't told anyone here about the car accident because it feels like it happened to someone else, but it was nice being able to share that with someone.

I showed her the scar on my forehead and laughed uncomfortably, and Sasha understood that I didn't want to get into it any further. You'd like her. She's our kind.

We talked about this for a while until the waiter came by and we ordered two more coffees.

Then, to lighten the mood, Sasha brought up Olivier.

"Too bad he couldn't come this weekend," she said slyly.

"Yeah . . ." I said.

"Everyone always loves Olivier," she continued. "He's so charming, girls just can't help it."

"Oh," I said. I had thought it was just me.

"But he never talks about women. He never has crushes or anything," she explained. "He's dated a little, but never for that long—I think his longest relationship was for like a summer back in high school."

"Are you sure he's straight?" I asked.

She laughed.

"He's definitely straight. At parties, I've seen him leave with women." She didn't directly say anything about my crush on Olivier, but I knew then that it was understood.

She added, "Jacques and Marc keep asking, 'What is his problem? Why doesn't he make a move on Rachel? When are they going to get together?'"

I ask myself this same question every day.

Basically, the rest of the weekend was windy walks along the beach under gray skies. I slept in the room that used to belong to a little girl, so it was full of unicorns and flowered wallpaper and felt very 1950s French to me. In the mornings, I woke up before anybody else and went to get us coffee, croissants, and Nutella.

Jacques would wake up and say, "You would be the best girlfriend ever."

I know, Jacques! TELL OLIVIER.

Love,

Rach

## Jess to Rachel

How is this Tall Sasha so sure Olivier is straight if she has no real proof and he doesn't date women? The evidence belies her statement. Maybe she has confused the words in English?

Anyway, it's official—I got into my program in Melbourne! Did you know that Melbourne is the Paris of the Southern Hemisphere? Some people say it's Buenos Aires, but they don't know what they're talking about. Maybe we'll lead parallel lives in our respective Cities of Light. I'll be a day ahead of you in Australia, so I'll know everything that happens first. If you're nice, I'll tell you. You can pay me in bonbons.

Oh God, this is really going to happen now.

I know I'm going to miss Beijing's unpredictability and weird charm (where else can I see a group of older Chinese people practicing Tai Chi in the park next to a sprawling construction site?), but I'm glad I'm leaving before I become a hardened expat. I'm always going to have a soft spot for this city in my life. This is where I sort of grew up. So many romantic mistakes.

But I'm ready to go. Isla will take my job, and I trust her with the magazine. I trust that she will love it as I have and as Victoria did before me. I can't believe I grew to care so much about it, but I really loved that job. Best summer camp ever. I told one of the mothers who I often work with that I was quitting, and she said, "You're quitting your job? You're twenty-four, you run your own magazine, and you're going to quit?" And then she looked at me like I was insane.

I'm still going to do it, although another acquaintance told me offhandedly that she couldn't believe I was the kind of girl who was going to follow a man all the way to Australia. When she said this, I didn't even recognize myself in the comment. Then I felt stung. Despite the evidence that I am going to do this, am I the *kind* of girl who does this? This is an entirely different question. Here's what I think, after some deep pondering: I do ALL KINDS OF STUPID SHIT (jumping into countless unexplored bodies of water, imitating Santa for thousands of Chinese children, dating an old man), and following the best guy I've ever met is actually one of the saner things I've ever done.

I hope. If Sam had given me any hesitations about his affection for me or his integrity, then I wouldn't know what to do, but right now, I believe in him.

Besides, I don't have time or room for doubts, because this is really happening now. When I get to Australia, am I going to forget all of my Mandarin and suddenly start talking like Isla? Not good. I'm going to call my sunglasses my sunnies and my chewing gum my chewy.

I've started saying good-bye to all of my closest friends in Beijing. I'm not throwing an elaborate going-away party, because I wanted to say good-bye to my friends privately and then sort of disappear from the rest of the Beijing scene without a fuss. Like if I slip away, no one will notice I'm gone.

See you on the other side.

Love,

Jess

JULY 18

## Rachel to Jess

OMG CAN YOU COME HERE?
SERIOUSLY, COME HERE.
Olivier kissed me.
He kissed me.
Like most Saturdays, I met Olivier and Sasha at the café at the

Swedish Institute for lunch and we sprawled outside on the terrace, where we drank super strong coffee, the best I've found in Paris so far (and the cheapest). Europeans don't seem to be affected by caffeine; I get jittery after only two cups, whereas Sasha and Olivier had three cups and were still laid-back and calm.

We were talking about IKEA, which is what we always seem to talk about at the Swedish Institute, when Olivier abruptly changed the subject.

"Whatever happened to the super tall Swedish guy from that party last week?" Olivier asked, still looking up, not meeting my gaze.

"What Swede?" I asked.

"That guy you were talking with on the stairs all night," he said.

"Anders?" I said. "He's a filmmaker who has been shooting on location in Lyon or something like that for the past month. His girl-friend has the lead role and is very famous in Sweden."

He grinned. "Oh well," he said.

Then Sasha went up to get another coffee. Olivier and I talked about my family and how my sister is pregnant. His eyes focused on me, and I felt it again: his total attention on whatever I am saying, and his thoughtful replies. His bright blue eyes on mine. With him, it's like conversing with your biggest fan, who also happens to be brilliant and handsome. *So* handsome.

The sun started fading and I shivered.

"I think I'm going to go home, guys," I said, and I stood up. Olivier scraped his chair back over the cobblestones.

"I'm walking that way too," he said quickly.

"Okay!" Sasha kissed our cheeks, and Olivier and I left. We walked up the street and when we reached the corner, he took my hand. I looked at him, waiting for him to explain. Why did he have my hand? Was he giving me something?

"Rachel," he said. "I . . . want to kiss you."

My heart started pounding so loudly I was afraid I'd misheard him.

The caffeine and adrenaline rush made me start shaking like a scared rabbit. Was this really happening? Every time Jacques or Sasha teased me about dating Olivier, I always brushed it off while secretly daydreaming about him whenever I wandered alone through Paris. For months, we've flirted and had so many close calls, and it was moving so slowly that I had almost given up on him. But finally, here it was, his perfect face so close to mine, his eyes so starry.

I couldn't stop shaking.

"What?" I said.

I had to make sure my brain wasn't playing tricks on me. I thought maybe he was confused about the English word for *kiss*, and that if I went in for his lips, he'd go for cheek kisses instead, then push me away and call me a lusty whore.

I did not know how to respond to his request. I swallowed and squeezed his hand.

And then he'd pushed me back against the wall we were standing in front of, and we were kissing. I'd never been kissed like that before, softly and passionately. The entire time, I was still shaking, fluttering, barely present.

And then he pulled away and took my hand. I opened my eyes.

We walked around the Marais, swinging hands. We wandered into an exhibit about Paris architecture, holding hands and grinning at each other the whole time.

He left me with a kiss on the corner of Vieille du Temple, with a promise to meet up later tonight for a loft party up in the Nineteenth.

Every time I think about it, I can't believe it.

Olivier kissed me. I'm in Paris. It is all too good to be true.

Love,

A Vindicated Lusty Whore

## Jess to Rachel

Rachel! OMIGOD HE KISSED YOU. He kissed you. I actually do not know how to convey how exciting this is for me as well! Why *am* I so excited? I don't know, but I am! Finally, Olivier! HE KISSED YOU!

Okay, now that I have finally gotten all that out of my system, I'm just left wanting more. What happened next? Do you think this is it? The moment when our Ones are revealed to us?

Either way, I'm in Australia!

Didn't even think I'd make it here because my Beijing apartment was such a disaster. I had 113 books in my apartment. What the hell was I supposed to do with 113 books?

Note to future selves: Never buy anything. You will just have to pack it in a suitcase one day and be at the mercy of airline attendants and their draconian weight regulations.

But . . . Olivier kissed you! And you kissed him back, you lusty whore!

I want more information and I want it immediately.

I'm in Melbourne! It's winter here! I flew from a Chinese summer into an Australian winter, but the sky here is blindingly blue and the sunlight is so white.

I'm writing this outside from a café on a street in the north part of the city, Carlton, where I used to spend most of my time when I studied abroad here. I love revisiting parks and bookstores where I have so many memories, but as I wandered through familiar streets to get here, I felt, very strongly, that I was no longer twenty. At twenty, everything here felt new and exciting. Every adventure felt like a life-changing experience. And now, at twenty-four, it feels slightly muted. Has it changed because of life experience? Is this what getting older is?

Even though I stood out more in China, it was more as a general foreigner, but here I feel so self-conscious as an American. My first day here, I gave a homeless woman my change, but when she discovered my origins, she recoiled in disgust and spat out, "You're American?? I *hate* Americans. You're all taking over Australia." Then she wandered off with my money. I had literally given her two cents for her thoughts. I want a refund.

She may have a point—our pop culture is the dominant culture here. But even so, I've been in Asia for so long that I feel I missed out on a bunch of things. I have no idea what's cool anymore. All I know is that all jeans are now supposed to be skinny, all lipstick is now supposed to be red, and everyone wants to sleep with some guy named Don Draper.

Last evening I wandered around Melbourne's Chinatown, which is just one street long and crammed full of tourists eating dim sum. It did not feel like real China to me. Disappointed, I walked by a Starbucks and saw hordes of Chinese students sitting outside together. That was slightly more like it.

Real China is so far away, but parts of Beijing linger with me. It was normal to shout in Mandarin, "Waitress!" at the top of your lungs in a busy restaurant. Try doing this in Australia, especially in an American accent, and it's the quickest way to have all of the Australians in the restaurant turn on you. And you have to be aggressive in China to get anywhere. I'd forgotten that outside of Asia, it isn't normal to run onto a bus pushing everyone out of the way and if someone steps on your foot, *you* have to apologize passive-aggressively. I hope I don't become too soft here.

When I ride the tram outside the city, I see the silhouette of gum trees on the horizon instead of the construction cranes of China. The sky here is enormous, just as big as it is in Texas. Melbourne has a small bustling city center, but about half a mile outside the center, it becomes sprawling suburbs.

It also feels so quiet because I know no one here. I'm staying in a hostel and have been searching for a place to live. I went to register for my classes yesterday at the Royal Melbourne Institute of Technology, and half of the students seemed so young because they enrolled straight after college. Classes begin next week, and I'm still trying to adjust to the fact that I'm going to be a student again.

All I want to do right now is have coffee with you and Astrid and Rosabelle. I'm tired of meeting new people. I want to say something wildly inappropriate and not a single one of you bats your eyes. Rosabelle will order black coffee, and for old times' sake, Astrid will light up a cigarette, even though she quit last year.

Being back here is making me sentimental, but I SEE SAM SINGER TONIGHT! The last time I saw him, we were standing on a dock in Malaysia—it feels like a lifetime ago.

I'm flying to meet him in a few hours and I'm nervous. Really nervous. Like can't-sit-still nervous. Beijing and my old life are a million miles away, and Sam is waiting for me in Sydney.

WISH ME LUCK!

Love,

The Most Excited Passenger on the Airplane

**JULY 20**

## Rachel to Jess

Melbourne sounds so shiny and new and far away. But here, reality is setting in. Everything felt so perfect, so dreamy, and now . . . I don't know anymore. Something feels off with Olivier. I'm trying to make us be in sync again, like we were every day when we were just friends. I want this to work so badly.

After Olivier kissed me, we met up later that night and went to a loft party. We had to wait in line for a long time with Jacques and

Sasha and Marc, but they suddenly started treating us differently. They left us off on our own. But I didn't know how to act like his girlfriend! I wasn't his girlfriend yet! What do girlfriends do?

Standing in line with Olivier, I didn't have anything to say to him. He kept squeezing my hand with a soft look in his eye, and yet I couldn't think of one thing to talk about. We're so far past all of the initial background that you usually share on first dates, and I've seen him so frequently lately (like just earlier that day and the night before) that there was no news to share. We're not at the point where we talk about deeper subjects. Also, we were waiting in line for a party, so I wasn't about to ask his opinion on the origins of the universe or when he sees himself getting married. The silence made me so uncomfortable. I felt infinitely boring.

Finally we were inside the party. One big smoky techno party. We immediately made a beeline to get drinks. Then I dropped mine as Olivier grabbed me around the waist and kissed me hard, passionately, his arms tightly holding me as the room danced crazily around us in the dark, with only a slideshow on the front wall providing any light. Worries gone. We did this for two hours.

Finally, when it was over, Sasha and Marc split off to take the bus back to their place, and Jacques went to meet up with some other friends. Once again, Olivier and I were left to our own devices. And Olivier went along with the whole "We are now an established couple" thing, holding my hand and waving good-bye to everyone as we walked away from our friends.

He walked me to the subway, and then we made out in the Metro station. But once we were on the subway, he asked, "Are we going back to your place or mine?" But we had just kissed for the first time that very afternoon! This felt so wrong to me. We were friends before and it took us so long to just get to the next level. Why did everything have to happen the very same night? I was completely confused about what was happening! WHERE WAS THE SEDUCTION? Where's the subtle angling to see if I *want* to spend the night with him? Where's the rascally look in his eye?

Basically, compared to my romantic fantasies, he might as well have looked me in the eye and said, "Where does the penetration begin? At your place or mine?"

I kissed him good-bye and told him that we should go home alone.

I am freaked out over how fast everything is moving. Is that how it felt in the beginning with Sam?

I went to bed that night feeling like I should have agreed to go with him and just accepted the blunt overtures as the way he is. Like I should forget about seduction. I was scared I had somehow made him feel rejected.

But then he called the next day to see how I was, and I was so relieved that he still wanted to see me. That afternoon, I met up with him and Sasha and Marc even though I felt run-down and had the beginning of a cold. They were all standing in front of a lingerie store waiting for me when I got out of the Metro. Subtle choice, guys. I cheek-kissed Marc and Sasha and had to go in for a real kiss with Olivier. A short one, but Sasha and Marc were literally a foot away watching.

We hung out in cafés all day, switching to a restaurant and then a bar in the evening. We acted exactly like we always did, except this time Olivier had his hand on my back. But when it started to get dark, Olivier once again asked, "Your place or mine?" I still didn't understand why he was rushing everything, but I agreed on his place because I wanted to redeem whatever I may have lost the night before.

So even though it was a Sunday night, even though we were both tipsy and I felt like I was getting sick and even though we were both exhausted from staying out so late the previous night, we went back to his place.

We got to his place and we made out on his bed. It was so sexy and exciting . . . for the first hour. And then it just went on for too long.

Although I'm so attracted to him, it still felt like I was kissing a good friend. I'm so timid when it comes to initiating the physical, but I thought he would be more aggressive because of all the arm brushing and knee touching of the past few months. It turns out we are equally physically reserved.

Somehow we had gotten far enough that my cardigan had come off but he was still fully clothed. Lesson of the evening: One of you has to be the aggressor or you both end up just lying on top of each other, still fully clothed, staring at each other.

I was just too shy to take off his clothes. It felt like at any moment, he'd be like, "Stop! What are you doing, you fucking weirdo? Why are you taking my shirt off?"

My cold was getting worse. I kept having to get up to get water. Finally we both decided to get some sleep. He told me I should sleep over, and even though I was so stuffy from my cold and his apartment was about a million degrees, I felt like if I left right then, the night would be a failure. I wanted a chance to salvage everything.

So we both lay there, staring up at the ceiling, like a terrible sitcom. A terrible, hot, sweaty sitcom.

In the morning, things were still awkward. All of a sudden, it was like I was his guest in his hotel, with him offering his shower and cereal. Finally I left, kissing him good-bye and turning to go home. And then he pulled me back and said, "Can I see you again tonight?"

WHAT? He wants to see me again tonight? Don't we need some space? But he must still like me? I felt both dread and relief.

Jess, I don't know what's going to happen tonight. I do know I'm going to enjoy my seven hours without him before he comes over tonight after work.

He obviously likes me, right? Advise me, please!

Love,

Panicked

## Jess to Rachel

Oh God, your ordeal with Olivier sounds like total hell. Ahh, I feel so awkward right now! Like I need to take a shower or something. Alone. I also feel thirsty when I think about making out for hours and having a cold. I think you should sit back, relax, and rehydrate.

First of all, why are you guys cramming eight dates into one? An afternoon in a café, a jaunt in the park, a loft party, another café, another bar, another party—tell Olivier that this is just so much, too much, and way too soon! The only reason Sam and I had an acceler-ated relationship was because of the constant sense of urgency that he was leaving. Also, we had just met, so every conversation revealed something new.

I would like to grant you permission (because I feel like you are waiting for someone to give it) to remove the clothes of someone you are kissing, especially if the kissing is going on for more than one hour. If you still don't like being that forward, just request him to take off your clothes. You don't even have to be coy about it. Just shout, "Take off my shirt!" Trust me, it works like a charm every time. Al-though I don't know how to say this in French. The only thing I can say in French is, *"No mas touche pas!"* or "Do not touch me!" Useful for the Metro, maybe not so useful when trying to seduce your crush.

In all seriousness, the beginning of a romantic relationship is deli-cate. It's always the trickiest. When Sam and I were reunited in Ma-laysia, things felt strange for the first few nights. I suddenly felt shy and nervous. Even now, we are still so new, and the balance is fragile sometimes. Sometimes it still feels like we are flirting. There are still awkward silences. What I'm learning is that if both people are willing to make an effort, that discomfort goes away, and you can't view a few clumsy encounters as a sign of incompatibility. You both just have to have that blind faith that someday you will stop feeling awkward. My current theory is that's the test of true love—waiting out the awkwardness.

Who knows? Maybe everything will flow perfectly tomorrow. Maybe all he needs is Sasha to take him aside and say, "Romance her, you fool!" And relax! Everyone just needs to relax.

Please, whatever happens, just make sure something changes before you two end up lying next to each other fully clothed and sexually dissatisfied for the next twenty years. I have to say, I'm very disappointed in Frenchmen right now. What, they think the accent is seduction enough? *Non.*

I mean, take my advice with a grain of salt, since I did plan my whole life on a whim. But a whim that I don't regret.

I spent the entire hour-long flight to Sydney tapping my fingers, thinking about Sam, and staring into space. When the plane landed, I was the first one off. I jumped onto a train to central Sydney and when I stepped off the platform, Sam appeared from behind a column, grinning. His hair was slightly longer and he wrapped me in his arms and then we looked at each other, stunned that we were both finally in the same place. It was one of my top ten moments ever.

He took me to a tiny authentic Chinese restaurant because I've been missing Beijing's food. Days in Sydney were spent lying on Bondi Beach, and at night we watched the fireworks at Darling Harbour.

You've never been to Australia, so let me overgeneralize, although this will anger the natives. Sydney is like Melbourne's hot blond sister who likes to fake tan and wears high heels to breakfast. Melbourne is the artsy, intellectual sister who makes her own clothes and listens to underground rock. She is, sadly, not as popular. It's like Sydney's always flicking her beach-blond hair and calling her sister "Mel-boring."

Melbourne is full of hipsters. Entire neighborhoods feel like they've been transplanted from Brooklyn. Yesterday, I walked by live window mannequins who were shaving each other's beards off. There seems to be some sort of vintage resurgence here as well, because all of the girls I'm meeting love baking cupcakes, knitting scarves, and wearing secondhand clothes.

Sam told me that if I start doing any of these things, he's not going to recognize me. I left him in Sydney after the weekend. Saying goodbye with so little time together was hard, but I know he'll be visiting me in two weeks. He's currently working at a magazine in Sydney that is struggling, so he's considering making the move to Melbourne if things don't change. I'm really hoping this happens soon.

So after a weekend in Sydney, I'm back in Melbourne alone, drinking a coffee outside. My classes have weekly local news quizzes, and I don't recognize a single politician's name, so I'm cramming. (Australians resent how little everyone else knows about their country, so I'm trying to prove them wrong, although failure seems inevitable.) You're welcome to join me at this café, but good luck finding me in the sea of other black jeans and newspapers.

Let me know what happens with Olivier. I'm here if you need me. I mean, I'm in Melbourne, which is basically the bottom of the earth. If you look at a globe, I'm about half an inch away from falling off the planet. But I'm still here.

Love,

Jess

**JULY 22**

## Rachel to Jess

Please send me that sad album you had on repeat when Sam left. Send it immediately. Before you even finish reading this. You are not at the bottom of the earth. I am. And also, Olivier and I broke up.

I can't even. I can't even write this.

It's over.

I had Olivier. And now it's over.

I lost him.

I don't know what I did. Or I can think of a million things that I did.

Jess. We dated for three days. A *friend* of mine dated me for three days and then decided that he didn't want to anymore.

I'm not sure my self-esteem will ever recover from this one.

It hurts too much to write about it. But I will. I have to tell you. I've just called you four times, but it's 6 A.M. in Melbourne.

Tonight, he came over. He wouldn't take off his coat. He wouldn't accept a glass of wine.

We sat down across from each other at my kitchen table.

"I want to talk," he said.

"Oh, thank God," I said, scared about what he was going to say but also hopeful that maybe we could figure out why things were so strange. If we'd both been so freaked out about the intensity of this— three consecutive days together—maybe we could find a way to act more natural. "I'm so glad you said that."

"You are?" He was visibly startled.

"Yes! But you go first."

"No, you go first."

I was growing suspicious. "No . . . *you* go first."

"Rachel," he said, "I only like you as a friend. I don't want us to date anymore."

I swallowed hard. I felt like I'd been hit in the chest. What was the deciding factor? My cold—the snoring—the prolonged kissing—my sleeping over—our awkward morning? WHAT HAD HAPPENED?

I started jabbering. Just going off in random phrases about how intense it had been, and I'd felt it too, but maybe we could just slow down and maybe that would work and maybe it was the intensity and maybe—

"Rachel," he said, "I don't think we should date."

It felt wrong to throw him out suddenly, so he stayed for another half hour. This is why we are both perfect and terrible for each other. I'm too timid to throw out someone who's dumped me, and he's so polite that he'll pretend that he didn't just dump me. Suddenly, it was like we were both pretending we were just chatting. I have no idea what we talked about, only that it was not about us. I cannot name one thing we discussed. I just wanted him to go, but I knew that the second he left, he would be gone from me forever.

And finally he walked out the door.

As soon as he did, I couldn't stop crying. And I can't stop trying to find the reason why it didn't work. Sasha said she was so excited that we were finally together because she'd never seen him flirt with anyone like he did with me.

He liked me for six months, I know he did. I know he supposedly doesn't have crushes on people, but he *did* on me. I know it from the way he looked at me and the way he always found a way to brush against me and the way he always found a way for us to be alone.

The core question of what happened is something I will never know.

Was I not good enough to wait out the awkwardness for? I was going to do it for him! I feel like he didn't fight for me.

What now? What do I do now? I got what I wanted and then I lost it. I don't know what to do now. Please help me. In fact, I'm dialing you again right now.

Ugh, it was the Chinese lady on your phone telling me that you "are power off." Jess! Turn the power on!

Oh, shit. You have a new cell phone now in Australia.

You call me.

Love,

Rach

## Jess to Rachel

Okay. I know that I just hung up with you, but still. I am shocked, even rethinking it now. And I *know* that it is not about you. Sasha warned you about Olivier, didn't she? "He never seems to like girls. He's never had a relationship." There's something off about him if she said that. Maybe he doesn't like real women, only ideal women he puts on pedestals. Or maybe he doesn't like women at all.

I think you should avoid him at all costs. This is going to take some time to get over. Remember, wallowing is perfectly respectable. Some may say admirable. Shows you are in touch with your feelings.

You want someone who is going to stick around and give you half a chance. Olivier is not this. At least you didn't waste years on him. It's better to know the truth about someone sooner, rather than later.

But honestly. Three days? I want to punch him in the face. I want to take a fish and slap it across his face, while yelling, *"NON! NO MAS TOUCHE PAS!"*

You are going to be okay. I promise.

If you visit me here, I'll take you to the farthest place from Paris: St. Kilda. It's the closest thing to a beach in Melbourne—a strip of sand on a bay. The streets are lined with fish-and-chip shops, cyclists, and bakeries. We'll lie in the sun, and I'll make sure your pale skin is completely covered in SPF 50 sunblock. I'll find a strapping Australian guy named Jono to rub it in for you. He'll say your name like this: *Rye-chull.*

Love,

Jess

## Rachel to Jess

I wish I'd gotten on a flight to Melbourne instead of what really happened.

I gave in. I had to see him.

Up until yesterday's debacle, I was still operating under the assumption that I was a character in an epic romance who had made a mistake. I could think of a million comparisons where, if people had talked things over honestly, so much heartbreak could have been avoided.

All of these thoughts, by the way, came to me after several days of stewing in confusion and frustration while eating frozen pizza in my apartment, and it felt eerily familiar to my nursery in Brooklyn. Did I come all this way just to be exactly the same? I can change this. I'm going to change this.

At the very least, I have to try. I was desperate to see Olivier again, desperate to undo what had been done. So I made Olivier get a drink with me.

He arrived at a crowded bar, and nodded at me. We did the cheek kisses. He wore an expression like I was about to open a jack-in-the-box in his face and he just didn't know when.

I felt like he thought I was a crazy rejected girl. But the thing you have to remember is that even though I *like* him, I still didn't want what we had a few days ago. I thought if we discussed it, I could get what I actually wanted—falling in love slowly. Learning about each other romantically without the pressure of immediate coupledom. Surprises.

Maybe it's not possible with friends, but I still wanted that and thought that maybe, if we tried, we could get it back.

We sat down. We made small talk. Finally he said, "It's late, Rach. What is it?"

Normally we talk in English or French, but I was definitely taking the upper hand on this one. English it was.

"I just don't understand what happened."

"Well . . . I think we'd be better as friends," he said tentatively.

"But you didn't think we were just friends when you kissed me," I said.

"I hadn't thought it through?" he said.

But this made me madder than almost anything else he could have said, because it was a blatant lie. "So . . . you didn't feel anything toward me before then?"

"No more than with anyone else."

"Olivier. We flirted for, like, months."

He shrugged. "We flirt with everyone."

I felt stung and like he was trying to make it seem like everything was in my head.

"I just don't think we should waste this! I was scared too! Neither one of us was being ourselves! Why do we just have to throw everything away?" I asked.

"Because I either really like someone, or I don't care," he said. "And well, with you . . ."

I couldn't believe I was hearing this. Why do you kiss someone you don't care about? Why do you seek them out in the middle of the day to kiss them? Why do you ask to see them three days in a row? I tried to figure out what to say next.

"So the door is closed, then," I said.

"For now, yes."

"For now? So in the future, the door might be open?"

He squinted at me, confused.

I repeated: "For the *future*, it's *open*? Or it's *closed*? Is it *closed*?"

206 | GRADUATES IN WONDERLAND

"No . . . not necessarily."

"So for the future, it's open?"

"I guess . . . but the door in the future is open for anyone. Like it would be open for you and Jacques or you and Marc."

"But they both have girlfriends."

"Exactly."

"*Exactly?* Exactly *what?*"

This is the point where I leaned across the table and screamed, "WHICH IS IT, OLIVIER? IS THE DOOR OPEN OR IS IT CLOSED? IS IT OPEN OR IS IT CLOSED? WHICH IS IT?!?!?!"

And I saw the look of horror on his face, and all of a sudden, I saw myself in his eyes.

I muttered an apology and left immediately. I did not care about the bill. I just had to get out of there.

Because that was the moment when I realized that we were not in an epic romance. Right now, we're nothing. But at least I tried. At least I know now.

Tell me what it's like where you are. I just realized that I can't picture your life in Australia at all. I'm so used to imagining you perched at a desk inside your high-rise apartment building in Beijiing. Distract me. Tell me what real love looks like, so I can be sure that it didn't just walk away from me.

Love,

Kray Kray

P.S. "*No mas touche pas*" is mostly Spanish, with some badly conjugated French thrown in. It's okay, though. The sentiment still stands.

## Jess to Rachel

Dear Kray Kray,

The only thing that walked away from you was a juvenile French guy with commitment issues. And I actually don't think your yelling was so bad. Everyone goes crazy on guys at some point. I remember Astrid once broke up with a guy because he refused to bring her ice cream one evening. And a friend of mine from home always pretended to be at some awesome party whenever she answered the phone from a guy. She'd blast Jay Z alone and yell into the phone, "Hello? Oh, sorry, I can't hear you! It's so crazy in here!"

Olivier just doesn't get it. You don't want someone who is indifferent to you. Don't waste any more of your life on him. It's better that it ends now than drags out for months—now you can move on and start to get over him. Don't see him again anytime soon.

Even though I'm finally in a relationship that's stable, it's definitely not perfect. Right now with Sam, we only see each other every weekend, when he flies here or I fly up to Sydney. I thought everything would be so much easier when I moved to Australia, but not being able to spend every night together is hard.

I dread Sunday mornings, which is when he leaves. Today, as I watched him get dressed to go, I felt a heaviness just like in Beijing, when I thought that I would lose him forever. Even though we now live in the same country and we're committed to each other, there are still so many days and nights alone. I hope it won't be like this forever.

But one of the best things about being in Australia is that instead of living in a high-rise building, I get to live in a real house. I'm renting the front bedroom of a two-story house with wooden floors and a small courtyard in the back. When I walk home from the nearest train station, I walk down leafy residential streets that are so quiet.

I moved in with an Irish guy, a Venezuelan guy, and an Australian girl. The Irish housemate, Dylan, has red hair and very pale skin and is growing potatoes in our backyard. This pleases me. He's cranky because he fell asleep with his curtains open, and when he woke up this morning, he had a sunburn across his forehead.

I'm bonding with the Irishman and the Venezuelan merely because none of us gets the Australian sense of humor at all, especially when we're watching local TV. We stare blankly at it while the laugh track plays in the background. Emily, the Australian girl, has to explain nearly every joke. I am suddenly part of an immigrant family that doesn't know what's going on.

I think most of the people in Melbourne are like this, though, because it's packed with so many different nationalities: Chinese, Malaysian, Indian, and Vietnamese, and large Italian and Greek populations. I finally have access to really great curries and authentic pizza for the first time in years. (In China, Pizza Hut offers a thin-crust pie with mayonnaise, fried shrimp, and mini–hot dogs. I'm glad this is not an option in Australia.)

Meanwhile, I've started my broadcast-journalism and news-reporting courses and today, for an assignment, my classmates and I took out video cameras to interview people on the street. I held a microphone and ran up to strangers asking them random questions. It was an exercise to make us loosen up and get used to humiliating ourselves in public, which is particularly easy for me, since the Australians call me out for mispronouncing nearly everything here. (I can't even pronounce *Melbourne* correctly. Why even *have* the *r* in it if you're not going to use it?) But we're also learning how to edit footage and put together reports—something I've always wanted to learn.

Since I signed up for my program so late, I'm in the afternoon tutorial with all of the slackers who didn't want to wake up for the early section. Everyone is relatively friendly, but nearly everyone grew up here, and I feel older than most of the students. I hoping there's close-friend potential somewhere here. I'm one of two Americans in the entire program, and the other one is married to an Australian guy.

I spend my days in class and my nights on the phone with Sam. I'm still trying to figure out what my life here is going to look like.

Love,

Sometimes Australians Laugh at Me and I Don't Know Why

## Rachel to Jess

It's strange to read about your new beginnings, when I feel like I just arrived in Paris yesterday. However, it was almost a year ago when I first moved here, and I even have my first French ex to prove it.

I want my attitude right now to be, "Onward and upward!" But it's not.

I'm not transcending this, not even a little. The other day, I was convinced I saw Olivier on the Metro. All of a sudden, my mouth went so dry and my heart started beating fast. I haven't had a panic attack in so long, but the signs are unmistakable. I fumbled for my medication, which I always carry with me, and waited for the feeling to subside.

But I've been walking around slightly worried for the past few days because the scariest thing about a panic attack is what it could set off in the following days. It's like the trigger for a potential avalanche. Tomorrow, I could still feel down, so I'll sleep a little late. The next day, I might feel worse and crawl into bed immediately after class. And before I've realized what's happening, I'm right back to where I started, at the bottom of a hole in New York. This chain of reactions always starts with a bad or upsetting situation, but then it's an incredibly slippery slope into a depressive episode.

Now, even though I've averted this for the moment, I still don't know what to do. I feel fine physically, and calmer and healthier. But I'm still confused about what to think about what happened with Olivier. The doubts just keep coming back in droves, bringing their friends with them.

If I'd been more interesting or aggressive, would I still be dating Olivier? If I looked like a French model, would he love me? If I hadn't gossiped so much with Sasha about him, would that have changed things? I hate that these doubts consume me, and that I want to understand something that doesn't have an answer.

Even though I tried to avoid him, we have the same friend group. The last time I really saw Olivier, we were all hanging out in a group at Sasha and Marc's apartment, and we were very polite to each other. But actually, it felt like we hated each other and were just hiding it. There was a coldness to every interaction. I could tell he didn't want to kiss my cheek. I didn't want to get close to him. At one point, I became totally lost as the guys discussed politics and their favorite candidates, but when the group broke into laughter, out of habit, I joined in. Olivier frowned at me and said, "Rachel, there is *no way* you understood that. It was about a suburban politician from the 1980s."

I turned red and tried to brush it off. I left soon afterward.

Olivier is known for being the "nice guy" in this group, and he's always given me preferential treatment, but now I feel like I've fallen out of his favor. For what? For kissing him when he asked me to? I'm starting to think that he actually isn't so nice. I'm not sure he's the pure-as-gold "good guy" he presents himself as. He has a cold side that he's not showing anyone else, and it's pissing me off.

I'm not going to see him for a while. I think I need to be with people who don't know Olivier.

I've become restless from one year of hanging around cafés and libraries all the time—Parisian life gets repetitive and the idleness seems to feed my neuroticism. I saw a job opening in an expat forum to teach English and the SAT that pays pretty well. Yesterday, I went in for an interview, where I was greeted by an American guy, Josh, who runs the academy (American Prep). He shook my hand and was very blunt. "Rachel, Classroom A. I'll meet you there in five minutes." Finally, no ambiguity.

He wore baggy jeans and a blue baseball cap, so even though it felt like we were peers, I had to audition for the teacher's role. This meant that I had to pretend that this thirty-year-old guy was actually a class of fifteen teenagers. He asked me to teach the math section. Cube roots? Exponents? I forgot these things the second I finished high school.

I had crammed for the past week and miraculously, the lesson seemed to flow and I solved all the problems correctly on the first try. This may be because Josh is bearlike and comforting, and I did not feel threatened by him at all. Thank God he's not my type—curly dark hair, very tall and stocky, and wears sneakers. Very American.

My final step to securing the job is retaking the SAT. This Saturday, I'm going to spend four and a half hours being seventeen again.

It's the moment of truth: Did Brown make me smarter or dumber?

After I passed the audition, Josh sat with me and gave me recommendations for the city, even though I've been here for a year. I only remember two things he said:

1.  Don't date Frenchmen. I don't trust them.

2.  You'll get a lot of shit if you speak English loudly in
    public, so suppress it the best you can.

Thanks, Josh. However, that advice was too little, too late.
Love,
Rach

# YEAR THREE

## Jess to Rachel

I just spent the last hour cowering away from my window because it sounded like there was a wheezing old man dying on my porch. Or people with emphysema having sex. Either way, I did not know how to handle the situation. Finally I ran to get Dylan, my six-foot-five Irish housemate. I pushed him outside. He looked around and figured out that the noise was coming from a tree outside my window.

"It's a wombat," he said. "They're like little Australian bears that live in trees and hiss."

I've never seen one before. In photos it looks like a cuddly bear, but all I know is that its moan sounds like a raspy death rattle. So many new animals in Australia.

I had to fetch Dylan instead of Sam because Sam flew back to Sydney this morning. We're still trying to see each other every other weekend and every time he leaves, I always pull him back for one more kiss or try to keep him in my bed for a few minutes longer. After he's gone, everything seems bleak and lonely for a few hours.

We are living two lives. On the weekends we get to be together and I tell him everything about my week as we walk around trying all the delicious brunch places in Melbourne, and at night we fall asleep in each other's arms.

The remainder of the time, I'm alone, listless, texting him from my unmade bed about how much I miss him because he is all the way in Sydney. But I get over it eventually, because this is what normal is for us when he lives five hundred miles away.

I'm still getting used to calling him my boyfriend. Even saying *boyfriend* just sounds foreign to me. That is something else that other people say. I've just realized that I've never really been a girlfriend before and I have no idea how to do this. Is it just kissing and sex as well as going to dinner? Birthday presents? Bringing them chicken soup when they're sick?

I've spent my life with long spells of being single interspersed with very short relationships, and then being single again, looking for someone new. Now I'm committed to Sam, and it feels serious and real for the first time in my life. But despite all the loving feelings I have for Sam, I still don't know if I'm doing this right. How do other people in relationships feel? I know that I feel safe with him. He calls me, without fail, every night, and always texts back.

My days in Melbourne are spent at class, and then my nights are spent alone. The only people I really see on a regular basis are people from my program. One guy, Callum, always tries to sit by me. He's extremely loud—the kind of guy who will walk across a crowded room and try to fall down to get attention. The kind of guy who gets pantsed and finds it hilarious. The kind of guy who will raise his hand to purposely deliver the wrong answer in a deadpan voice. When I first met him, I felt like I was in high school and the class clown was sitting by me.

Lately, I feel like all of his gags are within my sight line and are for the sole purpose of getting my attention. He has taken to calling me "America," in my program full of Australians, especially during class debates during our journalism ethics class. "Uh-oh," he'll tell the class. "America's getting riled up again." When I'm walking through campus, he'll appear from nowhere, running at me at full speed, yelling, "Calm down, America!! It's just me, for Chrissakes." And then he'll linger, accompanying me to wherever I'm going. I feel like he is thisclose to offering to carry my books.

I haven't told Sam about this. I don't know what I would even say. "There's a guy at school who likes to fall down in front of me. I thought you should know." So instead I say nothing. And so it goes on: Callum always tries to sit by me in class, and I let him. He knows I have a boyfriend—when he overheard me talking about Sam, he jumped into the conversation and asked hundreds of questions about Sam: "What does he look like? What does he do? Where does he live? How did you meet? What color is his hair?" He asked so many questions that I ended up walking away from the conversation feeling like I'd somehow done Sam a disservice by answering Callum's reductive questions.

I could also see what Callum was doing. I've done the same thing myself—trying to find out everything about some disagreeable situation, because if I can break it down into a handful of facts, there must be some way to reverse it. It's just strange to suddenly be on the receiving end of this.

Sam's on a flight back to Sydney as I write this. Every weekend Callum invites me out with him and some of our classmates. "Come on, America. I know you don't know anyone else in this city." And he's right. I have no friends. I've resisted going so far, but that's also because I'm usually with Sam.

I'm so confused right now. I like Callum's attention. Callum both confuses and enhances my feelings for Sam. He's irresponsible and not as kind as Sam, but he does make me laugh so much. And yet, when Sam left this morning, I wanted to follow him to Sydney and never come back here.

Do other girlfriends feel this way?

Love,

Jess

P.S. My Australian housemate just came home. I told her there was a wombat in my tree and she told me there was an idiot in my brain because it's actually a possum (wombats live in the countryside and can't climb trees). It turns out Dylan knew all along. Stupid Irish humor.

## Rachel to Jess

I also have no idea how to be a girlfriend. I love sleeping alone and I avoid sick people at all costs. I don't even cook for myself, so I need someone who appreciates a lovingly baked frozen pizza. In exchange, I would like somebody who would chase a fake wombat out of a tree for me. Is Dylan available for travel?

However, it has been a long time since I have been a girlfriend, but, based on my observations, you just have to add friendship to a torrid romance. Or a torrid romance to an existing friendship. Hence, girl friend.

Okay, I don't actually know. That formula totally failed for me and Olivier. I keep thinking that the second Olivier considered me his girlfriend, he immediately saw everything bad about me and found me wanting.

So . . . I'm not over him yet. To try and move on, I've taken to ignoring him. Please adopt this same "He does not exist" attitude toward Callum. I feel like you and Sam are still trying to figure out your own version of normal.

Everywhere I go in Paris, I see couples. Even now, I'm sitting across from a doe-eyed pair in a café called Merci, which is full of books, oriental carpets, and chandeliers, eating a tartine, which you would love (French bread with butter and jam).

I'm about to begin classes again. Marie has graduated, the exchange students I knew last year have left, but I now know things like where the bathroom is and that French professors never answer their e-mails. I'm spending more time alone now because I'm avoiding run-ins with Olivier, which means I haven't seen Jacques, Marc, and Sasha lately either. It's a fresh, if slightly lonely, start.

Last week was my final session of teacher training at the American Prep center. On my way there, I always pass a bunch of American establishments, like the Hard Rock Café, Starbucks, and McDonald's. It jolts me out of my French train of thought when I walk by. "New York? Is that you? You look *bad*."

Whenever I walk in to meet my boss, Josh, an actual New Yorker, for a while, I do forget I'm in Paris. Last week, he grinned at me as he tried to coax me into teaching my first official class. I thought I would be training to teach the SAT, but instead I was assigned to teach English . . . for the Ministry of Defense. Instead of fifteen-year-old boys and girls, I have to teach twenty-five French military men who need to pass an English test to be promoted to lieutenant.

Josh saw my face when he broke the news to me and tried to make it out that I was tough enough to handle them. I had pictured myself teaching awkward teenagers, and now I was supposed to face rows of soldiers? But it was the only class that hadn't been filled, and I figured it was now or never.

When I walked into my first class, I realized that I was younger than all of my student soldiers by at least ten years. Thank God they didn't come in uniform, but they did all have the same haircut, with the sides of their heads shaved. They were all chattering away in French, and I cleared my throat. They didn't realize I was the teacher and kept talking. I wrote my name and the syllabus on the board and cleared my throat again.

Finally, I just shouted, "Hey!" and they shut up. As soon as I started the lesson, it wasn't scary anymore, because I can speak English and they can't.

Their English is at the level where they can string together full sentences when put on the spot, but when I ask a question, it takes . . . a lot . . . of time . . . to get an . . . answer . . . ? (This is exactly how I used to speak French.) Also, when they ask some questions, I struggle to answer, because teaching English is like being asked to describe how breathing works. You can do it, but you don't know how to *describe* how. The lungs? Try to suck the air in and then push it out. In . . . and out . . . and that's why we use the past participle! No more questions.

Nevertheless, I didn't think that I would have this much fun teaching. I like seeing them get better at English. It was satisfying when during our lesson on animals, they finally stopped talking about the different "races" of dogs and started saying "breeds." And also, I like having all the answers for once. I like teaching something in which there *are* correct answers, as opposed to writing vague essays about French film philosophy.

I know it's hard to believe, but I'm not shy when I'm in front of a class, holding a black marker and writing on a whiteboard. In class, I get great reception and consider becoming a stand-up comic for about thirty seconds before I realize that my jokes are all about gerunds versus infinitives.

Josh asked me how long I think I'll be in Paris for, and I've been thinking about this a lot lately. I have nine more months left in my film studies program and then what? What the hell do you do with a master's degree in film?

The idea of being a professor has slowly taken root in my mind. I really like being in front of a classroom of students, and in my fantasy, I'm a professor instructing a lecture hall about *Casablanca* and *Singin' in the Rain* and *Blow-Up*. I like that idea. A lot.

Professors have always seemed like magical keepers of knowledge, and I know that I'll feel young and over my head, at least at first. But then I remember that visiting art history professor at Brown who kept tripping over the microphone and kept confusing Manet with Monet. I know I'm at least as good as her, right?

I think film might be something I want to study for a long time. Film itself is only a century old, and there's still so much to add to the field, unlike English literature or art history. Lately, I've been thinking a lot about an area that nobody's researched fully yet—the fluctuating popularity of European actresses in 1930s Hollywood due to complex relationships between America and Europe. The idea came to me after watching Greta Garbo in *Ninotchka*, when she plays a ridiculous Soviet comrade; after this movie, her Hollywood career plummeted because tensions in Europe made Americans start to distrust Europeans and immigrants.

Maybe I could even trick somebody into paying me to research it.

So I met with my advisor, Pierre, to discuss pursuing a PhD in film studies.

"Do it," he said. "But don't do it here."

"Why not?" I felt panicked. In my mind, I'd already planned my next decade in France. I would have a nice little summer house in Normandy (nothing ostentatious—wouldn't want to be *gaudy*) and a horse named Maurice, and eventually marry a Parisian director who makes perfect crème brûlée.

"I wouldn't recommend that anybody do their PhD in France if they don't have absolutely bilingual, beautiful, academic written French." He leaned forward over his desk. "Think about where the academic thought is exciting and new. Where it really fits your specialty. And go there."

As soon as he said it, I knew that Pierre was right about my having to leave France if I really want to continue this work. But I want my life here to last forever!

For the moment, I'm talking a lot more about split infinitives than about Gene Kelly, but maybe that will change one day.

Love,

Marlene Dietrich, showing her legs to the troops

## Jess to Rachel

Teaching military men sounds scary, until I imagine you making them do push-ups every time they misconjugate a verb. "You *TELLED* him the command? NO. Get down and give me *vingt* push-ups!" (I just had to Google "twenty" in French.)

I haven't seen Sam for two weeks and even though we talk every night, the distance is wearing on me. I really am starting to feel like we are leading different lives, and it's so frustrating when all I want to do is just be in the same room for once.

I can't stop thinking: Can I be with one man for the rest of my life? Is one person ever enough? And why am I just now thinking of these things? Maybe it's because my friend from home Paige is engaged. I felt like that was something other people did, and now that my oldest friend is taking the plunge, suddenly it feels like I need to suddenly get my shit together.

Callum has started texting me. He began by sending me questions about our writing assignments, but now his messages have progressed into funny asides that are really specific to me. I don't know what to do. I don't know the boundaries! And he's funny, so I text him back.

He's the kind of guy I used to like. The kind of guy I used to date. The kind of guy I thought I'd outgrown.

Last night, a bunch of my classmates went to a pub. Australians can drink, and I have no hope of keeping up. I drink about half a pint for every three they can down. My classmates like to gossip about everyone in our program and make wild projections about our lecturers (we like to imagine most of them have had scandalous affairs with politicians and media moguls here). Australians have a very laid-back attitude and everyone is always over-the-top with teasing, but last night things might have gone too far.

Callum got very drunk and announced to everyone at the table that he likes to pretend that I am his girlfriend. WHAT THE FUCK? The only reply I could think of was, "But I have a boyfriend," and he said, "Yes, I know. But I also like to pretend that he does not exist."

Everyone at the table awkwardly shifted in their seats and then changed the conversation.

I was stunned by his announcement, but the absolute truth is also this: I felt flattered. I felt acknowledged. Especially because I've been feeling neglected by Sam's absence. And more than that, though—I felt a flickering attraction toward Callum. This was immediately snuffed out by overwhelming guilt. I didn't talk to him for the rest of the night, but when I got up to leave the pub, he jumped up to offer to walk me to my tram stop. On the walk over, he said, "I'm just going to pretend that we're holding hands."

Finally, I stopped him.

"You can't say shit like that. I have a boyfriend."

"I know, I know! I'm sorry. I'm really sorry. Look, I just . . ." He trailed off before he feigned stealing my purse, which he thinks is a funny joke for onlookers. He laughed a lot, and so did I, because it *was* funny, and laughing made the flirtation feel harmless again. My tram arrived and I got on it alone.

We do not hug good-bye. We do not touch at all. And yet, I have to keep telling myself that I've done nothing wrong, which makes me feel like I have done something really wrong.

He's getting to me.

How do I know if Sam is The One? Why do I even think there is a "One"? Sam's the first guy I've ever made a real commitment to, but I don't actually know if I can even keep a commitment. I don't yet know what kind of girlfriend I am—the kind who stays forever or the kind who could leave her boyfriend for another man.

Not that that man is necessarily Callum. Callum's just fun. He loves to make a fool out of himself, but I'm not sure there's more to his personality than that. What I do know is that Callum looks at me like I'm the shiniest object in the room, like he's never met anyone like me before. Maybe he does this because I'm an American girl, maybe because he's never left Melbourne in his entire life, maybe because he sees me as a challenge. I'm not really sure why. He even enjoys it when I tell him to fuck off when he's annoying me in the library. In turn, I find his unflappability attractive, even though I'm not naturally attracted to him physically. He's losing his hair and he chews his fingernails and he has very thick eyebrows that look like caterpillars, but I find him amusing. I find myself looking forward to seeing him at class.

How do I pretend he doesn't exist when he constantly seeks me out?

J

**OCTOBER 11**

## Rachel to Jess

You know, what's strange is that I can easily put myself in Callum's place. I can hear what he is thinking: "I make her laugh. We have the same interests. I just need to push hard enough. That boyfriend will fade away at some point—most boyfriends do."

But I think that you are falling into the trap of "Love the one you're with." If you really think about it, would you prefer Callum to Sam if both of them lived in Melbourne? Either way, if you keep flirting with Callum, things with him will progress.

Even if it feels harmless, these things always turn serious fast.

Here, I'm back to hanging out with Jacques and Marc and Sasha, and see them on the weekends, when we go to house parties. Whenever I see Olivier, I try to be extra friendly to eliminate this coldness that's developed between us, but he's having none of it. Finally, I just ignore him as he ignores me.

To prep for my upcoming SAT classes, Josh gave me extra training sessions, and so I've had to spend hours with him as he teaches me things like, "If you don't know the answer, just act like you do but make them figure it out." The one-on-one sessions are pretty intense. We're becoming really good friends—it's great to finally have someone get all of my cultural references and jokes. We joked about how we thought we'd spend our time in Paris becoming great writers, but instead we're teaching snobby teenagers how to get into our alma maters. We also cried a little about this.

Josh is such a sturdy, levelheaded presence. He's so straightforward and blunt. After Olivier and the subtlety of the French, it's refreshing. I once told him that horses are people too, and he said, "Well, then why don't I get to shit in the street?" If I had asked Josh, "Is the door open or is it closed?" he would have responded, "The door is locked and you will never have the key." Still not the nicest thing to hear, but at least the ambiguity is completely gone.

By the end of our intense teacher training, we started having lunch together and I told him all about Olivier, whom I'm still hung up on. When I reached the part about the last time Olivier kissed me, I couldn't keep it together and started crying. He put a hand on my shoulder, but it didn't feel out of place. It just felt comforting.

Anyway, he has a girlfriend. Whom he lives with.

He also buys me coffee all the time when we bump into each other before work. His rationale: "I am your boss. I know what I make, and I know what you make, and I know who can afford this more."

We then go and drink them on the steps of a big nineteenth-century government building around the corner, where we share a cigarette. I have officially given them up(!), and his girlfriend has made him give them up too, but somehow I always have one or two in my purse. And he says witty things and basically we pretend we live in the Jazz Age and have lives as public intellectuals, in which sitting around drinking coffee for half the day is an acceptable occupation.

Quitting smoking (which I have now done four times since

graduation) is not my only self-improvement effort. I joined a gym and went curtain shopping. I just reread that and realized I am on my way to being a trophy wife who is really good at taking the SAT.

That's pretty much the most plausible future I can think of right now—everything else is hypothetical. Now that I know my time in Paris has a definite ending point because I can't pursue my PhD here, I'm growing anxious about moving to a new country. I hate thinking about starting over in a new place again. To start a PhD in the United States, I would have to repeat my last two years of coursework—and I'd have to pay US tuition fees, which are enormous, especially compared to here.

I started asking everyone I know where they thought I should go. Josh: "New York!" Sasha: "Vienna!" Olivier: "Anywhere but here!" (It was implied.)

But there is one other option that sounds feasible: England. Pros: I speak English. I wouldn't have to pay US fees. And most important, my French coursework would still be accepted, because both France and the United Kingdom have the same postgrad system.

I'm starting to think England might be the only solution. I've been researching programs in London and I'm going to send off some applications to see what happens. If I don't do anything right now, I'm going to end up back in Wisconsin, trying to explain the point of a film studies master's degree to recruitment agencies and my father.

But that means no more Sasha, no more Josh, no more Seine and cobblestones and champagne-colored light. I'm already reminiscing about my present.

Anyway, I'm off to go teach sixteen-year-olds. I had my first class yesterday, and in case you have forgotten, sixteen-year-olds are assholes. One kid dropped other people's coats on the floor, dumped out the contents of the girls' purses over lunch, and basically made my life miserable. Good joke, future psychopath.

Love,
Rach

## Jess to Rachel

That future psychopath sounds like Callum. Whom I can't stop thinking about. That is, when I'm not hating myself for doubting my relationship with Sam. What is wrong with me? I care so much about Sam, but I'm getting frustrated. I've finally found someone and yet I sleep alone most nights. I moved here so we could be together—but we're hardly ever together. In my darkest, most selfish moments, I think that he could find a way to see me more if he really wanted to. If he loved me more.

That's when my mind wanders and I wonder what it would be like to be with Callum. I want to know what it would be like to kiss him just once. I want to sleep with him just once. And then I'd know what it was like and it would never have to happen again.

Do you think I met Sam when I was too young? I'm beginning to think this. Although I'm always on the lookout, I never imagined myself finding The One until I was at least thirty. Sam arrived earlier than I expected and maybe I need more time to explore, to be alone, to be less serious, to learn about what I want from my life. To be with other people.

The extreme fluctuation of my feelings is beginning to scare me. Last year I was in Beijing. I fell so hard for Sam and all I wanted was him. I would have done anything for him, and then I did. And now here I am in Australia, part of a real relationship for the first time, and yet I'm thinking about some guy who makes me laugh by pretending to fall into a trash can.

I feel sick thinking about it. I don't know what to do. At this point, I seem to be trying to stand very still balancing these two relationships. I want everything to stay as it is, where I can flirt with Callum during the day and come home to my boyfriend, Sam, on the weekends.

Last night, a group of my classmates stayed late at the computer lab working on our final assignments for the semester. At midnight, Callum walked me to the closest train station. He asked what I was doing that weekend and I told him that Sam was coming into town. Callum nodded and grew serious. He said, "You're holding two fortune cookies. One says, 'Stay with Boyfriend Sam.' The other says, 'Date that asshole from your program.'"

I couldn't believe he was really saying this. Why did he have to push the boundaries and be so bold? Why was he ruining everything?

I'd never seen his serious side before, and didn't realize that he liked me so much. Am I only doubting my relationship with Sam because Callum appeared in my life? Now that he's presented himself to me so seriously, it seems like I really do have to make a choice.

I think you and I are in similar situations: Life has once again handed us ultimatums. In six months, we could both have completely different lives. You might be in England on your way to becoming a fancy professor, and I could be . . . breaking up with Callum.

I feel like my choice is less "Choose Callum or Sam" and more "Choose an unpredictable life of many loves" or "Choose a stable life with one love forever."

But instead of confronting these feelings, I simply shook my head in disbelief at Callum's audacity—and also at my own. I don't stop him from saying things like this, and I did not immediately leave. I did not say, "Don't talk to me this way ever again." I tried to laugh it off. I waved good-bye.

Moments later, when I was on the train, Sam texted and I did not reply until I was at home.

He's flying into Melbourne tomorrow for the weekend.

Fuck. Fuck. Fuck.

Rachel, I'm holding two fortune cookies.

Which am I going to choose?

Jess

## Rachel to Jess

You need to make your decision before a fortune cookie does it for you. You have the rest of your life to think about.

If you want something new and exciting, then you should break up with Sam now and pick Callum. But excitement always fades eventually. Is it still going to be funny when Callum falls into garbage cans as a forty-five-year-old man? I feel like there will always be new Callums. But honestly, I'm not sure if there will be other Sams. You love everything about him. His living in Sydney is temporary, but I've never heard you describe any guy the way you talk about Sam.

Sam could be the wrong choice, but remember that even though you didn't meet him when you were thirty, it did take twenty-five years to find him. On the other hand, Callum's only real pro seems to be that he lives in Melbourne and is new. He sounds like most of the guys you've ever dated—hilarious and unpredictable—but Sam is the first guy who you've actually considered a real future with.

Look at the guys you've dated since college. Bruno Who No Speak the English and George Who You Don't Want To Touch and Old Man Ray. Next up, Trash Can Callum? Or Sam? Whom you loved so much that you left China for him?

Let me know what you choose.

Love you,

Rach

P.S. If you pick Trash Can Callum, I'm really sorry about this e-mail.

## Jess to Rachel

Too late.

Sam has left me. He knows. He knows everything.

On Saturday, we had a great dinner out in the city and walked home arm in arm. We fell asleep spooning and I was so happy we were together. And then at 3 A.M., my phone rang. I couldn't find it immediately, and the ring woke Sam up. I finally found my phone at the bottom of my purse and I saw that it was Callum. I hit ignore.

"Who was that?" Sam asked.

"No one," I said and got back into bed. "Go back to sleep."

Then, the phone rang again. Callum. Sam looked at my phone and saw this.

"Why is he calling you at 3 A.M.? Why is someone else calling you at 3 A.M.? Why is a GUY calling you at 3 A.M.?"

I pressed ignore and then a minute later, the phone rang again. I shut it off and turned to look at Sam. I was frozen with guilt and fear and horror. Sam lay next to me and began shaking uncontrollably. I tried wrapping my arms around him, telling him it was nothing, it was nothing, but he was shivering. Shaking.

He kept asking me, over and over again, "Why is Callum calling you?" And then he began asking, "Does he call you often? How much do you see him? What's going on with him? I thought he was just some guy in your class whom you barely knew." I kept denying there was anything going on, even denying Callum's feelings for me. I was overcome with fear and such guilt unlike anything that I have ever known. I kept playing down Callum's feelings because I didn't want to worry Sam. I rested my head on his chest, and his heart was beating so quickly.

Suddenly at that moment, I wanted to have never met Callum. I wanted to undo what damage had been done. I didn't care if I ever saw Callum again. All I wanted was for Sam to be as loving and trusting as he was when we fell asleep earlier that night.

We both lay there in the darkness, not sleeping or touching. This morning at breakfast, I tried to be chipper and talk about a million other things, but Sam was quiet.

Finally, he looked at me and said, "Please tell me everything. Tell me everything that's ever happened with Callum. I'm asking you to be honest with me." I felt sick looking at him, scared of the truth, scared of what boundaries I'd broken.

I lied. I said that Callum was just a friend and nothing else. I said I did not think that Callum liked me at all. I said I definitely did not have any feelings for him. I said I had no idea why he was calling me at 3 A.M.

Sam asked me again, "Please tell me if you ever spend time alone with him. Please tell me what he says to you. Please tell me if you have ever thought about him romantically." And I lied again.

I couldn't bring myself to tell him the truth about my feelings and doubts. All I could think about was how I might lose Sam and that I would do anything or say anything to keep him.

I finally saw how everything really was. Callum meant nothing to me and Sam meant everything, but it was too late.

I loved Sam, but I could not tell him the truth about what had happened. If I told him everything, there may be no way back to where we were. I finally managed to end the conversation by saying I was going to shower.

When I stepped out of the shower, Sam and his bags were gone. My computer was open. Rachel, on the screen was my last e-mail to you. He'd read it.

It's over. I'm so shocked that I don't know how to react. I don't feel angry. I don't feel betrayed. He knew I was lying. And I had my computer open and my e-mail inbox open. I would have done the same thing.

I could barely bring myself to reread my words.

"I want to know what it would be like to kiss him just once. I want to sleep with him just once."

Oh God, can this ever be undone?

I really fucked up. He's been gone for a few hours now, and I'm going crazy. I didn't know what to do except write you.

I don't know what to do next. Call me.

J

OCTOBER 24

## Jess to Rachel

I can barely keep my eyes open, but before I crawl into bed and sleep for the next ten years, I'll let you know what happened after we spoke. I'm still trying to process the last few hours.

Sam wasn't answering his phone, and I had no idea where he had gone. I had nowhere to go. I didn't know what to do. I just lay on my bed staring at the ceiling for hours, intermittently numb with shock interrupted by stretches of misery when I realized that I may never be in the same bed with Sam ever again. I remembered how I had also lain in my bed in Beijing the morning he left, staring listlessly into space, and I didn't know how I had ended up right back where I had started, even though I had traveled halfway across the world.

There's nothing to do when you feel like this. Nothing that can be done but staring into space or frantically hatching plans to win the person back or wiping back angry tears. Fucking fucking Callum. Fucking me. Stupid fucking me.

There was also the crushing guilt. During the entire flirtation with Callum, I never really thought about what Sam would think or feel when he found out. I thought about me and what was better for me and whom I should be with, and now all I can think about is the look on Sam's face this morning.

We were slowly building something, and he is so good to me. He's the only guy I've ever been with whom I trust so much and whom I never get tired of being with. I can't believe I hurt him. I lay in bed for a long time.

And then hours later, there was a knock on my front window. Sam. I opened the front door and we both stood there, not daring to say anything. It was dark outside and I did not invite him in and he did not try to come inside. I knew that I could not reach out and touch him anymore.

On the porch, I told him everything, although he already knew it all from reading my own words. But I don't think he knew how much I loved him, because I didn't even know how much I loved him until last night. I think it was the most honest moment of my life, standing in front of Sam, groveling, desperate, and distressed, telling him how I needed him and how careless I was but how much I loved him. Finally, I stopped talking. He had been rapt the entire time I was talking, moving slowly closer, with an unreadable expression on his face. And then he reached out his arms and I stepped into them.

I think we stood together like that for twenty minutes. And then he turned my face toward his and kissed me. "No one has more love for you than I do," he said. "No one."

He came inside and we talked for a few hours and then he left to fly back to Sydney. He knows I didn't cheat on him and he knows I love him. I didn't lose him, but I know that Sam doubts me now. At the beginning of a relationship, everyone acts like the best version of themselves and is very cautious, but inevitably, someone is going to make a mistake. But I just happened to make a really huge mistake.

It's almost as if that ever-present lurking part of my existence that wants to stay up all night and smoke cigarettes and run away to different countries also wants someone like Callum to come along and ruin everything. Even when I am unsure of Sam, I still feel like he is too good for me in some ways. As in, he's actually good, something so rare. Everything Sam does is thoughtful and careful—the one thing he's ever done that seems brash is date me.

I don't know exactly what drove me to stray, but I think there's a certain sadness to finally getting what you want. I've wanted to meet someone like Sam my entire life, and then when I did, I felt too settled. There's a simplicity and sense of adventure to being alone, and I sometimes envy you for still having it, as you explore Paris. Even when you're getting your heart broken, you can still wake up and not know what's going to happen next. When I was single, I could hitch a ride on a whim or spend the night with an exciting stranger. I love Sam so much, but sometimes I wish I could have it both ways.

But after today, I know, I really know, that I can't.

But I pick Sam. Almost losing him made me know that he is worth more to me than exciting strangers. And I'm finding that again and again, I choose him.

We discussed that if this is going to really work, we can't be apart anymore and he's going to try to find a way to move to Melbourne. The magazine he was working for is about to fold, so it's a good time for him to leave Sydney. We'll finally be in the same city for the first time in our entire relationship.

It was unspoken, but definitely understood, that I can't hang out with or correspond with Callum again. Which might be hard as we have class together four days a week next semester, but as for actually cutting all ties with Callum, I don't care about him anymore. Any hint of feeling that I had for him is dead. I know that I am to blame for all of this, but to me, Callum represents the walking demise of my relationship with Sam. He could never seem attractive to me again.

I don't know how I'm going to handle next semester in class, but at least I still have Sam. For now.

Time for bed. Finals are next week. I can't believe we're almost twenty-five. Life moves fast. Don't be stupid like me.

Love,

Jess

*Four Months Later*

## Rachel to Jess

Do you remember that summer after freshman year when we felt so grown-up because we had summer jobs and snuck out to bars? And now here I am six years later, wearing a business suit, sitting on the Eurostar headed to Paris after a week in London, and writing thank-you notes to the professors I talked to about PhD programs. We were such babies that summer, and now I'm suddenly one of those adults who seemed so old to us back then.

All in all, I had two interviews with professors in London. And although I was nervous, I didn't know how formal they would be or how much I would have to prepare. Therefore, I prepared nothing.

For the first one, I visited a professor at King's College, which is right by the river. The professor was Scottish (so I could barely understand him yet was inexplicably charmed by him). We had an informal conversation in his office about my project, but I'm not totally convinced that our interests align. I want to study movie stars and their interaction with history, and he wants to add the element of city space, which doesn't really thrill me.

Afterward, I went back to my hotel in South Kensington and drank tea and ate scones to feel like a native. I also found the best magazine in the world, *Tatler*, which has approximately five pictures of Prince Harry per page. For my birthday, please get me a subscription.

For my second interview the following morning, a professor at University College London, Robert, arrived with a historian who he thought would make a good second reader for me. They both specialize in American film history. They played a little "good cop, bad cop" with me, but with posh English accents. ("Why women? Why Hollywood? Why the 1930s?" I resisted saying, "Because if you take those elements away, I have no thesis?")

I liked them a lot. Robert was so encouraging about my project, but there are a limited number of students he can take on, so it might not go anywhere. I'm supposed to hear back from both universities within six to eight weeks.

It was strange to speak English to locals and have everyone understand me. I felt inconspicuous for the first time in over a year. London is so much bigger compared to Paris and it's easy to feel invisible. In Paris, it always feels like everyone is examining you, and I'm not sure which one is more unsettling. But compared to Paris, London is gray and elegant and gritty.

In less than two hours, I'll be back in Paris, maybe for the last time in a while.

Tonight, it's back to apathetic teenagers—it is prime SAT season and apparently every person ever, even in France, wants to go to Harvard. The teenagers actually get my jokes, probably because they can all speak English (most have slutty American mothers with a weakness for Frenchmen). They also check their cell phones and flirt with each other incessantly.

I like the students who actually work hard, but some of them talk over me, refuse to take notes, and laugh at sly French jokes I usually don't get. When I called one of them out on it today after class, she looked at me and said, "My parents make me come here. I just want to go to art school and then open up my own gallery in New York, so this doesn't matter." After my third day with girls like this, I want to hiss, "Well, it does matter *a little*. Just wait until everyone asks you about your SAT score at orientation and you have to say five."

There's something unnerving about being so close to the life I was living as a seventeen-year-old. Have I changed at all? I remember my own dreamy beliefs about the incredible unknown, but I know the realities of going out into the world by yourself. They're shiny (literally) and wide-eyed, but I don't envy the seventeen-year-olds who have yet to discover the truth about what happens when you find yourself in a new place without any of your friends or when the perfect boy closes the door on you forever. And that's when I really see that they are seventeen and I'm twenty-five. And that there is more than just the eight years between us.

Despite my best efforts, though, I actually do regress into my teens sometimes. At American Prep, Josh and I go out behind the building at lunch to smoke cigarettes, which are still forbidden to us (him by his girlfriend, me by my promise to myself that I have quit).

I see Josh nearly every day and he's started to talk about the future, and has mentioned New York so many times I want to slap him with a fish (French style). I don't want my favorite part of my work life to leave! I want to say: "Don't you love it here? Couldn't you wrap a white scarf around your neck and walk gallantly through the Paris wind for the rest of your life? Spend your days finding tea shops and tracking down antique maps to see the city as it was in the eighteenth century?"

Even though I don't know how much longer I'll be in Paris, I can't believe he would leave, but when I try to tell him, it comes out: "New York, Josh? Like, really?"

See? Teenage talk. I'm back to saying "like" a hundred times a day.

Another sign of regression is that I can't help but look to astrology. I know. I know. I KNOW, JESS.

Not like you care, but Josh is a Pisces, which means he is very kind and sensitive, but also goofy. He has picked up all kinds of French mannerisms, which he exaggerates to make me laugh—like blowing out his cheeks when he doesn't know the answer to something, or saying, "ehhhhh" instead of "ummmm."

But he's taken.

I know for sure now that I am not a teenager anymore because I realize that this great guy belongs to someone else, and I'm hoping that mine is still out there. Maybe in London.

Love,

Rach

**MARCH 1**

## Jess to Rachel

Teenage girl, I can forgive. Astrology queen? No. But my birth date dictates that I would say that, doesn't it? The last time we argued about the validity of astrology, you told me that the defining trait of Aries is that we are assholes.

Your potential move to London is very exciting. I told Sam that you were visiting his mother country and he told me to tell you to make sure you eat a bacon sandwich for him. Obviously, I am telling you this too late, but who cares. Who makes bacon the main ingredient in a sandwich?

Do you think we're going to be seventy-five and still going on interviews? Still putting on stupid blazers and checking our teeth in hand mirrors before we walk into offices and justify our life's work and choices in twenty minutes? And if so, when is it our turn to have the kind of interviews on *Ellen* where we can eat cupcakes and dance?

School is back in session in Australia. I thought you should know that if there was any way to handle the Callum situation with dignity and grace, I did not find it. In class, I always make sure to sit by someone else and avoid Callum's looks. I refuse to engage in conversation with him and I turn down social outings when I know he'll be there.

My system worked perfectly until yesterday, when I was walking across campus and I saw him walking toward me from fifty feet away. I . . . okay, I pretended like I did not see him and then turned left into the nearest building. But he had seen me, and he caught up with me.

"Jess. I hate that you're avoiding me. Can't we still be friends?" he said.

"I know. I'm sorry. I just . . . can't. I almost lost my boyfriend because of you. I know I was part of this too, but it's over," I said.

And then, before he could say anything else, I left.

I felt sick after this confrontation, but I don't have any real regrets about it. I wonder if this is how guys who have ended things with me felt. Um, I am going to try not to think about that, actually.

Sam is finally moving to Melbourne, so we will get to give our relationship a real chance. I tried calling you to let you know but you aren't picking up! However, I have to sleep now—I have been up all night writing assignments for my classes. This is the best kind of grad school, though, because it's definitely more fun to turn in journalism pieces than to write academic essays. For my radio final assignment, I sat inside a computer lab in a basement for fifteen hours editing a radio segment about a punk band's tour through Asia. And I kind of loved it the entire time.

This work is so much more stimulating than writing about expat families and city sights in Beijing even though Melbourne is a peaceful, quiet, and relatively unexciting place in comparison. I also appreciate that I can run outside here without coughing up my lungs.

I'm flying to Texas for Paige's wedding at the end of the month. I'm going to be the worst maid of honor ever because I missed the bridal shower, engagement party, and bridal luncheon. I did not throw a bachelorette party. Basically, I have done nothing to get this job except put in a lot of hours of my childhood.

Sam can't accompany me to the wedding because he wants to save money and spend that time getting settled in Melbourne. But I wanted to test him out in Texas waters! See if anyone in my town could understand his English accent. Take him to classy burger joints called Buns Over Texas or show him that gas stations called Toot'n Totum really exist. Maybe make him drive a pickup truck.

But mostly, I need someone like you or Paige, someone who really knows me, to meet him and size him up. I recently realized that it's strange that no one close to me has met him.

Is he even real? What if I made him up?

Love,

Jess

MARCH 12

## Rachel to Jess

So, Olivier just called and asked to get a drink tonight so he can get the keys to Sasha's apartment (she and Marc are out of town and I'm taking in their mail). I wanted to find a way out of this, but he's moving to a bigger apartment nearby and has lots of boxes that he needs to store in Sasha's apartment between leases.

Still, though. HATE HIM. Advice on how to act tonight during this exchange?

MARCH 12

### Five minutes later

## Jess to Rachel

Throw them in his face and say, "Have the fucking keys!" And then run away, in heels, so it makes a good noise on the ground.

*One minute later*

## Jess to Rachel

Sorry. Just rewatched a French film, with a super dramatic opera soundtrack. A very loud emotional movie. Put me in a melodramatic mood. My life definitely needs more opera music.

*One minute later*

## Rachel to Jess

Or I could just drop them on the ground in front of him and stand there until he picks them up. Cold. Only works if I have super confidence. Like a cruel ice queen.

*One minute later*

## Jess to Rachel

No, no, you really can't be crazy! You have to just be normal. Not jokey and smiley, but not mean either. Just say something like, "Here ya go, how's moving, oh yeah? Well, gotta go screw my Italian boyfriend, who I forgot to tell you about. Tick tock."

If you really say that, I will pay you thirty euros.

*Two minutes later*

## Rachel to Jess

Um, the cold ice-queen thing was a joke! But the fact that you said that makes me think that you think I'm a little crazy.

*Tick tock?* Stupid Australia.

The worst thing is, I know when I see him, I'll melt. I wish I could hold on to the hatred.

*One minute later*

## Jess to Rachel

Tick tock is not Australian! That was just some dismissive nonsense to say to confuse him.

When you see Olivier, just pretend you are Audrey Hepburn and he is a flea. No, you are a powerful vampire and he is Bella. Wait, now you love him again. NO. I don't know.

You are YOU and he is Olivier the Loser, who will be remembered for absolutely nothing.

Love,

Jess

P.S. Also, I need fashion advice! There are no bridesmaids dresses for Paige's wedding. The wedding invitation says that the attire is "ranch formal." Not really sure what this means. High heels with my overalls? I want to wear my most comfortable outfit, which is Levi's, a plaid shirt, and a tiara.

## Rachel to Jess

I've never been to a fancy party at a ranch. In fact, I did not know that those two things were compatible. What that means to me is full equestrian show gear. Please go wearing a black jacket, white collared shirt, riding pants, high boots, and a hard hat. Maybe a pair of pearl earrings.

Every day I do an hour on the elliptical (one hour! Self-improvement kick is official! BOOM!) while listening to an audio-book about Grace Kelly. And she, a Scorpio like me, almost backed out of her marriage when she found out that Prince Rainier was an incompatible Gemini.

HA NOT ALONE IN MY CRAZY!

Anyway, I gave Olivier his stupid keys. I tried to be calm and controlled, with just a touch of condescension. Slid them across the table. "Oh, how's my life? It's amazing. I'm having such an amazing time. Life is so amazing right now."

I've been spending my days with Josh, who is the polar opposite of ambiguous Olivier. Josh indulges me at my worst, and today we were sitting on the steps of an old church and I asked him why he came here in the first place.

He said, "I came here to be Hemingway."

"You *did*?"

"And to marry a French girl."

Oh.

"So do you write?"

"I keep a notebook," he said. "I've got some ideas."

I have always placed adult Hemingway lovers who come to Paris as walking clichés, but when Josh talks about Hemingway's life, I can tell he wants some kind of epic life, epic romance, epic adventures.

I thought I did too, but the only thing is, I think it's too late to have epic adventures in Paris now. It's too polished. For epic, you need China (as you know), or India, or some place other than Western Europe. I would say this to Josh, but I think he already knows this. I also think he knows that he is too much of a real romantic to have the same kind of laissez-faire attitude of the Lost Generation.

The longer I'm in Paris and the more I think about leaving for London, I'm discovering that I love the sheer cinematic aspect of just living here. Paris is so movie-like in its way, where every walk along the cobblestones, beneath the nineteenth-century streetlamps, along the steep staircases, could all be taken from a romantic movie made in the 1890s or the 1950s or yesterday. All of it makes you feel part of something epic, in your own way.

Of course, I actually spend so much of my time at the library watching old movies about Paris for the final stages of my degree. It's the best homework in the world, but being tucked away in a corner watching classic movies set a block from my apartment can feel surreal. After I leave the library, I can see an imaginary red balloon floating over the city in the same way that I can see Gene Kelly dancing along the Seine.

I haven't spoken to a single person today, and wandering along the Seine all day has made me a little too dreamy. You would snap me out of it in a second, probably by pushing me into a river every time I start singing "La Vie en Rose" to myself.

No word from the universities in London yet, which is kind of good. Suddenly, I like not knowing. I like not having to be sure that I have to leave this all behind—knowing that Paris is still my home, right now, at least.

What is living with Sam like? It's the first time that either of us has EVER lived with a boyfriend. Feels very serious suddenly.

Love,

Rach

## Jess to Rachel

Whenever I imagined living with a guy, I also thought that it would feel really serious, but actually it's just sort of a game where I try to mask or conquer weird habits. When someone's suddenly just there all the time to witness you falling asleep in your jeans for a mid-day nap or only eating crackers all day because you felt too lazy to go get groceries—suddenly you don't want to do these things. Just the extra pair of eyes makes me act like a real person. Sometimes when I lived alone, I would have phases where I wore pajamas all day and had no outside contact. I basically did not feel like a person at all.

I've always had this anxious fear of what would happen if a guy saw me at my worst—hungover at 6 A.M. with dirty hair and panda eyes from the previous night's mascara. But Sam and I are working through it together. So far, I don't really care about how sweaty he is after playing soccer, and he doesn't seem to mind panda eye too much.

And after a while, it just gets too exhausting to pretend I look good all the time. Laziness eventually wins out over pride, and I figure it's better he knows what he's getting into sooner rather than later, but maybe I'm getting a little too comfortable too soon. I wore the same baggy T-shirt to bed five nights in a row and found it at the bottom of the laundry hamper when I got home today. I did not put it there.

Before Sam moved in, I was worried because we skipped the whole casual dating thing and went right from fling to moving in together, which could have gone horribly wrong. But he's easygoing and rarely grumpy, so, it's actually going really well. Mostly, I can't believe we get to spend every night together. There's relief in finally having him here for good. All those terrible good-byes that I had to dread and endure are gone.

We cook dinner nearly every night. He's teaching me the basics. And after dinner, Sam washes the dishes and I dry them with a dish towel. He's a little shocked at how undomestic I am, but I tried to explain how none of my friends are. You aren't. Astrid definitely isn't. Paige is good at drawing houses, but not cleaning them. We all have our different talents, but live in rooms covered in clothes piles that reach our knees.

Sometimes I look at Sam chopping tomatoes in my sunny kitchen in Australia, and I can hardly believe that we are leading this low-key, coupley life when just a few months ago, I was his boss and he was my intern in Beijing, and not a soul in the country knew we were a couple. Ten months ago, we were on our pretend honeymoon in Malaysia, frolicking on the beach. I feel the urge to write a flow chart of how I got from Point A to Point B just to try to make sense of it all.

I have never felt this settled before. Yesterday, I saw a baby cactus, and I had to buy it. I had to have it right then. I brought it home, and Sam and I decided it was definitely a male and named him Brian Flanagan, because we felt like Brian Flanagan was the name of a scrappy guy. One small cactus against a big world. It's also the name of Tom Cruise's character in *Cocktail*. It was all very symbolic.

I can't seem to get enough of Sam. We bicker sometimes, but it's the first time that I've ever been in a relationship where I feel that, no matter how big the fight is, it won't lead to the end of us. We've already survived one of the worst I can imagine.

You always said we had to be honest, so I feel like I should tell you that sometimes we write entire e-mails that only consist of rows of xoxos. Please slap me in the face with a fish. We have a Sunday-morning routine, which involves mochas and newspapers and discussing ideas for my news articles. It does not involve teary good-byes.

So, I lead a boring, coupley life. Finally. I had one brief panic-stricken moment after we spent seventy-two hours together nonstop where I told him I needed to go for a run. I just needed to be alone with my own thoughts. I put on my shoes quickly and sprinted through the park thinking, "I am a stallion! I cannot be tamed! I want to roam free!" An hour later, panting, I walked in the door and found Sam in the kitchen, cooking dinner. He smiled at me and kissed me even though I was sweaty. Then he told me he had a great idea for a feature article for one of my assignments. I actually can't imagine my life without him now.

Sometimes I remember that I almost lost all of this. That's also when I decide, okay, maybe I'll shave my legs today. Better not push my luck too much.

Anyway, what's going on with Josh now? Have you met his girlfriend? Are you positive you aren't attracted to him? You definitely sound more than a little enamored. Send me a photo of him so I know if you are actually just friends, or you are "just friends" and he looks like a Calvin Klein underwear model. You're talking an awful lot about him. . . .

Love,

Jess

APRIL 5

## Rachel to Jess

Pass this message on to Sam: Living with you is like living with a cat. Sometimes the cat wants to play with you and it's super fun, but when the cat doesn't want to play with you, you have to leave it the hell alone. Also, it sleeps during the day in short bursts and prowls at night. Does Sam realize this?

Honestly, I don't know what's going on with Josh. I'm trying to figure this out.

I can ask him anything about men. Anything. Having no brothers, I am definitely lacking in knowledge about how men think. I asked him what his first sexual experience was, and he told me (although he did add in that he didn't remember some parts of it—is this even possible? I could reconstruct mine second by second if I ever had to). He doesn't hide anything. In fact, we talk about sex all the time, because he's so open, which makes me open. He doesn't have defense mechanisms the way other people do.

Josh is the first guy I've ever been this comfortable with. He's always bringing me things, like coffees or chocolate. We laughed so hard because a French bulldog snorted all over us in the park and walked away when we offered him part of our sandwiches. This led to a routine where he brings me coffee and I pretend to be a French bulldog who hates generic coffee. And I feel like I can tell him anything.

And sometimes when we sit on the steps during lunch, I lean on his shoulder.

Is this what dating somebody should feel like?

I don't have any photos to send you, but Josh is cute—losing some hair, which doesn't seem to bother him much. He has the perfect build, though, and really pretty green eyes with brown flecks.

Sigh. That does sound like I love him, but he still lives with his girlfriend.

Last night, my closest friend from work, Anne, and I went over to his place for his housewarming party. I was a little nervous to meet his girlfriend, Sylvia—the girl who has the perfect Pisces. From Josh's description, I was imagining a waiflike French beauty.

Anne and I were full of hypotheses on the way up to his apartment. We rang the bell. Sylvia answered the door.

And, she just looked like a normal girl! Very long brown hair, normal green eyes, average size, jeans and T-shirt. I thought we were going to walk in on a young Carla Bruni with pouty lips and legs up to her eyes. Instead she could have passed for some girl at Brown during finals week.

Of course, I had nothing to say. "I'm Rachel. And so . . . you're half-Portuguese! Do you . . . go to Portugal often? . . . I like to talk to your boyfriend about sex?"

There were also several French couples there, meaning that Anne, Josh, and I were the only Americans at the party.

The party's background was bad French pop, six simultaneous French conversations, and Sylvia on the phone to someone in loud Portuguese.

Josh and I ended up in a corner together, controlling the music, as we got drunk and sang along to old pop songs and fought over his iPod. Sylvia remained in the opposite corner with her friends while occasionally glancing at us.

Josh and I sang along some more. We drank together. We laughed a lot.

I walked home thinking, "I had no idea this was possible! I have such a great connection with this guy and I love how we can just be friends and his girlfriend doesn't care. This is just a really great friendship." I couldn't wait to see him the next day.

When Josh walked into work today, I said, "Last night was really fun."

Josh smiled halfheartedly. "I know. I had fun too, but that's the last time that's happening."

"What? Why?"

"Let's just say that Sylvia is not happy with—" He gestured between us.

"But Josh, that's ridiculous! There's absolutely nothing between us! Just air! Less than nothing! No air!"

[Thinking: "PICK MY FORTUNE COOKIE!"]

"Maybe when you get a boyfriend you've been dating for a year or more, we can all hang out in a group. Until then, though, we can't hang out at all anymore socially. We're just colleagues."

I didn't know what to say. It hurt. What was I thinking? Of course you can't be friends with guys. Guys with girlfriends are supposed to have inside jokes with their girlfriends. They are supposed to talk about sex with their girlfriends. They are supposed to bring their girlfriends coffee. They are not supposed to do those things with some random woman at work.

Oh, fuck. I am Trash Can Callum. I AM TRASH CAN CALLUM!
He is you. Sylvia is Sam.

Oh God. And now I must mean less than nothing to him, as Callum did to you. Just a mere distraction he seriously regrets.

The only way he can save his relationship is to drop me.

I feel stupid. I feel like if it had stayed a little more on the correct side of the line dividing platonic men and women, I wouldn't have lost my friend. We shouldn't have talked about sex. We shouldn't have had inside jokes. We shouldn't have gotten drunk together at the party. And I am old enough to know better.

I'm going to go fall into a trash can now.

Seriously. If you need to find me, look for the green bin next to the American Prep center with smoke coming out of it.

Love,

Trash Can Rachel

**APRIL 13**

## Jess to Rachel

No! You aren't Trash Can Callum. First of all, until now, you've never deliberately fallen into a trash can! Second of all, Callum really did seem to be trying to break Sam and me up, and I think you just slowly found yourself growing attached to Josh, especially after being burned so badly by Olivier. It's just too bad that he was already taken.

Please get out of the trash can.

So what's going to happen with Josh now?

I wish I could come rescue you, but I flew into Texas a few days ago and am back in my old bedroom. After I arrived in Amarillo, I was immediately swept up in the wedding madness. I don't know how weddings always manage to do this. They seem like such simple affairs. A white dress, some friends, some vows, cake. Done.

Then the groom's sister misses her flight and has to catch a late plane the night before the rehearsal dinner and, as maid of honor, you find yourself in an SUV with four other bridesmaids at 3 A.M. on the way back from the airport driving along dirt roads when a DEER REPEATEDLY DARTS IN FRONT OF THE CAR and you nearly kill half of the bridal party by swerving into a ravine.

It doesn't help that I haven't driven a car in years. I kept trying to remember if it's more likely for a buck to crash through my windshield or wound passengers with its antlers if they puncture the roof of the car.

Anyway, we all survived.

There are twelve bridesmaids. Twelve. I kept trying to get Paige alone, but her peppy friend from summer camp always showed up right when I was about to get five minutes alone with her. The three of us ran wedding errands while my thoughts alternated between those of a sane twenty-five-year-old and those of a crazy woman about to throttle the summer-camp friend.

*Can't believe Paige's name is changing. . . . If this stupid camp friend calls her Paige Bear one more time, I will push her out of my car. It's my car. I must have rights. . . . I wonder if I need note cards for my speech. Wait, did the camper just ask if she could give a speech at the wedding too? That's it. I'm going to push her out of my car at the next stoplight. She'll be fine. Campers are very resourceful.*

Okay, maybe it's mostly the crazy woman in my head.

God, weddings make me emotional. What's it like in non-wedding land? Remind me what that place is like. Right now, I've already been in Texas long enough that I'm carrying around a gallon of iced tea in a Styrofoam cup everywhere I go and considering the benefits of a fake tan.

Love,

Jess, Who Is Barely Keeping it Together

## Rachel to Jess

I feel like you should embrace the chance to be as crazy, emotional, vulnerable, and nostalgic as you want, because there are so few
times in life when we can get away with it without feeling awkward
or being judged. However, this is also a special occasion, and you don't
want it colored by memories (or photographs) of your wild descent
into kray kray. So keep it together a little bit.

I walk by French weddings all the time, and now they make me
think about you and Paige and how different her ranch-formal wedding is from these quiet ceremonies in the district hall. At my sister's
wedding, which was in a big garden in Madison, we had to wear pastel green, and I had to hold her bouquet in 105-degree heat—nobody
tells you how heavy those bouquets are, but if I were you, I would
start building my upper-body strength now. In all of the pictures, you
can see my wrists drooping.

I did get to walk down the aisle with a very handsome best man;
however, he was the brother of the groom and had been married for ten
years, with two children. I am not going to tell you the fantasies that
came to mind when I saw the pictures of us together after the wedding,
but I think you can imagine them. We made a very cute couple.

Okay, in my mind, we are married.

DON'T FALL IN LOVE WITH THE BEST MAN.

Anyway, while you're in sunny Texas, I've been walking to school
in the rain, even though it takes me about an hour. I get to pass
through tiny winding passages and Notre Dame, climb bridges over
the river, and remind myself that I really am here, but not for long. I
still live in Paris. For now.

I had just gotten back into my apartment after one of these wanders when the phone rang. I answered it and heard a faint English

accent on the other line. I could barely make out the words until I finally heard:

"Rachel? Rachel? It's Robert here! From UCL!"

And that's how he told me that I'd been accepted into their doctoral program! He said my topic fits exactly what they are looking for and that he's interested in my research and that he'd love to see me in London in September!!

Finally, some relief and validation after all of these months of writing film essays, going to lectures, and loving what I was studying but not knowing if I had a future with it. I have two months to decide whether to accept his offer.

I would love to live that life, of a London doctoral student, but the programs, along with the living expenses of living in London, will put me two hundred thousand dollars in debt. All of this talk may be moot. I'm putting off this decision until I find out about funding.

I have five euros in my bank account. My ten thousand dollars in insurance money got me through exactly one year in France, and it's been paycheck-to-paycheck from teaching ever since.

I wish I could talk to somebody here about it, but Sasha's away for a few weeks. Everywhere people and friendships are changing. I'm starting to wonder how many friends I've made here will still be friends for the long haul. How many places can you leave people behind and still expect to keep in touch with all of them? Even without going anywhere, I've already managed to lose Olivier and now Josh.

It's created a big void in my life, so instead of spending six hours a day thinking about Olivier or loitering around cafés, I've started writing my novel again. I've missed writing and I'm actually beginning to enjoy the time alone. Kind of. Rewatching *The West Wing* helps too.

So, did you make it out of the wedding alive? Did the summer camper?

Love,

Rach

## Jess to Rachel

I survived the wedding. It was so hot that the cake melted. It was an outdoor morning ceremony, and I wore a short black satin dress while standing next to Paige during her vows. She stared into her fiancé's eyes, and so did I, because I had the second-best vantage point.

I think I was looking for some sort of sign about my own relationship with Sam. Do grooms have some sort of magic quality that unmarriable guys lack? I didn't have much time to mull this over, because even though I tried my hardest to will them not to, my eyes welled up and the tears had free rein to pour down my face because my hands were clutching two bouquets. My heels began to sink into the grass. The entire wedding party now has sunburns across their cheeks and shoulders.

That's all I can really remember about the event, even though it was this morning. There's been so much buildup, and once it was official, the rest of the day was a blur spent under a tent in the shade, poking at wedding cake and drinking warm champagne during toasts.

I should raise a glass as a toast to you, as well, because you're in! I knew you'd get into London. They say that education debt is the best kind of debt (*they* is universities). I know you think you aren't ready to leave Paris, but if there's nothing left for you to do while you're there, then it makes sense to move on. At least, that's one of the reasons I left Beijing after two years. That, and Sam.

Other than my parents, most of the men and some of the women at the wedding wore cowboy boots, and I spent a considerable amount of time avoiding the dance floor because I did not want to be cajoled into dancing the two-step in public. I watched Paige dance with her dad and then her husband, and I even let her summer-camp friend sit with me for a while.

Paige seemed really happy. I've met all of her previous boyfriends—

knew her when she had her first kiss (at hunting camp), first boyfriend (he was the worst), first breakup (he cheated on her), and all the boyfriends in between then and now, actually. It's exciting being part of the wedding and seeing up close how in love she is, but also, it feels surreal to see her in a wedding dress after all these years. Does everyone feel a little bit sad at their oldest friend's wedding? Because I do.

I wished that Sam was there, but I was also glad he wasn't, because I don't want to invite any questions about our own future. He makes me happy, but is that the only requirement? How does everyone at their own wedding always seem so sure? As much as I love Sam, weddings feel so definitive. So final.

Last night on the car ride with Paige to the ranch, she and I were finally alone. I asked her how she knew, how she really knew that Henry was right for her to marry. She's a serial monogamist and has had three or four serious boyfriends. Why not them? She said, "I think that we can be happy with any number of people. It's also about timing and finally being willing to settle down with just one person."

This didn't seem like enough, so I asked, "But how do you know which one to choose?"

She thought about it and said, "You know when you can imagine being as happy with someone else, but you can't imagine anyone making you happier."

And then she turned into the side road that leads to the ranch and the barn, where I put on a pair of cowboy boots and gave my rehearsal dinner speech in front of one hundred people and thirty-five mounted deer heads. (I've repressed the entire memory of this because I hate public speaking so much. It helped to focus on the deer heads.)

I caught the bouquet this morning. I leapt into the air above the nine other single bridesmaids. There's a photo in which I can actually see my calves flexing as I leap into the air. If you can't tell, I'm so proud of myself.

I wonder what Sam's reaction will be when I tell him.

As the afternoon faded, Paige and her new husband got into a car and drove away toward their honeymoon. I got into a car with my parents. As my dad drove us home on the familiar roads, I felt very young again, until I looked down at my lap and the bridal bouquet. We drove past the local bookstore where I imagined my alternate homebody self working the cash register—my dad told me that it was now closed. Also, my favorite field is now a used-car lot. Life back home has not stood still without me as I had hoped.

I don't know what to do with myself at this moment. Wish you were here right now. I miss you so much. I'm flying back to Australia tomorrow, which isn't any closer to Paris at all. The world feels too big tonight.

Love,

Jess

**APRIL 20**

## Rachel to Jess

Today, after I got back from my film class, Josh came to my apartment. He's borrowing my air mattress for when his parents visit Paris next week. Sylvia does not know this, though. We are still not supposed to be alone together per her instructions, but Josh initiated it, and I've missed him. Missed our conversations about Hemingway and grand adventures.

We sat down to talk for a moment, and I offered him some wine that was on the table. He refused but reached past me with one arm to pick up the bottle and examine it. For a second, seeing his face coming toward me, I thought he was going to kiss me. The blood rushed out of my face and I lost all feeling in my hands. Then he said something about the wine and I laughed super hard. I don't even know if he made a joke.

After that, he stayed just long enough to get the mattress and browse my books.

His eyes immediately fell on my copy of *Fiesta*, the Cuban edition of *The Sun Also Rises* I bought on a class trip to Havana ten years ago.

I told him its story: I spent one hot morning at the book markets, where I found this volume and zeroed in on it. I opened the cover and saw that it was published in 1964. First Cuban edition. And it had a name scrawled in the front.

My heart racing, I asked in Spanish, "Hemingway write here? HEMINGWAY WRITE HERE?" pointing to the signature on the front page.

"Si, si."

So I bought it for what seemed like an amazingly cheap twenty-five dollars. When I got home, I showed it to my father, who immediately pointed out that Hemingway died in 1961 . . . three years before this book was published.

Side note: Also during this trip, a prostitute asked me if my breasts were real. And I got food poisoning and had to have an antinausea shot in my butt in front of a bunch of Cubans. It was also the first time I ever drank rum. I take this book on all of my travels, because it was my first real adventure. I almost never open the book anymore, but I carry it around with me when I travel. I guess that I also had dreams of being epic.

Josh listened to my experiences in Cuba, laughing a lot in his big-hearted way. The story of the book seemed to touch some chord in him. Then he stood up and left my apartment in order to make it home to Sylvia on time.

I sat on my bed thinking for a long time after he left. I would still have bought that book today, full of the illicit pleasure of being in Cuba, but I no longer believe that people actually live the way they do in its story—all pithy words and dramatic adventures.

In a way, that's what London would be for me: embracing a feasible life even though it may not be as grand as I had imagined when I was fifteen. I find myself hoping to get the good news from England that my

PhD will be funded. But the idea of living in a larger-than-life Hemingway, Hunter S. Thompson, Janis Joplin kind of way is hard to let go.

All my love,

Hemingway Write Here

**APRIL 24**

## Jess to Rachel

I like that story. You've never told me any of those things about Cuba. Sort of makes me want to go. I'm kind of up for anywhere right now because it's getting harder and harder to settle here.

Since I've been back from Texas, Sam and I have been talking about our future together. We might want to stay in Melbourne—Australia is our shaky middle ground. He can't work in America; I can't work in the United Kingdom. I can stay here for a few months after my program ends, looking for someone to sponsor my work visa. We've been talking about this a lot lately and there's been a very sudden, bizarre development. As a UK citizen, he can stay here too, under one very big condition.

The only way to extend Sam's current visa is if he spends the next three months doing manual labor or agricultural work in the country. There's a shortage of willing agricultural workers in Australia and so the government's solution is to put sad Englishmen who want to stay in the country for their girlfriends to work on farms, cattle stations, and vineyards. Apparently, most farms have a few Irish or English guys doing anything from picking fruit to working with livestock for minimum wage, just so they can stay in Australia for another year.

Doesn't this sound so old-timey? Ye shall sow, ye shall reap, and ye shall be rewarded with . . . another year in Surfers Paradise!

We'd both been trying to avoid this option, but time has run out.

If Sam wants to stay in Australia with me, he'll have to leave next week for the countryside. Every online description of the dull, physically taxing jobs, like fruit picking, is tempered by the phrase, "but if you are working with fun people, it'll be a laugh!" The photos are all of guys picking oranges or shoveling manure, doubled over with laughter.

It's winter in Australia, and Sam has figured out that the least taxing work would be to go to Australia's wine country and work trimming the branches or stems of the grapevines on a vineyard (known as pruning). He must head to the bush (the countryside) or the outback, because the final condition of his visa is that he can't work near a city.

He made a few phone calls to some wineries and is headed to a town in New South Wales called Canowindra.

Canowindra, population 1,500.

Sam spoke with the owner of the organic vineyard, which is on the outskirts of the town, and mail only gets delivered once or twice a week. To get food other than basics, they have to drive to a town three hours away. The closest big city is Sydney, which is two hundred miles away.

And so this is our only option if we want to remain in Australia together. Sam seems very stoic and resigned to the manual labor that I just know will ruin his good hands.

Three months feels like an eternity to me, especially because we'll be apart for most of it. After he gets settled there, I'm going to visit him in Canowindra for a week.

Unfortunately, everything I know about the country comes from *Little House on the Prairie*: the dog dies, Mary goes blind, and I need to hoard all of my food.

Love,

The Pruner's Girlfriend

## Rachel to Jess

What? Pruning to stay in the country? That is the strangest rule I've ever heard of. Are you sure it's real? Did your Irish housemate tell you that?

I'm from Wisconsin, where *Little House on the Prairie* is from, and I read the entire series, so here's some advice: If rural Australia's anything like those books, you can look forward to spending your nights listening to fiddle music and sitting around in sewing circles.

It feels like just yesterday that you two were secretly in love with each other from afar, and now he's willing to sacrifice three months of his life for the good of your relationship. It's kind of amazing, actually—three months of manual labor is like nine years doing anything else.

It's impossible to think that far in the future for me. In three months, I might be gone from Paris if my funding comes through.

Oh—and so will Josh.

Yesterday Josh and I went to sit on the steps of the stock exchange. This is, of course, forbidden, but we have the same lunch break and he wanted to talk to me. But instead of laughing at the tourists or gossiping about the teachers at work, he got weird—quiet and excited at the same time—and told me that he is engaged.

He asked Sylvia to marry him last week. It wasn't that it was out of nowhere, but it still took me aback. I had to suppress a gasp and then compensated by acting a little too happy for him.

"Eeek, Josh, how exciting, omigod, I can't believe it! That's amazing! When is the wedding?!?!"

It was me on fifteen cups of coffee.

His fiancée's dream is to move to New York, and they've been planning their life there for several months. And now their departure is only a few weeks away.

I can't believe that he's leaving.

And also—Josh! I always said Paris was worth a million New Yorks!

He's going to work for a competing education company, and he already gave his notice at American Prep. I had no idea. Was he afraid to confide in me at all, having been forbidden by Sylvia?

I do kind of hate Sylvia for that. I know that if I were her, I would act the same way, but Josh and I were good friends and I feel like she kept something really important from growing between the two of us. At the same time, though, I know that whatever he and I could have had would only have infringed upon what they have together, so I guess I understand why she had to stop it. Even if I don't like it.

It's hard to say good-bye to someone when you haven't realized the full friendship potential. When we left college, we knew all of our close friends so well. The kind of closeness that grows from spending day after day in six-hour-long conversations. The friendships were intense. And now I've met—and am losing—somebody who had the potential to be this kind of friend, but who will now never be one to me.

Anyway, the wedding is next summer, in Bordeaux.

I think if you can make plans that far in advance, you are officially in the adult club. My current life has the same expiration date as my student visa.

Love,

Rach

P.S. A student of mine from an English class for adults asked me out. I finished teaching the class this week. Ethical/unethical to go out with him? Please write your answer in fifty words or less.

## Jess to Rachel

Rachel, I'm the girl who pursued, dated, slept with, and then followed her intern to Australia (but let's make sure this doesn't go in my obituary). Do you really have to ask me what I think about dating one of your students?

I've started interning at an evening news show at a national TV station here. I shadow reporters all day and after filming interviews during the morning and afternoon, I sit with them as we edit and put together the video packages. So much of putting together TV reports involves going through the archive, looking for stock footage to fill up airtime while making it somehow relevant to your story. We once resorted to using footage of a man eating a donut for a report on a drought that wiped out the sugarcane crop. Today, I spent all morning with a reporter trying to figure out how to show postpartum depression on the screen.

"Would a shot of a woman furrowing her eyebrows at her child be over-the-top? Should we stick to a generic woman sitting on a park bench, looking out into the distance?"

But I like the actual reporting aspect—finding stories and interviewing people. I wonder if I could actually get a job as a TV reporter in Sydney or Melbourne. I worked with a reporter our age and she said it took her three years of grunt work at the station to even get an interview to be a reporter.

But I'm already twenty-five! The second-oldest person in my journalism program! Oh God, I spent my requisite entry-level time in China editing at a magazine and now it feels like I have to start over again climbing the ladder in the Western world.

It's also strange to be an unpaid intern again who doesn't want to get in anyone's way. I miss being the one who told the interns what to do. As in, "Write this. File that. Date me."

I'm also creating and editing my own TV news stories for school. I sit in a dark editing suite rewinding and fast-forwarding the footage over and over to cut it just right. I'm slowly losing my mind watching myself on-screen. After my radio course, I'm finally capable of listening to my own voice—but this is like watching a news anchor that I really want to make fun of.

The worst part, though, is filming in public. Whenever I try to look into the camera to say something really serious, a crowd of people gathers around to watch me. It is total hell.

Maybe I should stick to radio or print. I'm still scrambling to find my next step because my program and my internship finish up in a few weeks. What next?

I'm trying to book my journey to Canowindra to visit Sam, but I can't go for some time—school is still in session. Every night, he calls from the vineyard's landline and logs our conversations so that he can pay back the vineyard owner for the long-distance calls. Apparently it is 1900 there.

I wonder if I'll show up and he'll open the door wearing overalls with a wheat stalk hanging from the corner of his mouth and have a twangy Australian accent. I kind of think he'd look dapper in overalls. . . .

Love,

Jess

P.S. If you really do become a professor, though, you can't date your students. It must be strange to have that rule hanging over you—at least on TV, you can sleep with anyone, including your boss. Wait, did I just figure out my way to the top?

## Rachel to Jess

You know you're truly in love with someone when you think they look good in overalls. (Or maybe you're just from Texas.)

I agreed to go out with the guy from my English class. Although he speaks English with a heavy French accent, it turns out he's Spanish and his name is Pablo. He's about four years older than us. He has dark hair, a medium build, and brown eyes.

For our first date, I met him outside a theater, where we saw a musical comedy show in French and I understood nothing. Literally nothing.

We were headed back to the Marais together because he lives near me, when all of a sudden, he just pulled my shoulders toward him and dove in for a kiss, but I was smiling and it was unexpected, so we hit our teeth together in the process.

"Now it won't be awkward later," he said, smiling, even though it was totally awkward at that moment.

It was exciting to finally be kissing someone who seemed to like me so much, but other than that, I just felt disappointed. I had thought I was attracted to him until he kissed me. But first kisses can be weird, so I gave him the benefit of the doubt.

Then he invited me back for dinner at his place. He fried up some scallops and then we sat on the couch and we kissed some more, because we didn't have much to say to each other. We spoke in French, which is the second language for both of us. It feels like 40 percent of the time, I say what I *can* say, rather than what I really think. What if he is doing the same thing? We could end up married and half of our personalities and thoughts could be obscured because we simply couldn't be bothered to look up the right word.

Still, I kept reminding myself that he's a nice, cute guy. A genuinely good guy who seems to like me a lot. So I agreed to see him again.

That second date consisted of Pablo making me dinner (again), and then us making out on the couch (again).

I mean, I *like* both these things, but I kept being pulled out of the kissing by thinking that Pablo was the Spanish version of British George. And thinking this while we were making out can't be a good sign. We then slept together, because I was curious, and I really wanted to salvage our relationship with mind-blowing sex. But it was unremarkable. Only missionary. Sweet but brief.

He saved the tickets from our first date and ever since I told him that I love pistachio macaroons, he always brought me some. And if someone else did this, I might melt. But with Pablo, I was flattered but indifferent.

What would the stock footage be for a mediocre relationship? Two people on a couch, staring into space? A guy kissing a woman's neck while she checks her watch?

I cooked dinner for myself the other night and ate it sitting at my table, and looking out into my courtyard, I could only think: This is so much better than being with Pablo.

But I wanted to give him one more chance. He called me and invited me over to his place, where . . . he made me dinner again. It flashed before me: This could be the rest of my life. Waiting for Pablo to get off work, come home, make me dinner, make out on the couch, and climb into bed. He is so set in his traditional ways that he will not make out anywhere except on the couch or have sex anywhere except his bed.

Did someone tell him that women love it when you cook dinner for them, make out with them on the couch, and then assume the missionary position?

After the third date of his cooking dinner, and predictable vanilla sex, I ended it. We went out for coffee, and I had to look him in the face and tell him that the sparks just weren't there.

Because Pablo and I speak only French together, I'm not sure the breakup was as subtle as I would have wanted it to be. In English, it's easy to read the other person's reactions and respond appropriately—

but in French, instead of saying, "I love spending time with you, but sometimes I have the sense that the spark just isn't there—or, if it was there, it's tapering out," I have to say things like, "I think we should end our relationship."

And, of course, he was nice about it and now our brief courtship is over. I'm not sad, just regretful that the relationship couldn't be what we wanted it to be. I want fireworks from the start. Pablo told me that he had a crush on me for the entire six weeks I was his teacher. It's not a good sign when I think, "You were in my class for six weeks and I didn't even notice you until you asked me out." (Though this isn't true with friendship. Remember when you used to confuse me with the ultrareligious good girl down the hall in our freshman dorm? I can't believe that ever happened.) It's not like Pablo was going to wake up one morning and turn into a bounding, charismatic, witty Olivier who is madly in love with me.

If I could pick and choose their best traits, together they would make the most perfect guy (with one AWFUL guy left over).

Last night, I went to a party at Jacques's house. Olivier showed up, a little late, and we made light conversation. We're back to a guarded friendship, and I see now that he will be happy someday with a wife who cooks and makes puns and knows about French culture. He just wants someone easygoing. Olivier shut down every time I showed strong emotion of any kind. He might, actually, be very happy with Pablo.

Love,
Rach

### One Month Later

JUNE 1

## Jess to Rachel

I'm packing to leave for the bush to see Sam for the first time in more than a month! I turned in my final assignments and now I have to catch a flight to Sydney, then a train, then a bus, and if I miss the first leg, I am totally screwed! I'm throwing things into a suitcase as I write this, but I wanted to say good-bye before I go off into the wilderness.

For one of my final journalism assignments, we had to write our own fake obituaries. Really makes you realize how little we've done with our lives. Mine was basically three hundred words long, and the experience of writing it was so morbid. The hardest part is choosing how you die. I didn't have the nerve to off my fictional self on a vineyard in Australia. Trying not to think about poisonous spiders and snakes. Kangaroos. I'm thinking about kangaroos.

WHAT IF I NEVER MAKE IT BACK?

WHAT ARE YOU DOING AND WHAT ARE YOU WEARING AND DID YOU EAT LUNCH?

JUNE 1

---

*Five minutes later*

## Rachel to Jess

Jesus! No pressure or anything! I ate a bowl of Frosted Flakes for lunch! I'm wearing jeans, a T-shirt, and flats! Would you prefer me in business casual for your potentially last e-mail on earth?

I've been living inside the library, but I am finally done! DONE! I turned in my master's thesis. I went to hand it in—the illustrated, photocopied, proofread, and bound document that has hovered over me these past two years—and, of course, I was relieved, but I was already starting to formulate plans for my next research project.

I've decided I want to go to London, no matter what happens with the funding—but give me some reasons to justify two hundred thousand dollars in debt. Or at least tell me some good things about England before you head off!

Right now all I can think about is rain, meat pies, and coal miners. This may be because I just watched *Billy Elliot*. But there was a dancing ballet boy in that movie, so that's one good thing? I need a few more.

Love,

Rach

*Two minutes later*

## Jess to Rachel

The Queen. Wimbledon. Crumpets. Guards who wear fuzzy hats. Moors to run through. Emulating scenes from Jane Austen's books. A surplus of tea. Clotted cream. Rich history. Getting to wear a stupid hat to a wedding without being judged. Fog. Oasis. Kate Moss. Hugh Grant. Phone hacking. Suddenly acceptable to act superior to Australians. Irony. Never sweating again. Charles Dickens? Jack the Ripper? Bacon sandwiches?

CADBURY CHOCOLATE.

Love,

Jess

P.S. THIS IS SO EXCITING!!! You know, I hear the men in Britain have a certain, eh, how do you say, je ne sais quoi.

P.P.S. It is their proximity to Topshop.

*Two minutes later*

## Rachel to Jess

Ohhh, I like this game!

Red buses. Polo matches. Horse races. Fox hunting. Pimm's. Finger sandwiches.

I want you to visit me! I want to go to Royal Ascot with you so we can listen to poncy British people and imitate their accents. I want to lie in Hyde Park on the occasional sunny day! I want to see Shakespeare at the Globe Theatre! I want to stroll around the grounds of Windsor Castle in a floaty dress!

Okay, maybe I am getting excited and can leave Paris. Maybe.

Going to go eat *pain au chocolat*. I'm going to have to call this a chocolate croissant in London. Doesn't sound as delicious.

I had a tarot reading today (yep) that said an arriving girl with dark hair will make my life better. Seriously. Six of Cups (someone from the past with good news) modifying the Queen of Swords (a dark-haired woman). So I think you'll be fine in the country. But be careful anyway!

Love,

Rach

## Jess to Rachel

I'm alive!

I'm writing this from a house on the vineyard called the Straw Bale House, which the vineyard owner built. (I misheard him the first few times and called it the Strawberry Bale House.)

After a long train-and-bus journey, I finally arrived at Canowin-dra. I was the only person to get off the bus at the small stop. I say "Can-of-Wind-ruh," but the bus driver yelled the stop out as, "Ka-NOUN-dra." I'm never going to say it right.

For the first few moments in the empty town, I didn't see Sam and was terrified about what I would do if he didn't show up. Our phones don't work here! But then I saw him wave to me from the driver's seat of a truck on the side of the road. He now has longer hair and stubble and was wearing a plaid shirt.

He looked at me like he hadn't seen another person for ten years and threw his arms around me. He smelled different—wood fires and the outdoors. He had ruddy cheeks from working outside every day. No overalls, but he wore boots like a lumberjack.

He drove us back to the Strawberry Bale House and I love how blue the sky is here, especially against the green fields and vineyards. It was the bluest sky ever. On the drive, Sam explained our sleeping arrangements.

The family has two large houses on the vineyard, and the family's French ninety-three-year-old grandmother, Lily, lives in one of them. The only spare bedroom with a double bed is in Lily's house, so that's where Sam and I are staying.

Lily's actually very spry but has a memory problem. Sometimes when I appear around a corner, she'll be startled to find a random Asian girl with an American accent, and she doesn't quite remember who I am. She always smiles and reintroduces herself to me in French, be-cause she does not speak English. We communicate only in miming and it reminds me of my time in China. When she tries to say some-thing more complicated than "It's cold today" or "You have crumbs on your face," I want to call you so you can translate the French for me.

Sam wakes up at six every morning and then goes to collect the eggs from the chickens. Then he heads out into the cold weather and prunes vines all day. While he's working, I'm left with the endless rolling hills and fields and sheer space. Since Lily and I can't communicate, the loneliness is getting to me.

I spend most of my days outside, and I'm so lonely that I'm turning to animals for company. Today, I went running and came across fields and fields of sheep. I stopped in front of a herd of them to study them more carefully and see if I could maybe pet one, but they took one look at me and, terrified, hundreds of them stampeded away. Kind of insulting, really. Earlier that day, the owner kept trying to stress to me that sheep aren't dogs. If I've ever had some fantasy of wanting to live and work off of the land, it has been shattered. Sheep make terrible company.

After my run, I came back to the house and hung out with the chickens. Sam and I have a favorite one who is a different breed from the archetypal chicken. It's a fat hen with long black feathers that go all the way to her feet, so that she walks clumsily and trips over them. It's basically the equivalent of wearing false eyelashes and sequins, and I call her Liza Minnelli. She is also pretty bad at jumping onto things and often misses the target, ending up in a cloud of flying black feathers and dust.

And then finally, Sam comes in and takes off his muddy boots and together we lock up the chickens to protect them from foxes and then we make dinner for us and Lily. Sam goes outside and I watch him chop wood (when I attempted this, I nearly cut off my own leg and scared the shit out of Liza Minnelli in the process).

And then we sit around the fire trying to stay warm. It's still winter in Australia and freezing cold at night inside the house, especially without radiators or central heat. At night, we sleep under ten million blankets while the wind howls. The only familiar thing here is Sam, and I hold him so closely at night, not just because the sheets are icy cold. I can't believe he lives this life every day and night, all for us.

We spent one night away at a bed-and-breakfast. We drove for a few hours and Sam brought wine from the vineyard and we sat on big lawn chairs at the top of a hill and ate cheese and crackers while we drank it. I like those moments when you are in nature with someone and it feels like nobody else exists. I like that I can imagine spending an infinite amount of time with him and it doesn't freak me out.

Do you remember how many times we sat with Astrid and Rosabelle and talked about guys and what we wanted and how we would know, really know, if someone was right for us? We assumed it would be some sudden moment, like it would just reveal itself to us in one fell swoop. I don't know what it's like for other people, but with Sam, when we lie in bed together and his arms are around me, it's a growing visceral feeling of attraction and comfort and being content.

The future doesn't scare me anymore, the way it used to. I like that Sam saw my life in Beijing—that when I mention Isla, he knows exactly who I am talking about. There's something very comforting about that. We already have history, despite being relatively new.

I'm here for less than a week and then I'm going back to Melbourne and he'll be alone again. I always knew Sam was good, but I didn't know anyone was this good. Even though we'll be apart again for a short time, I have to remember that he'll be joining me soon.

Right. I'm off to have tea with a chicken.

Love,

Jess

JUNE 20

---

## Rachel to Jess

Liza Minnelli? And I'M the old lady between the two of us?

The country life sounds so far away from Paris. It's like an elaborate test from a fairy tale or something. Josh left yesterday, and I was really sad to see him go. I'm realizing that no matter where I go, I'll always be missing someone. It helps me to think of the world like this, though:

Buenos Aires = Rosabelle

Oslo = Astrid

Beijing = Old Jess

Melbourne = Current Jess

New York = Josh and Platonic Nick

These cities house my favorite people, and I find it reassuring. It makes the world feel smaller.

On Josh's last day at work, we walked out of American Prep together to a café to spend our last few hours together. I think he told Sylvia that other people would be there too, but it was just the two of us.

I decided to give him my Hemingway book from Cuba. He's a traveler, and I want him to remember how much he believed in his epic life here. He needs it, and I don't need it anymore, and more than all of that, I want him to remember me.

As we stood up to go, I handed him the book, *Fiesta*.

"I want you to have this," I said. "I want you to remember why you came to Paris."

He said, "This is the best present I've ever gotten." Then, because he is the most honest person ever, he added, "Well, one of the top ten presents I've ever gotten."

In terms of the fortune-teller Astrid and I saw, I think that Josh might have been The One before the One. He knew me, even before he got engaged to Sylvia, and he still chose her. For some reason, I can understand that more than what happened between Olivier and me. I know the reason why Josh isn't with me (obviously, Sylvia), while Olivier's reasons remain completely opaque.

Josh walked me home, and when we reached my building he gave me my first (and last) bear hug. It was as good as I always thought it would be. I can't believe I won't be seeing his face every day anymore. It's so strange how people become so tied up with your experience of a place. I won't be able to remember Paris without thinking about him. It really makes me realize how different the experience of living here has been from what I thought it would be.

I got an e-mail from Platonic Nick. He and his best friend, Tyler, (remember him from across the street senior year?) are traveling through Europe and staying with me next week. I haven't seen either of them since New York and can't picture their jovial, loud bickering on my quiet street in Paris. It'll be nice to be around some goofy American boys again, but if they get into one of their three-hour-long conversations about Spider-Man's superego, I'm going to give them a basket of croissants and two cheek kisses each, and then I'm going to swiftly drop them off at the American Embassy.

Love,

Rach

**JUNE 27**

## Jess to Rachel

??????? ARJKFJKLDJFDKLS

That's how it feels inside my brain right now.

I've applied for several reporting jobs because my journalism program ends very soon, but I haven't heard back from any of them. I also e-mailed a journalist at the Australian Broadcasting Company who liked my radio piece on the punk band touring through Asia. He referred me to an executive producer who works for a news radio program that specializes in Asian affairs. I sent the producer my résumé and went in for an interview, and after half an hour, he said he'd love to get me trained and started on some radio shifts right away. I could barely sit still. My mind was racing.

"I'm going to be a paid radio journalist reporting on Asia. I might even get sent to Asia sometimes. I can't believe this is happening. Don't blink too hard at him. Oh God, I cannot believe this is finally happening."

Then he took me around the building before steering me to the head of the department, an older blond woman named Dana. She looked me up and down and the only thing she said was, "So you're an American? You're far from home. . . . How long are you planning on staying here?"

I reassured her that I was going to stay in Melbourne and couldn't wait to start the job.

Then the producer walked me out, saying he'd e-mail me the shift schedule and a contract that afternoon. I left the building and left a message for Sam, telling him that I had big news. Great news.

While sitting on the tram, I stared out the window but saw nothing. I kept thinking, I'm finally going to be a real journalist, and I get to report on China. Maybe even get sent there. Everything is aligning.

Then my phone buzzed.

It was a text from the executive producer. He was rescinding his offer.

"I'm really sorry, Jess, but Dana wants to go with someone who is permanently based here. It's difficult to process your visa and we've spent too much time on international recruits who have left Melbourne very shortly after training. I'm really sorry about the misunderstanding, but we can't take the risk. Good luck."

And that was it. The five-minute dream was over. I immediately replied asking for clarification or another chance, but he did not respond.

I feel so deflated and frustrated. I wanted this job so much. When Sam called me back from the vineyard and I told him what happened, he seemed to think about it for a long time. He said that when he gets back to Melbourne in a few weeks, he wants to have a talk. My heart is sinking. I don't know what this is about, but he told me not to worry.

All I want to do now is put on pajamas and hit things.

Love,

Jess

P.S. I hate Tyler. I sent him a Facebook message three years ago and he never replied. Tell Nick hello.

## Rachel to Jess

Wow, seriously?! I'm so sorry. What do you think you're going to do now?

When we live abroad, we aren't just trying to be young entry-level workers, but we're also competing with, and trying to catch up with, people who have lived here for years. We have to work ten times harder than we would back home, but I think the thrill of living in different countries is irreplaceable, even if it is intangible. But it's also hard to see while you're in the midst of the struggle.

Nick and Tyler left the other day, and I can say with certainty that everybody's life is confusing right now. Tyler has just decided to return home to Ithaca to go to medical school—after spending the past two years working in publishing—and Nick wants to leave his gallery job, but doesn't know what he wants to do next. Seeing them was just confirmation that staying in New York wouldn't have made my life better.

Meanwhile, here are some highlights from the week Nick and Tyler spent ruining my life:

- I had to sleep on an air mattress and they shared my bed. However, they were too "manly" to sleep side by side so they slept head to toe. Every morning Nick woke up to Tyler kicking him in the face.

- Snoring. My God, the snoring. And yet they made fun of my snoring! Not okay. Tyler tempered this by saying it sounded feminine, but Nick laughed and said I sounded like a hibernating bear. I wanted to yell, "Fine, Nick, so get out of my fucking cave!" but instead I silently cursed them and their hipster glasses.

- I had to show them around the city like they were children. "Look! Big church!" "Look! River!" "Look! A French policeman!!!" This was very frustrating after having spent so much time trying to assimilate here, only to become the kind of tour guide I avoid.
- They were both so picky about food and they only ate what they referred to as "baguette sandwiches." This is not what they are called. And also, you are in Paris, and you only want to eat sandwiches?

Finally, on their last day here, I sent them to a rock climbing gym in the middle of nowhere even though I knew it would take them half the day to get there and back. They didn't love the gym, but it was totally worth my three-hour nap of uninterrupted bliss. Then we all went out for some baguette sandwiches.

They both still love comic books and ironic T-shirts. I wished that I could fall in love with them because it was fun being with witty American guys and being able to banter fluently. That said, I was thrilled when they left.

New measure of love: letting someone stay with you for an extended amount of time and not having it drive you insane.

But my biggest news is: I got the funding for UCL! Now I'll only be *one* hundred thousand dollars in debt! This means I'll be living on twenty-five thousand dollars a year in London—not enough for celebratory champagne, but enough for cheap boxed wine. I'll still be working for American Prep, though, so I'll get to teach wealthy British teenagers how to write like straight-A American students (they can teach me how to address a duke).

Oh! And Rosabelle e-mailed me—she's coming back from Argentina for law school in the States. Are we ALL just putting off our inevitable destinies as attorneys by staying abroad for a few more years?

Love,

Ithaca is Gorges

P.S. Tyler says he's sorry he never replied to your Facebook message.

**JULY 18**

## Jess to Rachel

Careful what you wish for—you could become a lawyer in London, and if you do, you have to wear one of those stupid wigs.

But seriously, do you think you'll be in London for a long time? I don't know how many more times I can uproot my life. I'm beginning to think that all of the energy we've taken relocating to new places should be put toward creating a life that's sustainable. Otherwise we're going to be sixty and all of our possessions will still be floating around in one giant purse.

Sam finally came home to Melbourne from the vineyard, weary and super scruffy. He reached into his backpack and said, "Here. I bet you've missed him." And then he handed me Brian Flanagan, whom he had wrapped carefully in a T-shirt. Sam had taken Brian all the way to Canowindra and then packed him up again and taken him on the bus, train, and the flight to Melbourne. Here he was. Spiky. Green. Stumpy. Still alive.

Sam arrived in the evening, and in the middle of unpacking, he said he wanted to talk, really talk, about what we are doing in Melbourne, since my program is ending in a week. He told me that while he was on the vineyard, he realized he was tired of messing around with his life.

"I just started to wonder why I was in the middle of rural Australia doing manual labor. I'm English, and I have a university degree. My friends back home have already been promoted multiple times while I've been pruning grapevines and living in the Strawberry Bale House with Lily."

I had nothing to say to this. Was he breaking up with me? Was he going to leave me and go back to England? Did he want to move on without me?

I stared at him.

"So what does this mean?" I asked him.

He said, "I'm nearly twenty-seven and I've been traveling for over two years. I was happy to go to the vineyard because I love you and this was the only way to stay together in Australia. But even if we find jobs now, it will be difficult to get long-term visas—like what happened with your radio job. And if we're both going to struggle to find fulfilling work in Australia, then why are we here?" he asked.

"Because we have nowhere else to go?" I said. "Maybe we could move back to China?"

He shook his head. I could probably find journalism work in Beijing now that I have experience, but he doesn't know Mandarin and we'd be in the exact same position a year or two from now—trying to decide where to go next.

I can't work in the United Kingdom. He can't work in the United States. We'll both eventually be kicked out of Australia if we can't find work. We both sat in silence until he said something that I had always feared he would say.

"I would love to move to London. It's a great city and all of my best friends live there. I've been gone from England for a really long time," he said.

During this entire exchange, we'd been sitting together at the foot of the bed, and at this point, I stood up.

"But what about me?" I asked him. I picked up Brian Flanagan. "What about us?" I asked, trying to smile.

"There are ways for us to move to London together," he said.

He and I both knew the only way. Marriage. Neither of us said the word.

"We need to think about what we want for the future," Sam said. "If we have a future, it's either in America or in England. We both like New York and London. We can't keep floating around forever," he said. "I need to start my real life now."

This went on for a while, until we decided that we should think separately about what we wanted, and sleep on it.

Right now, he's fast asleep in our bed.

But I can't sleep at all. Rachel, what do I do? What do *we* do?

He was right about a lot of things. I'm tired of starting over in new countries. The first two times were exciting, but the next place I go, I want to stay for a long time. Each time, it gets harder and harder to leave behind my friends, my work, and all of my connections. I'd love to be in a place where I can have 113 books without giving them all away in a year or buy something that weighs more than five pounds.

Tough life questions. Shit. New York or London for the rest of my life? Annie Hall or Bridget Jones? The West Village or Notting Hill? Being a lowly intern at the *New York Times* or the *Guardian*? BAGELS OR SCONES?

It's so hard to factor someone else into my life decisions. I never thought I could be with someone for this long, and yet Sam always surprises me in good ways. When I met him, he was a fun backpacker, and then he became my boyfriend. And while I knew he loved me, I had no idea he would work for three months in the country for our relationship. But still. Time to choose.

Sam's always believed in us, even when I had doubts.

I'm so confused about what to do. The only thing I really know is that I love Sam. But is that enough?

Love,

Jess

## Rachel to Jess

I know that everything still feels so uncertain, but you love Sam—whether you go to the next place together or not, you know that you love him and that's a truth. But what do you want most of all?

I completely agree with the idea of being somewhere long-term. When we first made the choice to move abroad, it was a random and exciting decision. But each time, it takes a little more out of us. I thought that we'd have inexhaustible inner resources, but I'm finding that I don't. I really don't.

I'm leaving Paris in one month. I'm sad to be leaving my life here, but I know that it's time to move on. I'll be in London for at least the next three years, and I feel like I could really be there for a long time.

As I'm sitting here, I can see the little old lady across the courtyard pruning the vines around her window. I can't believe I never saw how much the little old lady is like Sam Singer.

Of course, I'd love you to come to London, but with you, where you go next is anyone's guess. I'm not going to get my hopes up. I also don't want to be the one to tell you what to do.

Do you realize that it's now been almost THREE years since we graduated? So long ago, I remember choosing New York because it felt like the only place to go—a non-choice. I remember choosing Paris because it felt like the perfect place to go—an easy choice. And now, I finally feel like I'm choosing the right place for me and what I need to do.

During my time in Paris, I:

Fell in love and dated the love of my life for three days
Learned to not be friends with engaged guys

Finished my thesis

Met Picasso's grandson (forgot to tell you about this; he was
    completely normal)

Wrote 31,000 words of a 50,000 word (and growing) novel

Gained ten pounds (croissants are delicious, buttery saboteurs)

Taught hundreds of teenagers about right triangles

Saved $5,000

Spent $4,000 on my credit cards

Netted $1,000

Fell into the best group of French friends in the world

Published two short stories

Got much better in French and then, somehow, suddenly
    overnight, much worse

Got accepted into a doctoral program

Did not get hit by any cars


This coming year, I will:


Move to London

Lose ten pounds

Find love (although it seems psychologically bad to connect it
    to the previous thought)

Watch every movie Greta Garbo ever made

Find a secret London library

Publish one academic paper

Ride horses again

Learn polo

Finish my novel

Save up enough money to visit you wherever you are, even if
    it kills me

Join the Daughters of the American Revolution (I just want
    to, okay?)

YEAR THREE | 281

I can control most of those things, except love. Love being, of course, the one thing that I want now. But at least I have the certainty of knowing what I don't want: someone who won't fight for me or someone who leaves me feeling lukewarm.

And I'm getting better at dealing with how I approach life. I don't think I'll ever be able to stop myself from freaking out at inopportune moments or having dark lapses in my life, but I know that those moments rise and fall like waves, and then they're gone.

After it all, you're still the only person I would send this e-mail to. I miss you like crazy. We are too far from Brown for me to want to go back there. Think of how different we are from how we were then. I am glad we are different, but I miss us. And I miss the current you too.

I think no matter where you go, you'll be happy as long as you know why you're there.

Love,

Rach

**JULY 25**

## Jess to Rachel

Rach,

A few weeks ago, Sam and I walked by a poster for *Amélie*, the French film, which showed her reading in bed, with Chinese characters instead of French or English in the background. I thought about how if you combined your life and mine, it would look something like this picture in this shop in Melbourne.

I think you are right about England being the place for you now. We've both moved our lives across the world, and when it comes to what we are looking for, I think we're getting warmer—although you are still terrible at making life lists. Give up polo and learn how to fry an egg or change a tire! Be useful for once in your life!

I'll let it slide for now, since you did manage to have two years of kissing Europeans, teaching soldiers, and inventing new French phrases.

So, did Oprah tell you to make these lists? Fine. (This worked for me once before.)

I thought that you should know that during my last year I:

Fell in love with Sam Singer
Nearly lost Sam Singer
Produced two radio stories
Fell in love with an Australian hen named Liza Minnelli
Learned how to make chili
Didn't meet a single wombat
Had three journalism internships
Scripted and voiced three TV reports
Gained and lost my dream job in same day
Met Buzz Aldrin (I interviewed him. He talked about the
   moon too much.)
Began running again
Caught the bouquet
Sheared a sheep (worst experience of my life)
Wrote you 4,000 times

I think I live almost too much in the present moment, because everywhere else I've lived feels so incredibly far away that it now feels made up. Every time I unpack my suitcase, I start again. My childhood in Texas is one self-contained blur of family and flat plains; my second life at Brown was pretending to be an adult, as we watched plays in black box theaters but still lived in the dorms. I flew into my third life in Beijing, where I spoke Mandarin with taxi drivers and fell in and out of love, and now my fourth life, in Melbourne with Sam, is fading.

Now, my next step. The most miserable I've ever been was when

I thought I had lost Sam—first in Beijing, and then here. And the happiest I've ever been has been with him. I still don't know what my career's going to look like, but I've met reporters from all over the world, so I know that it is possible to have the kind of career I want anywhere if I work hard enough (although New York is still oversaturated with journalists and writers).

Last night, Sam and I spent all day at a nearby park that was playing movies on an outdoor screen. We spent the day discussing how most of my friends are scattered across the world and how all of his friends live in London and some of mine will now too. We walked home with our arms around each other and kept arguing about who could imitate an Australian accent better, and I just kept trying to say "Pineapple coconut" in an Aussie accent and failing. It kept coming out "Peen-apple." It reminded me of our first date, except I already love him so much. So much, too much.

When we came home, he handed me a long poster tube. He said, "This will look good no matter where you live."

I ripped off the wrapping paper and reached my hand inside and found . . . nothing. And then . . . lots of tissue paper. And then . . . a ribbon. And more ribbon. No *Amélie* poster. I kept tugging and found a card that had four Chinese characters on it. I kept pulling on the ribbon until I found another card attached that had more Chinese characters on it and then I kept pulling until another note had a giant question mark. And there, at the end of ten feet of ribbon, was a small black box. I put the cards in order, and basically understood this: "You ——— me —?"

Sam thinks I'm better at reading Mandarin than I actually am.

And then I opened the box. He got down on one knee. Then he slipped a platinum ring with my birthstone, an aquamarine, onto my finger.

Rachel. RACHEL! I've figured out my fifth life.

This coming year, I will:

Marry Sam Singer

Move to London

I mean, we've got visas and life plans and logistics to figure out, but ultimately this means you're finally going to meet Sam! Look out for a crooked English Tom Cruise carrying a baby cactus.

Call me back. Immediately. I can't wait to see you in London. Together again! At last!

Love,

Jess, A Girl with Dark Hair Arriving in London

P.S. You're really going to miss getting 437 e-mails from me a day.

# EPILOGUE

Before her wedding, Jess spent nine months in Beijing while her UK visa was processed. Back in China, she worked as the worst TV reporter in the world.

Jess married Sam Singer in the Lake District. It rained the entire weekend. Rachel cried approximately five different times that day. Platonic Nick held her tissues.

Jess now works as a freelance writer. She lives with Sam in London.

Rachel will finish her PhD in 2015 and has become a partial magical keeper of knowledge. She has had five different apartments since moving to London.

Rosabelle is on her way to becoming a top human rights lawyer. She married Buster, who became a neuroscientist and then a consultant.

Astrid moved back to Norway and is an entrepreneur who will run the world in five years.

Brian Flanagan was murdered in a bathtub when he was mistaken for a bath toy by two children.

Now that they live in the same city, instead of writing e-mails to each other, Jess and Rachel text each other random nonsense approximately forty-three times a day. It is un-book-worthy.

For the rest of their story, visit www.graduatesinwonderland.com.

# Acknowledgments

We'd first like to thank Allison Hunter, who saw something in our project and took a chance on us. We feel so lucky to have you on our team—you are definitely our hot twin cousin forever. Without you, none of this would have been possible.

We'd also like to thank our editor, Marisa Vigilante, who really understood our vision for this book and helped bring our creative grammar, dumb jokes, and haphazard storytelling into a real narrative. We're so glad we got to work with you, although it was mostly from opposite sides of the Atlantic. A big thank-you also goes out to everyone else at Gotham Books who worked on this book behind the scenes—we know it's a team effort.

And special thanks to Jori Thompson (Paige), who was our very first reader and believed in this book from the beginning. Thank you to Imogen Kandel (Isla), whose early comments on our first draft were invaluable.

We also wanted to recognize all the people who appear in this book: Thank you for the crazy years of our early twenties and for giving us these stories. Jess would personally like to thank the real Sam Singer for his infinite love, support, and patience and say: xoxoxo.

And to our dear friends and family who do not appear here but were very much part of our experiences during these years—just because you didn't break our hearts, employ us, or live with us, we still want to thank you for being part of our lives and our journeys.

*Photograph by Ian Cook*

**Jessica Pan** *(right)* has a BA in psychology and literary arts from Brown University. She holds a master's degree in journalism from the Royal Melbourne Institute of Technology. She was the editor of a magazine and a TV reporter in Beijing. Jessica lives in London.

**Rachel Kapelke-Dale** *(left)* is pursuing a PhD in cinematographic studies at University College London. She has a BA in history of art and architecture and comparative literature from Brown University and a master's in cinema studies from the Université de Paris VII. Rachel also lives in London.

www.graduatesinwonderland.com